IL 77|607 Due=890420
IL 32977/79 Due = 871112

APR 0 6 2018

DISCARDED

HIGHSMITH 45-220

ENTERED NOV 1

ADVANCES IN THE STUDY OF ENTREPRENEURSHIP, INNOVATION, AND ECONOMIC GROWTH

Volume 1 • 1986

ENTREPRENEURSHIP AND INNOVATION:
THE IMPACT OF VENTURE CAPITAL ON
THE DEVELOPMENT OF NEW ENTERPRISE

ADVANCES IN
THE STUDY OF ENTREPRENEURSHIP,
INNOVATION, AND ECONOMIC GROWTH

A Research Annual

ENTREPRENEURSHIP AND INNOVATION:
THE IMPACT OF VENTURE CAPITAL ON
THE DEVELOPMENT OF NEW ENTERPRISE

Editor: **GARY LIBECAP**
Director, Karl Eller Center
University of Arizona

VOLUME 1 • 1986

 **JAI PRESS INC.**

Greenwich, Connecticut   *London, England*

CONTENTS

Part II: Research in Entrepreneurship and Innovation

LIST OF CONTRIBUTORS

Willard Carleton

Department of Finance
University of Arizona

John Freeman

Johnson School of Management
Cornell University

R. Mark Issac

Department of Economics
University of Arizona

Arne L. Kalleberg

Department of Sociology
University of North Carolina,
Chapel Hill

Gary Libecap

Director, Karl Eller Center
University of Arizona

David C. Mowery

Department of Social Sciences
Carnegie-Mellon University

Almarin Phillips

The Wharton School
University of Pennsylvania

Stanley S. Reynolds

Department of Economics
University of Arizona

Nathan Rosenberg

Department of Economics
Stanford University

David A. Tansik

Department of Management
University of Arizona

Gerrit Wolf

Department of Management
University of Arizona

FOREWORD

The annual business/academic dialogue, sponsored by the Karl Eller Center in the College of Business and Public Administration at the University of Arizona, is designed to promote communication and exchange of ideas between the business and academic communities. Such communication is clearly needed. Despite the importance of private markets in allocating resources and in defining incentives for economic activities, the processes involved are too little understood and appreciated. Many public policies have been adopted in ignorance of their impact on market functions and have been counter-productive. The effectiveness of markets in channeling resources for efficient uses has been blunted and incentives have been dulled. As a result, productivity and competitiveness have declined in many industries. At the same time, foreign competition has increased.

A new understanding of private markets is clearly in order. To accomplish that, academics must become more acquainted with the real, day-to-day market activities that are well-known to business. Knowledge then can be incorporated into scholarly analyses of markets. On the other hand, business needs the broader, more detached perspectives of academics on the value of markets to see beyond the immediate issues facing their firms in the marketplace. With these issues in mind, the Eller Center dialogues provide the setting for a valuable exchange of ideas and viewpoints between business and academic leaders.

This volume contains papers and discussion from the first business/academic dialogue on entrepreneurship and venture capital. It also includes four papers, representing ongoing research in the areas of innovation, technological change, and entrepreneurship. This is an exciting endeavor that will benefit both the business and academic communities.

Karl Eller

PREFACE

This is the inaugural volume for a new JAI series titled, *Advances in the Study of Entrepreneurship, Innovation, and Economic Growth*. The series includes scholarly papers and business/academic discussions of critical issues affecting the American economy. The discussions are from the annual business/academic dialogue, sponsored by the Karl Eller Center at the University of Arizona. Each year, the dialogue brings together approximately 30 business and academic leaders throughout the United States to discuss specific questions regarding markets, entrepreneurship, and innovation. The discussions are organized around three papers prepared by nationally-recognized scholars.

The 1984 dialogue topic, "Entrepreneurship and Innovation: The Impact of Venture Capital on the Development of New Enterprise," is presented in the first part of this volume. Financial support for the dialogue was provided by Citicorp, Deloitte, Haskins and Sells, and the Gannett Foundation. The three papers are authored by Nathan Rosenberg of Stanford's Economics Department, a recognized expert in technological change; John Freeman of the Johnson School of Management, Cornell University, an authority on organizational behavior; and Willard Carleton, Karl Eller Professor of Finance of the University of Arizona and a noted scholar of financial markets. Each paper is followed by a summary of the dialogue on the topics raised by the authors.

The Eller Center dialogues are organized on the belief that advances in the study of market behavior can be made through exchange of perspectives by business and academic leaders. These exchanges can provide new insight into market processes, such as entrepreneurship, which play a critical role in the United States' economy and require increased research attention and rational government policies.

The 1984 dialogue participants bring a broad spectrum of backgrounds and views on entrepreneurship, venture capital and technological change. The entrepreneurs represent both large and small firms, and include Norman Auerbach of Coopers and Lybrand, a big eight accounting firm; Tom Brown of Burr-Brown Research Corporation, a manufacturer of scientific instruments; Tim Day of Bar-S Foods, a processor and distributor of meat products; John Dorie of Dorie, Inc., a travel agency; Karl Eller of Circle K Corporation, a convenience retail chain; Ed Frohling of Mountain States Mineral Enterprises, a mining and engineering firm; Bennett Greenspan of Industrial Photographic Supply, an industrial photographic supply concern; Clinton Hartmann of RFM, Inc., a manufacturer of semiconductor chips; Warren Rustand of International Holdings, a boat construction firm; Alan Smith of Deloitte, Haskins & Sells, a big eight accounting firm; Richard Spencer of SLM Instruments, a manufacturer of scientific instruments; and Milton Stewart of the law firm of Robbins and Green, a small business authority.

There is similar diversity for the venture capital representatives. They include Lawrence Campbell of Campbell and Company, a New York investment firm; Charles James of Scientific Advances, Inc., the venture capital division of the Battelle Memorial Institute; Jack Thorne of the Enterprise Corporation of Pittsburgh, a venture capital firm; Thomas Whitney of Whitney Ventures, Inc., a Silicon Valley seed capital firm; and William Witter of William D. Witter, Inc., a New York venture capital firm.

The academic and press participants include Michael Block, Mark Isaac, Gary Libecap, Kenneth Smith and Edward Zajac, economists from the University of Arizona; Willard Carleton of the Finance Department of the University of Arizona; John Freeman of the Johnson School of Management, Cornell University; Soma Golden, Editor of the Sunday financial section of the *New York Times;* Robert Higgs of the Economics Department, Lafayette College; Morton Kamien, an economist from Northwestern University; Almarin Phillips, an economist from the Wharton School, University of Pennsylvania; Louis Pondy of the Department of Business Administration, University of Illinois; Nathan Rosenberg of the Economics Department at Stanford University; Paul Uselding of the Economics Department at the University of Illinois; and Gerrit Wolf of the Management and Policy Department at the University of Arizona.

In addition to the three papers and discussion from this varied group of participants, some final thoughts on research in entrepreneurship and venture capital are provided by Almarin Phillips of the University of Pennsylvania.

Each year the Eller Center will sponsor a dialogue on a new topic, with papers from leading scholars in the field and comments from business and academic participants. We are excited about the series and the opportunities provided by business and academic exchange for advancing our understanding of market processes.

The second part of the volume contains four papers representing research in the areas of technological change and entrepreneurship. David Mowrey, of the Department of Social Sciences at Carnegie-Mellon University, analyzes the impact of firm organization on innovation, with particular reference to the semiconductor industry. Gerrit Wolf and David Tansik, of the Management Department of the University of Arizona, continue with an examination of organizational issues and their impact on entrepreneurship and new technology adoption. Finally,

Arne Kalleberg, of the Sociology Department at the University of North Carolina, presents a field study of small business entrepreneurs and the characteristics of their businesses. A third paper, by Mark Issac and Stanley Reynolds of the Economics Department of the University of Arizona, uses an experimental approach to investigate the effect of differing property rights arrangements on R&D.

Welcome to the JAI series on *Advances in the Study of Entrepreneurship, Innovation, and Economic Growth.*

Gary D. Libecap
Series Editor

PART I

PAPERS AND DISCUSSIONS FROM
THE BUSINESS/ACADEMIC DIALOGUE

SPONSORED BY

THE KARL ELLER CENTER FOR THE STUDY
OF THE PRIVATE MARKET ECONOMY
UNIVERSITY OF ARIZONA
(November 29–30, 1984)

INTRODUCTION: THE DIALOGUE FORMAT AND A SYNTHESIS OF THE PAPERS AND ISSUES

Gary D. Libecap

The 1984 Eller Center business/academic dialogue, "Entrepreneurship and Innovation: The Impact of Venture Capital on the Development of New Enterprise," examines the role of entrepreneurship, venture capital, and technological change in the performance of the United States' economy. As Nathan Rosenberg points out in the lead paper, the United States' economy is in transition: foreign competition is displacing many American products; heavy industries, previously the heart of the U.S. economy, are declining while services and light high-tech industry are rapidly growing; and productivity growth by some measures, has fallen. For example, from 1948 through 1973 output per worker grew at an average annual rate of 2.4 percent, while more recently, from 1973 to 1981, productivity advanced only .1 percent. On the other hand, a more positive indicator is that since 1979 there has been an apparent increase in entrepreneurship and the availability of venture capital. Accordingly, this is a critical time to carefully

Advances in the Study of Entrepreneurship, Innovation,
and Economic Growth, Volume 1, pages 3-9.
Copyright © 1986 by JAI Press Inc.
ISBN: 0-89232-703-0

examine entrepreneurship, venture capital, and technological innovation to determine what they offer for the future.

For the topic "Entrepreneurship, Technological Change, and United States' Economic Growth," Nathan Rosenberg is concerned with the general performance of the American economy. Technological change, which he broadly defines as the innovation and dissemination of new products and processes, has been responsible for perhaps as much as 85 percent of American economic growth since 1869. Technological change increases productivity in numerous ways: by allowing more production from existing resources, by expanding the economy's resource base, and by providing new products so that the composition of the economy's production is changed. Entrepreneurs and venture capitalists are the center of this process. They are the people who seize opportunities to develop and market new products and processes; they are the ones who incorporate technological change into the economy.

Rosenberg provides four major points for understanding technological change. First, it is a continuous process that fundamentally alters the functioning of the economy. Historically, doomsday prophesies of impending shortages of basic raw materials have not materialized because entrepreneurs have provided new processes that conserve resources and use more abundant, lower-quality supplies. While these innovations have allowed the economy to expand and meet the demands of its growing population, Rosenberg is concerned that the rate of productivity advance has slowed. At the same time, there have been spectacular advances by the Japanese. Will the recent interest in entrepreneurship in the United States lead to a resurgence in technological growth? What policies can be adopted to encourage those activities?

Second, technological change is characterized by the slow accumulation of small, minor improvements, rather than dramatic breakthroughs. Entrepreneurs primarily refine existing products and processes to lower costs or capture new markets. The recent proliferation of microtech firms, using existing scientific knowledge to modify the products of their competitors and to seek new markets, is an example of this process. While the individual refinements may be small, their aggregate impact on the economy is large.

Third, the diffusion of new technology is critical. While new ideas are developed daily, they must be marketed to be considered by other firms and consumers. Entrepreneurs, as risk-takers, search for and promote novel products and processes and thereby play a critical role in the dissemination of technology throughout the economy. What determines the rate of adoption and the success of a new idea? Since many innovations ultimately fail, what are the characteristics of successful entrepreneurs? Are there social or cultural factors that affect the receptiveness to new technology?

These questions lead to Rosenberg's fourth point that technological change is interactive. The economic consequences of important innovations create further adaptations. Unfortunately, the market reaction to a new product or process cannot be accurately foreseen. Innovations disrupt existing market relations between firms and consumers. Those firms that rapidly implement successful new technology increase their market shares, while others incur declining shares. Additionally, labor and other inputs are displaced and consumer purchases are altered. Many of the negative distributive effects of new technology are narrowly focused on certain firms and groups, while the gains are broadly spread and may be more difficult to perceive. This asymmetry poses problems for entrepreneurs in two ways. First, if the benefits of a new innovation are difficult to forecast, while the costs are clear, the venture capital for the new enterprise will be limited. Second, the reaction of those adversely affected by the innovation may lead to formation of interest groups and government policies that restrict technological advance. Negative societal response to technical change poses serious implications for entrepreneurs and future economic growth. This is an area where universities and business schools, in particular, can contribute by promoting research and understanding of entrepreneurship and technology.

The conference discussion of Rosenberg's paper is summarized in Chapter 2. Two points absorbed most of the discussion: the definition of entrepreneurship and the role of business schools in encouraging the study of entrepreneurship and the associated problems faced in starting new ventures.

For the topic "Organizational Issues Affecting Entrepreneurship and the Supply of Venture Capital," John Freeman examines entrepreneurs who become dissatisfied in their existing firm and leave it to found new enterprises. He argues that in any large organization, there are people who can become entrepreneurs. Some organizations are successful in retaining those people so that innovation and intrapreneurship (entrepreneurship within firms) occur within the firm, while other organizations drive out such people. There is a life cycle for firms. As they become larger and more established, they become more inflexible and less responsive to new opportunities. Employment in large organizations provides potential entrepreneurs with knowledge of the technology, the market, and social contacts. With this potential, entrepreneurs can exploit the slow reaction of large organizations by founding firms and moving into new areas.

Freeman points out that entrepreneurship, defined as firm founding and failings, and the availability of venture capital seem to occur in waves of five to seven years. Why that is so is not clearly understood, though it may follow the business cycle. It may also be due, in part, to the life cycle of organizations. There is an entrepreneurial phase where start-up occurs and the firm experiences (if successful) rapid growth. As the firm becomes established and tied to particular products and production processes, a managerial phase begins where the firm is less flexible and innovative than before. This leads to conflict and frustration for some people, who eventually leave the firm to exploit new opportunities. Indeed, Freeman points out that many managers prefer to see such individuals leave the organization, rather than to respond to their complaints. As a result, organizations create their own competition by driving out those who start competitive firms.

This life cycle perspective and notion that entrepreneurs are misfits in many

large organizations raises two issues. First, are entrepreneurs always on the
fringe, exiting firms once they become established? Second, what strategies and
incentives could be adopted to encourage intrapreneurship and the creation of
new enterprises within large firms?

Freeman observes that organizations differ in the spin-off of entrepreneurs. To
see why, he examines the semiconductor industry in general, and Texas Instruments and Fairchild Semiconductors in particular. He finds that entrepreneurs
exit from parent organizations for three reasons: economic considerations, not
receiving equity commensurate with their contribution; dissatisfaction with firm
policies on pursuing new technologies and products; and dissatisfaction arising
from political processes that result in the replacement of supportive senior executives.

While the parent organization provides entrepreneurs with the skills, social
contacts, and reasons for exit, venture capitalists provide the funding to start an
organization. Freeman argues that venture capitalists look more at the knowledge
and experience of the founders than at their business plans. Their skills, provided
by the parent firm, decrease the probability of failure of the new organization.
This focus on the characteristics of the founder reflects the riskiness of new products and processes when there is little information for forecasting market responses. The problems of forecasting raised by Freeman are similar to the ones
raised by Rosenberg in discussing the social reaction to new technology.

The growth of entrepreneurial activities in the United States has coincided
with an expansion of venture capital. Freeman lists six different types of
financing, based on the stage of firm development. At the early entrepreneurial
phase, there is a personal relationship between the venture capitalist and the entrepreneur, and time horizons for investment payoff are long. Later, as the firm
becomes more established, greater amounts of money are required, and the firm
turns to less personal and more institutional funding sources. In those venture
capital relationships, time horizons are shorter. The conference discussion of
Freeman's paper is summarized in Chapter 4.

For the topic ''The Relationship Between Venture Capital Firms and Entrepreneurs,'' Willard Carleton examines venture capital issues as they affect
entrepreneurship and economic growth. He defines venture capital as investment
in new, small, and risky companies, especially those that are commercially applying the technological innovations discussed by Rosenberg. Venture capitalists, in turn, are those individuals who bring such new companies from infancy
to early maturity, when they can gain access to more conventional financial markets.

Carleton argues that the funding of new entrepreneurial firms differs from
financing more established firms, and examination of the process provides both
understanding of the problems facing entrepreneurs and venture capitalists, and
knowledge for forecasting the impact of government policies on entrepreneurship and technological change.

A distinguishing characteristic of venture capital funding is a long-term, sequential decision/investment process because of a serious lack of information about the new product or process. The venture capitalist initially invests enough to carry the firm through a development stage. During that time, additional information on the profit potential of the innovation is obtained. At the end of that stage, a decision is made to continue with new funding or to abandon the project. These contingent decisions continue until the firm can go public or secure other funding sources.

This sequential decision process is complicated by problems that distinguish venture capital financing from more conventional capital budgeting and financing decisions. First, there is general uncertainty regarding both the market potential of any new product or process and the firm's untried management. Second, that uncertainty is exacerbated by differences in the information available to the entrepreneur and the venture capitalist. External investors are in an inferior position to judge the true value of an innovation. They must rely upon the information provided by the entrepreneur. In negotiations, entrepreneurs may be reluctant to reveal proprietary information that might weaken their competitive advantage. In the early stages of development, much of the firm's identity is tied to the entrepreneur. This fact exemplifies Freeman's point that venture capitalists more closely examine the character of the entrepreneur than the business plan in their initial funding decisions. A third source of uncertainty is the long-term nature of the investment. It is difficult for the venture capitalist to accurately forecast either the capital market's response to the firm when the investment is liquidated, or the general market's response to the new product.

Carleton points out that in the sequential investment/decision process, there exists an important interpersonal relationship between the venture capitalist and the entrepreneur. Through this relationship, the venture capitalist can monitor the firm's performance, provide needed managerial advice, and minimize friction over contractual shares.

Because of this sequential decision process and the lack of good information, Carleton argues that venture capitalists prefer to provide funding only after entrepreneurs have significantly invested their own capital in the project. They will also specialize in certain industries that they can learn well, and favor risky projects with high expected returns.

Carleton argues, though, that recent institutional changes in the venture capital market may influence both the supply of venture capital and the nature of new enterprises undertaken. If permanent, these changes could significantly influence the pattern of technological change in the United States' economy. First, venture capital has become more impersonal as large institutions have begun funding new projects. Venture capital was previously provided principally by small, private venture firms. With larger organizations, the interpersonal relationship between venture capitalists and entrepreneurs may be lost. It is not clear whether this is a transitional phenomena that will change as new institutions learn about the venture capital-entrepreneur relationship. If it is not transitional, the decline in interpersonal relations may result in more poorly managed portfolios and a reduction in funds available to new firms.

Second, institutional venture capital may constrain entrepreneurial projects if large firms place strict controls on the new operations. These controls could include stressing short-term returns and requiring larger equity shares. Large investors, because of the lack of interpersonal relations and poor information, may have different investment objectives and time horizons than do small venture capital firms. Such constraints may limit risk-taking by new firms. This will affect the projects undertaken and the nature of technological development in the United States.

Third, Carleton conjectures that the resort to large institutional fund sources may result in greater fluctuations in the supply of venture capital. Venture capital is comprised of both *new* and *recycled* funds, and since they are likely to move together in the business cycle, they will amplify any fluctuations.

Besides these changes in the character of venture capital sources, Carleton outlines other factors that influence the supply of funds to entrepreneurs. He argues that venture funding moves inversely with the real rate of interest. When real rates are down, the high expected returns of venture capital are attractive, and money becomes available for new enterprise. This was the case in the late 1960s through the mid 1970s. When real rates rise, as they now have, there are alternative, less risky investments that compete for funding, reducing the money available to new firms. Carleton also notes, however, that recent changes in the income and wealth distribution in the United States may make more money available for new ventures, if the wealthy save more and are less risk adverse than those with lower incomes and wealth.

Carleton points out that new ventures are very sensitive to government tax and regulatory policies. Lower capital gains taxes are a subsidy that increases after-tax returns for venture capital. Lower taxes lead to more investment in long-term, risky projects. Another form of government subsidy is direct investment in new ventures. Carleton notes that there are social benefits and costs from both subsidies, and the results are hard to predict, making it difficult to determine the most efficient way of promoting new enterprise.

Finally, cultural factors appear to influence entrepreneurship, though the exact nature of that process is not clear; environments, where entrepreneurship is encouraged and valued, support innovators. What policies could be adopted to provide such an atmosphere? Given the controversial nature of many new products and processes as noted by Rosenberg, are such policies likely? Does the United States have a unique cultural and institutional setting for entrepreneurship? These are critical questions that require more research.

Chapter 4 outlines the reaction to the issues raised by Carleton. In particular, there is a clarification and a new understanding of the various levels of venture capital financing and the important role of risk in distinguishing venture capital from more conventional funding conditions. The participants also address some relevant policy recommendations.

Professor Almarin Phillips provides an afterword in Chapter 7 on the appropriateness of received theory for analyzing entrepreneurship and venture capital markets. He draws upon the "transactions cost" literature to briefly describe venture capital transactions and to point the direction for future research.

Chapter 1

TECHNOLOGICAL INNOVATION AND ECONOMIC GROWTH

Nathan Rosenberg

I. INTRODUCTION

This is a very opportune moment to be addressing the questions of technological innovation and entrepreneurship. The performance of the American economy, at least judged by certain important criteria, has been highly unsatisfactory. Even a casual reading of most newspapers throws up numerous reminders of the rapid displacement of American products from markets that United States manufacturers have dominated for decades. Our economic performance, as measured by recent rates of productivity growth, is truly dismal. That adjective is appropriate whether we compare our productivity growth to that of our major commercial competitors or to our own earlier performance.

Consider our productivity performance in the years since the Second World War. According to the most authoritative estimates, national income per person employed grew at about 2.4 percent per year between 1948 and 1973 (Denison, 1979). After 1973, national income per person actually declined. Between 1973 and 1981, national income per person employed declined at a rate of 0.1 percent per year.[1]

Advances in the Study of Entrepreneurship, Innovation,
and Economic Growth, Volume 1, pages 11-24.
Copyright © 1986 by JAI Press Inc.
ISBN: 0-89232-703-0

I would like, however, to set the background through a longer time perspective. My own view is that innovation and entrepreneurship are at the heart of successful economic performance. Candor also compels me to admit that modern economics has had relatively little to say on these critical subjects. In general, economics has been reasonably successful in identifying the conditions that must be fulfilled for an *existing* volume of resources to be utilized with maximum efficiency; it has been much less successful in identifying the conditions that generate longer-term economic growth and productivity improvement. It is useful, then, to clarify the connection between the innovation process and long-term economic growth.

II. INNOVATION AND LONG TERM ECONOMIC GROWTH

What is economic growth all about? How do we account for America's earlier rapid rate of economic growth in the first place? What were the main factors that generated the long-term economic growth that has given America the highest standard of living in the world?

Starting from first principles, it is obvious that we could have achieved this growth in per capita income in two different ways: (1) by using more resources, or (2) by getting more output from each unit of resources. How much of the long-term rise in per capita incomes is attributable to using more inputs, and how much is attributable to extracting more output from each unit of input?

You might conclude that this formulation of the question is so fundamental to an understanding of economic growth that the economics profession has been hard at work trying to provide precise quantitative answers since time immemorial. If you drew that conclusion, you would be wrong. For many decades economists approached this issue of rising per capita incomes as if it were primarily a matter of using more resources, especially capital equipment. The first serious attempts at providing quantitative estimates came during the 1950s. The answer suggested by these estimates came as a big surprise to the economics profession.

In the mid-1950s, Abramovitz looked at the quadrupling of United States' per capita income between 1869 and 1953, and asked how much of the observed growth could be attributed to the use of more inputs during this time period. Additional capital and labor inputs accounted for about 15 percent of observed growth.[2] The residual—the portion of the growth in output per capita that could not be explained by the use of more inputs—was at least 85 percent. Several other economists used different techniques and data and got roughly the same results. What seemed to emerge forcefully from these exercises was that long-term economic growth had been overwhelmingly a matter of using resources more productively, rather than simply using more resources.

Since growth has been primarily a matter of raising resource productivity, to what can we attribute that rise? The residual, after all, captured everything *aside* from the growth in inputs, as conventionally measured; it did not capture just the benefits of technological change.

Abramovitz (1956) was circumspect in interpreting his findings. He said the large size of the residual was "a measure of our ignorance," and of course he was correct. His study allowed us to say with authority that most of the observed growth in output per capita cannot be explained in terms of a growth in inputs per capita. But this was an important finding because "main line" economics had for a long time suggested that economic growth was accomplished by increasing the supplies of inputs into the productive process.

In the past twenty-five years or so, many economists have tried to calculate with greater numerical precision the contribution of technological change to the long-term rise in per capita incomes. These exercises in "growth accounting" have been fascinating, but, I believe, doomed to failure. The ultimate object of the search is, in my view, an unattainable "holy grail." The contribution of technological change cannot be isolated and sorted out as a separate contribution alongside capital formation and increasing resource availability. The inescapable truth is that these variables are highly interactive, and the contribution of any one will depend on the simultaneous behavior of the other variables.

Nevertheless, I believe that the growth accounting exercises have made at least one extremely important contribution to our understanding of the economic growth process, even though that contribution has been, in a sense, a negative one. They have shown that the old neoclassical view, which interpreted economic growth as primarily a matter of accumulating larger stocks of homogeneous inputs, is fundamentally inadequate. The growth in such inputs, by itself, only accounts for a small fraction of observed economic growth in the past century. What these exercises have demonstrated is that economic growth has been primarily *not* a matter of using more resources, but of generating more output per unit of resources used. And this, in turn, has suggested to economists that they should devote more attention to the contribution of technological change.

Although the economics profession has, as a result, paid more attention to the impact of technological change in the past two decades, I believe all economists would admit that the results have not been entirely satisfactory. This is partly because technological change is a collection of activities that is inherently very difficult to model. It is not a single activity; it is a wide variety of activities. Its form and content, for example, differ drastically from one industry to another, and in any industry it is probably very different in 1984 from what it was in 1954 or 1924.

Economists have responded to this bewildering diversity of technological activities largely by remaining aloof to the specific forms and content of technological change. They have adopted a ''black box'' approach in which technologies are treated in a highly abstract way—a given technology is treated as a specific quantitative transformation of inputs into outputs. Technological change is represented as an improvement in that quantitative rate of transformation of inputs into outputs that economists call a shift in a production function.

Let me emphasize my belief that this black box approach to technological change has been extremely useful and has yielded many important insights. Indeed, we could not get along without it. Nevertheless, we have paid a high price by operating exclusively at such a high level of abstraction. Specifically, we have lost contact with certain characteristics of technologies—characteristics that play a critical role in shaping the success or failure of new technologies and in determining the economic impact. More broadly, the abstract black box view of technological change is one which denies us some of the most critical ways in which new technologies shape the long-term process of economic growth and structural change in industrial economies.[3]

At the same time, the black box approach has encouraged an excessively mechanical treatment of a complex set of activities. The decision to introduce a new technology cannot be made by resorting to some straightforward calculus of costs and benefits. New technologies, especially drastically new technologies, represent voyages that are full of technological and commercial uncertainties. The essence of such decisions is that they are made on the basis of very limited information and involve a substantial degree of risk-taking. I will return to these issues later.

III.   EXAMPLES OF TECHNOLOGICAL CHANGE IN NATURAL RESOURCE USE

The approach to technological change that calls for generating greater output per unit of input (merely as a shift in a production function) understates the impact of technology in highly significant ways. The approach is, first of all, excessively static in nature. It fails to take into account that the definition of the word ''input'' in this context is not fixed and unchanging. The natural environment is fixed, but only in a geological sense; it is not fixed in terms of its economic significance. Indeed, one of the most important features of technological change is that it has continually expanded the resource base of the economy. This has taken several forms. Improvements in techniques of extraction have made it possible to recover oil from depths of 20,000 feet or more, an accomplishment that was physically impossible not very long ago. In general, advances in technological knowledge have led to the development of techniques for the exploitation of materials that were formerly unexploited. Uranium, for example, was only a resource in the geological sense and not the economic sense as recently as 1940. It was a very valuable economic resource in 1950. The same was essentially true of easily accessible petroleum deposits in 1800, but primarily as an illuminant. It was only with the development of the internal combustion and diesel engines around 1900 that petroleum became valuable as a fuel. Natural resources possess economic significance only as a function of technological knowledge, and improvements in such knowledge have regularly led to an expansion in the resource base in the economic sense.

Another dimension of this process has become particularly conspicuous in the twentieth century as the supplies of high quality resources have been gradually exhausted. A major thrust of twentieth century technology has been the development of techniques for the exploitation of low-grade resources. The gradual exhaustion of the high-grade iron ores of the Mesabi Range in America was followed by innovation to exploit the new resources, such as methods of concentration and beneficiation (a technique for enriching the ore before it enters the blast furnace) which made possible the exploitation of the immense deposits of hard, low-grade taconites. In a very meaningful sense, I would argue that as a result of the availability of the new processing techniques, the United States has larger iron ore deposits today than it did in 1950. The flotation process, originally applied to the exploitation of low-grade porphyry copper ores, has been applied to a wider range of ores, both of lower mineral content and more complex chemical forms; whereas the technology of 1870 required access to ores containing at least 3 percent copper, more recent technologies successfully utilize ores of only 0.4 percent copper content. Techniques of selective flotation have played a major role in offsetting the decline in the quality of available resources not only for copper, but also for such important materials as lead, zinc and molybdenum. The great advances in sulphate pulping technology during the 1920s liberated the wood pulp industry in America from its earlier bondage to northern spruce and fir trees and made possible the exploitation of the more rapid-growing, but previously unusable southern pine. Undoubtedly, a persistent theme in the future will be the search for technologies that will make it possible to rely on highly abundant resources for the supply of essential materials. Important examples are the nitrogen fixation process which fixes nitrogen from the atmosphere, and the increasing interest in sea water—already a source of magnesium—as a source of mineral inputs.[4]

The intimate link between technological innovation and natural resources can be readily observed in the iron and steel industry.[5] Since the 1850s, a series of innovations continually altered the economic significance of natural resource deposits for the iron and steel industry. The original (acid) Bessemer process represented a huge improvement in energy efficiency, but could only be used to refine materials fulfilling certain precise chemical conditions (the process required iron free from phosphorus). The later (basic) Bessemer process, by contrast, required ores of a high phosphorus content, but the United States did not possess large deposits of such ores; thus, the process never became significant in America. The basic Bessemer process, however, made possible the exploitation, for the first time, of the huge high phosphorus iron ore deposits of western Europe and literally changed the course of European history.

The basic open hearth furnace of the 1880s was capable of exploiting a wide range of inputs in steelmaking. In addition, it permitted a more precise degree of quality control than was possible with the Bessemer technique. In particular, it could utilize ore of almost any proportion of phosphorus content, and its availability made it possible to exploit a much wider band of the available spectrum of the gigantic Lake Superior iron ore deposits. Moreover, the process could also utilize a high proportion of scrap as a material input; a consideration of great and increasing significance in locations with ready access to such supplies. The growing abundance and declining price of scrap in the twentieth century induced research into methods of increasing the proportion of scrap used in oxygen converters. With the recent development of the electric furnace, we now have a technique for producing steel entirely without iron ore since such furnaces can operate with a 100 percent scrap charge. Thus, the potential supplies of inputs into the steelmaking process have been steadily widened to include the junkyards, and thereby make possible the large-scale recycling of steel products. The electric arc furnace also has made possible highly efficient recycling of aluminum, avoiding the energy cost of producing aluminum from the original bauxite.[6]

The point here is of basic importance in understanding the significance of technological change. Such change alters the economic significance of the physical environment so extensively that one cannot really discuss the role of natural resources in economic activity without first carefully specifying the level of technological knowledge and sophistication. In other words, the growth of technological knowledge generates information which makes it economically worthwhile to exploit resources formerly considered not worthwhile because of their poor quality. For this reason, discussions which ask how long it will take, at present or extrapolated consumption rates, to exhaust a particular natural resource are usually not very interesting. What the natural environment usually offers is limited deposits of resources of high quality and then a gradually declining slope toward lower grade resources that typically exist in abundance. It is a geological fact of life that there is usually a much greater profusion of low-grade than of high-grade resources in the earth's crust.

Thus, it is not enough to think of technological innovation merely as a way of increasing the productivity of available resources. It does much more than this. It takes natural resources that previously had no economic value, and converts them into inputs of great economic value. Technology, therefore, enables us to move down the slope from higher quality natural resources to poorer ones as the higher quality resources are exhausted. In general, technological innovation has served as a collection of methods to evolve with the changing patterns of resource scarcity. Basically, it has done this by vastly expanding the number of resources in our natural environment that we are capable of exploiting economically.

IV. CHARACTERISTICS OF TECHNOLOGICAL CHANGE

Let me now call your attention to some other characteristics of technology that play an important role in the link between technological innovation and productivity improvement. A large portion of the growth in productivity resulting from innovation assumes the form of a slow and often almost invisible accretion of individually-small improvements. Unfortunately, too much of the literature on technological innovation is preoccupied with the technologically spectacular, rather than the economically significant.[7]

It is useful here to think in terms of the life cycle of individual innovations. Major improvements in productivity often continue long after the initial innovation as the product goes through innumerable minor modifications and alterations in design to meet the needs of specialized users. Widely used products like the steam engine, the electric motor or the machine tool, experience a proliferation of changes as they are adapted to the varying range of needs of users. Consumer durables have typically gone through parallel experiences with special emphasis on expanding quality in catering to different income groups. Such modifications are achieved by unspectacular designing and engineering activities, but they constitute the substance of productivity improvement and increased consumer well-being in industrial economies. Indeed, the ability to execute these modifications is critical to the success of an industrial technology.

Much of the technological change which goes on in an advanced industrial economy is, if not invisible, at least of low visibility. Often it does not require any sophisticated scientific knowledge, but does require a detailed familiarity with the production technology and strong, effective incentives to reduce costs. It includes a flow of improvements in procedures such as materials handling, redesigning production techniques for greater convenience, and reducing maintenance and repair costs (as in modular machinery design). In iron and steel, major reductions in fuel requirements have been achieved by rearrangement of facilities to eliminate the need for successive reheating of materials. In metal-working, new and harder materials continue to be introduced in cutting edges, making possible a considerable acceleration in the pace of work. In electric power generation, where the long-term rate of growth of total factor productivity has been higher than any other U.S. industry, the slow, cumulative improvements in the efficiency of centralized thermal power plants have generated enormous long-term increases in fuel economy. A series of minor plant improvements including the steady rise in operating temperatures and pressures made possible by metallurgical improvements, new alloy steels, and the increasing sophistication of boiler design and resulting increased capacity, have sharply raised energy output per unit of input. The magnitude of this improvement may be indicated as follows: It required seven pounds of coal to generate a kilowatt-hour of electricity in 1910, but in the 1960s the same amount of electricity could be generated by less than nine-tenths of a pound of coal. Yet most people would be hard-pressed to identify any major innovations leading to this great improvement in productivity.

One of the important points to note about technological change and its economic impact is that it is seldom a once-and-for-all affair. The introduction of a technological innovation is not something that happens only once and then can be forgotten; it is a continuous activity. Most technologies are relatively inefficient when they are introduced and require a long process of improvement. Often, the later improvements in an innovation will be more important than the original innovation itself. Since I do not have the time to develop the point, let me merely suggest that you think of the steam locomotive as it existed in 1830, the automobile around 1905, the airplane around the time of the First World War, or the computer in 1950[8].

Let me make two further points. Since I have emphasized technological innovation, I would like to remind you that from the point of view of the economic impact of technology, it is the diffusion of the technology that counts. An invention acquires an economic importance only as a result of its utilization and exploitation. For this reason, technological innovation and its economic consequences must be linked to an analysis of the forces shaping the diffusion process.[9]

Secondly, it is important to realize that technology is not some kind of exogenous phenomenon that leads a life of its own and is unaffected by economic forces. Technology not only has economic consequences, it also has economic *causes*. Technological change is clearly the outcome of economic decisions; decisions of business firms to commit resources to the search for more effective products and processes. It is influenced also by larger social decisions to commit resources to certain bodies of science, whose findings, in turn, shape new opportunities for the innovation process in specific directions. And it is influenced by the whole set of forces embedded in laws, legislation, and government regulations that increase the incentive to engage in innovative activity or that create deterrents to it.

V. PREDICTING THE IMPACT OF TECHNOLOGICAL INNOVATION

I would like now to turn briefly to the question of what the impact of technological innovation is likely to be in the years ahead. I do so with considerable diffidence—a wise man once said that it is very difficult to make predictions, especially about the future! Nevertheless, since many such predictions have filled the media and the halls of Congress in recent years, a few cautionary observations are appropriate.[10]

There is widespread apprehension that we are now poised at one of those great discontinuities in history, where new technologies are going to have unprecedentedly large effects in generating a permanent pool of unemployed. This is because many new technologies—robotics, CAD/CAM, the growing capacity of the electronic chip, automation—are expected to have strong labor-saving effects.

It is, of course, always impossible to prove anything about the future merely by looking at the past. It is impossible to prove that we are not at some genuine discontinuity in history. Furthermore, it is painfully clear that the American economy is performing poorly and has been performing poorly for at least a decade. Productivity improvement has been particularly dismal, and unemployment levels have been unacceptably high. However, I do not believe the high unemployment rate has been due to the character of technological change, nor do I see any compelling reason to believe that new technologies will have an unusual job-reducing bias in the future. Some categories of employment will, of course, suffer. Technological change has always reduced specific categories of employment—e.g., farm workers, railroad workers, coal miners, lumberjacks. The electric light displaced the candle maker, and the automobile put saddlers and whip makerrs out of business. The crucial question is whether the thrust of technological change will reduce *total* employment, not whether it eliminates specific jobs.

Labor-saving innovations are not the same as job-reducing innovations. The reductions in cost and price associated with labor-saving innovations may bring in their wake vast increases in specific kinds of employment. When Henry Ford introduced the progressive assembly line to the American automobile industry in 1914, the result was a huge reduction in the number of labor hours required to produce a car. But the resulting ability to sell a Model T Ford for only $400 was a revolutionary event that resulted in an immense increase in employment in the automobile industry. The demand for cars turned out to be highly elastic. On the other hand, when demand is inelastic, cost reductions shift demand elsewhere. The impact of technological change cannot be confined to the sector where it occurred—it is a problem in general equilibrium analysis. I might add that, in the present international context, new steps forward in automation may increase U.S. employment by repatriating activities that have recently moved offshore. Thus, the automation of a variety of labor-intensive assembly line work may well bring jobs back to the United States that have recently migrated overseas in search of cheaper labor.

As a general matter, it is easier to anticipate the employment-displacing effects of technological change than the employment-expanding effects, largely because we don't have a good technique for dealing with product innovation. The anticipation of the employment-expanding consequences of innovations requires a much greater exercise of the social imagination—an ability to foresee uses in entirely new social contexts. Even a casual glance back into history confirms this. In the early days of the radio, people anticipated that it would be used primarily as a device for communication in places where wire communication was impossible, such as remote mountain locations and ships at sea—hence the term "wireless" (still used in Britain). No one seems to have correctly anticipated the immense commercial, entertainment and educational uses the invention was used for during the twentieth century. In the 1950s, when the computer was still in its infancy, it was confidently predicted that all of America's future needs would be adequately catered to by about a dozen computers. Even Thomas Edison, a genuine inventive genius, is said to have anticipated that the phonograph would be used primarily to record the death-bed wishes of elderly gentlemen! It is extremely difficult to anticipate the impact of new innovations because that impact is not something inherent in the hardware. It depends, rather, on social uses and cultural contexts which determine how society chooses to mobilize and to exploit the potential of a piece of hardware. No one seems to have anticipated how much computation would occur in our society when the productivity of the calculating technology was increased by several orders of magnitude.

Thus, I believe there is a systematic bias in our perceptions about the future. This bias sharpens our awareness of possible job-reducing consequences of technological change, but at the same time fails to identify the prospects for enlarged employment opportunities that flow from the ability to produce certain products more cheaply or to invent entirely new products with unanticipated uses and applications. A distinctive feature of western capitalism seems to have been the ability to produce very cheap variants of products that in an earlier age were consumed only by a small elite—nylon stockings for silk stockings and ball point pens for Parker 51s, recorded stereophonic music for court musicians.

I expect technological innovation to continue to require labor force shifts and reallocations as it has in the past. These shifts are extremely painful to the individuals and families concerned, and the magnitude of these shifts has been enlarged by drastic changes in America's position in world markets in the last ten or fifteen years.

What I want to insist upon is that I see no evidence to support the expectation that technological innovation is now poised to cause unemployment of a vastly enlarged scale when compared to our historical experience. I believe such fears are based upon a misdiagnosis, and that our present difficulties lie primarily in the macroeconomic sphere rather than in the sphere of technologically-generated unemployment. If that misdiagnosis led to measures that hindered our capacity to exploit a new generation of technologies, or to artificially prolong the economy's attachment to obsolescent technologies, or to protectionism, it would seriously damage America's viability in an increasingly competitive world economy. America's comparative advantage, I believe, continues to lie in the direction of the generation and exploitation of new technologies.

VI. CONCLUDING REMARKS: PRODUCTIVITY ADVANCE AND INCENTIVES FOR ADOPTING NEW TECHNOLOGY

I would like now to revert to the poor productivity performance of the American economy in recent years. I do not, to be perfectly candid, know how to allocate the causes of that decline with any pretense of precision; nor does anyone else know how to do that. Clearly there have been a large number of factors at work, some short-term and others longer-term. The double oil shocks after 1973 undoubtedly had a traumatic effect, especially on the willingness to make long-term investment commitments. The post-war "baby-boom" brought a vast increase in new entrants into the labor force. The extraordinarily rapid growth in the labor force through the 1960s and 1970s was, in some respects, the other side of the coin of the productivity slowdown, since the new entrants had, on the whole, limited job experience or extensive vocational preparation.[11]

At the same time, I do believe that a number of trends during the 1960s and 1970s had the effect of contributing to an environment that was at least less congenial to innovation and entrepreneurship than in earlier periods. Let me develop this point.

What really matters for economic purposes is not the capacity to invent or to perform high quality scientific research. These activities acquire economic significance only in the presence of a well-developed capability for selecting, adopting and exploiting the economic potential that is merely latent in research and inventive capabilities. To bring about this exploitation involves a range of talents and background conditions that are difficult to identify, much less to measure, with any real precision: strong incentive systems, effective managerial skills, and business people who are highly motivated and capable of making informed assessments of market opportunities—including the all-important matter of timing. Although the role of such capabilities cannot be identified with great precision, it is possible to learn something about their economic significance by looking at extreme cases. In recent decades, the British have continued to demonstrate a high degree of purely inventive ability, such as they showed in the cases of penicillin, radar and the jet engine. Moreover, their scientific community continues to do brilliant basic research. On a per capita basis, Britain continues to receive more Nobel Prizes than does the United States. Nevertheless, they have not done very well at coupling these great capabilities in the marketplace. In the post-war years their performance in bringing new inventions or new scientific insights to the point of successful commercial exploitation has been distinctly disappointing as has been their economic performance generally. The Japanese, on the other hand, while they have not been a source of major inventions or of the highest level of creative scientific research in the past, have achieved an unprecedented growth in their economy by learning how to exploit—and to improve upon—foreign inventions. It seems fair to say that differences in the environment for entrepreneurship between Britain and Japan are probably an important part of the explanation for the drastic differences of economic performance between the two countries.

I would like to linger on the point that inventive abilities are only a part of the story because it highlights another critical component of America's lagging productivity performance that is closely linked with our present interests and concerns. If, as I have been insisting, invention exercises its impact only when it is adopted and employed in the productive process, then capital formation is ordinarily the vehicle that delivers the benefits of invention to the economy at large. It follows from this that economies with high rates of saving and capital formation will derive the productivity-increasing benefits of invention more rapidly and reliably than economies with low rates. The bad news, of course, is that the American economy is generating rates of saving that are not only lower than at earlier points in our history, but far below the rates achieved by our commercial competitors in international markets. Thus, according to estimates by the Organization for Economic Cooperation and Development, net personal saving in the United States was 5.8 percent in 1978, compared to 16.9 percent for Japan, 12.0 percent for France, 12.5 percent for West Germany, and 11.9 percent for Italy. In the same year, American gross fixed investment, expressed as a percentage of GNP, was 18.1 percent, far below Japan's 30.2 percent, and also substantially below the 21.5 percent figure attained by both France and Germany. More recently, the United States figure for gross fixed investment has been even lower— around 15 percent.

The reasons for these low rates are complicated, but clearly they are closely connected with factors in the larger business environment that are intimately linked to the rewards that society offers to entrepreneurship. I include here (1) a tax structure that offers weak rewards for saving, (2) inflation and inflationary expectations that seriously distort the capital replacement process and raise the effective rate of taxes on business income, and (3) an unusually high degree of uncertainty that, combined with high interest rates, has had a severely dampening effect upon the willingness to undertake long-term capital investment projects. I should add that worry over the prospects for future inflation has been one of the most serious of all the uncertainties. I feel obliged also to record my view that economists have seriously underestimated the disruptive effects of inflation on the performance of the economy. The reason for this is that, when inflation accelerates, it does not do so uniformly across the sectors of the economy and, as a result, market prices become a less reliable guide to efficient resource allocation.

A final possible reason for the slowdown in measured productivity growth since the 1960s is the expansion of certain kinds of regulatory activities by the government—regulations that intend to reduce atmospheric and water pollution, and to improve the safety of the workplace and consumer products. Thus, beginning with the Delaney Amendment (1962), we have had a succession of congressional initiatives in these directions, including the Clean Air Act, the Clean Water Act, EPA, OSHA and the Toxic Substances Control Act.

The growth of government regulation in the past ten or fifteen years has had two obvious impacts. First of all, by raising the cost of certain kinds of R&D activities, and by deferring the flow of possible benefits, it has had the effect of reducing R&D spending. This impact is very uneven across industry lines. It is very clear in certain industries such as pharmaceuticals where FDA regulations have raised the cost of developing and marketing a new drug.

In pharmaceuticals, raising the cost and slowing the rate of introduction of new products has been the explicit goal of the regulations, which have required time-consuming and expensive testing procedures as part of a policy designed to protect the consuming public.

Secondly, and as a closely related point, government regulation has brought about important shifts in the composition of the reduced R&D spending. More money is now spent on activities which will be responsive to the new government regulations. Thus, much more R&D spending is now directed toward such activities as reducing air and water pollution, providing safe work environments, and improving product safety.

Estimating the impact of such regulations is an extremely complex exercise. Nevertheless, we can cite the estimate made by the President's Council of Economic Advisors. The Council estimate in 1979 that the growth of productivity since 1973 may have been reduced by about 0.4 percent per year as a result of the direct costs incurred in complying with environmental, health and safety regulations.

I am not especially interested in trying to pass judgment on whether any particular regulation is socially desirable. That calls for some difficult balancing and adjudication of costs and prospective benefits of the regulations. But it is clear that certain kinds of R&D spending and the thrust of business entrepreneurship in certain directions have been reduced or even discontinued as a result. For example, federal regulations now require that new contraceptive technologies be tested for 180 months before they can be marketed. As a result of this prolonged postponement of possible revenue flow, private industry has withdrawn from all research activity in the field of human fertility control. Given the potential dangers of new contraceptive technologies, it is easy to argue that such regulations are justified. On the other hand, in view of the immense social and economic benefits that flow from improved methods of preventing unwanted pregnancies, I cannot completely suppress the thought that perhaps it is possible for society to be too careful.

Here, as elsewhere, we may be failing to fully articulate the prospective benefits that may flow from more innovation and entrepreneurship. A single-minded determination to reduce risk, or policies that reduce the possible financial payoffs to those who are willing to assume risks, may deprive us of future benefits that may be extremely large. As a society, we therefore need to continue to ask ourselves whether we have the balance between risks and possible benefits just about right, and whether the incentives, the regulations, and the institutional mechanisms that we have devised for dealing with risk are presently as close to the societal optimum as possible.

NOTES

1. See Denison (1979). If we look at these figures more closely, interesting additional trends emerge. The point is that a measurable downturn in the rate of growth of productivity per worker shows up back in the mid-1960s. Between 1948 and 1964 national income per person employed grew at about 2.8 percent per year, but between 1964–69 it fell drastically to 1.8 percent per year. There was a further fall of 1.6 percent between 1969 and 1973, and then the numbers turned negative between 1973–81 (− 0.1 percent). Thus, although these figures confirm the truly dismal performance of the 1970s, they also call attention to the fact that falling productivity had commenced back in the 1960s.

2. See Abramovitz (1956).

3. For further discussion, see Rosenberg (1976), Chapter 4, "Problems in the Economist's Conceptualization of Technological Innovation".

4. Barnett and Morse (1963) outline an interesting discussion of related issues.

5. See Temin (1964) for an authoritative treatment of the American scene. Landes (1969), Chapters 4 and 5, also provides a useful survey of European developments.

6. See Rosenberg (1982), Chapter 4, "The Effects of Energy Supply Characteristics on Technology and Economic Growth".

7. See Rosenberg (1982), Chapter 3.

8. The entire flight of the Wright Brothers at Kitty Hawk in 1903 could have been conducted inside a present-day C–5A!

9. A more extensive treatment of this issue is in Rosenberg (1976).

10. See House of Representatives (1984).

11. Civilian employment increased by more than 20 million between 1970 and 1980, a truly remarkable performance for a single decade.

REFERENCES

Abramovitz, M. (1956), "Resource and Output Trends in the U.S. since 1870." *American Economic Review Papers and Proceedings* 41(2):5–23.

Barnett, H. and Morse, C. (1963), *Scarcity and Growth, The Economics of Natural Resource Availability*. Baltimore, MD: Johns Hopkins University Press.

Denison, E. (1979), *Accounting for Slower Economic Growth: The United States in the 1970s*. Washington, DC: The Brookings Institution.

House of Representatives, 98th Congress, first session (1984), *Technology and Employment*. Joint Hearings before the Subcommittee on Science, Research and Technology of the Committee on Science and Technology and the Task Force on Education and Employment of the Committee on the Budget. Washington, DC: U.S. Government Printing Office.

Landes, D. (1969), *The Unbound Prometheus*. Cambridge: Cambridge University Press.

Rosenberg, N. (1976), *Perspectives on Technology*. Cambridge: Cambridge University Press.

Rosenberg, N. (1982), *Inside the Black Box*. Cambridge: Cambridge University Press.

Temin, P. (1964), *Iron and Steel in Nineteenth Century America*. Cambridge, MA: M.I.T. Press.

Chapter 2

THE DIALOGUE ON TECHNOLOGICAL INNOVATION AND ECONOMIC GROWTH

In his paper, "Technological Innovation and Economic Growth," Nathan Rosenberg outlines the role of technological change as the major driving force of American economic growth. Of concern to Rosenberg are recent trends of declining productivity in the United States and the reasons for it. His concern is shared by others and has led to a reevaluation of the role entrepreneurs play in technological change. Entrepreneurs and technology are linked because they find opportunities for introducing new products and processes into the economy.

The conference discussion of Rosenberg's paper focused on two points: first, defining entrepreneurship and isolating the conditions necessary for it; and second, determining the role of business schools in training entrepreneurs.

Advances in the Study of Entrepreneurship, Innovation,
and Economic Growth, Volume 1, pages 25-31.
Copyright © 1986 by JAI Press Inc.
ISBN: 0-89232-703-0

I.   WHAT IS ENTREPRENEURSHIP; WHO ARE ENTREPRENEURS, AND WHAT CONDITIONS OR ENVIRONMENTS SUPPORT THEM?

To assess the impact of technological change and the role of entrepreneurs in promoting it, the dialogue began with an effort to define entrepreneurship. Given the variety of backgrounds of the participants beyond merely an academic/business distinction—small business persons, members of large corporations, entrepreneurs, venture capitalists—there was no final consensus on a definition. Many attributes and conditions facilitating entrepreneurship, however, were clarified.

Two issues were debated. The first was whether entrepreneurs could function within large organizations or only in small business environments. The second was whether entrepreneurship involved only the introduction of new products and processes or if it encompassed expansion of more traditional retail activities. In other words, does a definition of entrepreneurship require high-tech activities, and is the starting of a new small business an essential attribute?

To begin, Warren Rustand argued that the focus of the discussion should be on individual characteristics and the results of their actions, rather than on the environment in which entrepreneurs operate. For Rustand, entrepreneurs are characterized by an "indomitable spirit, the can-do, the self-esteem, the high self-confidence, the never-doubting-self kind of characteristic that runs through . . ."[1] Rustand argued that these personal characteristics are more critical than the environment, and they are necessary to successfully execute risky activities, such as introducing new products, starting new firms, and redirecting established organizations. He noted that because entrepreneurs are typically alone in seeing new opportunities ('visionary'), they cannot rely upon the support of others in their new enterprise, particularly at the initial stages. The uncertainty surrounding new ventures is directly related to Rosenberg's point that there are biases in predicting the outcome of technological change. The costs (the displacement of old products and firms) may be clearly seen, but the benefits are often less certain, except to the entrepreneur. Self-confidence plus perseverance are essential for new ventures. Those characteristics are also important because entrepreneurs must expect to fail. Indeed, Rustand estimated that each fails four times on the average before they succeed. Finally, Rustand argued that entrepreneurs don't have to be engineers or scientists, but they must be characterized by strong intellect, extreme flexibility, and ability to quickly assimilate new information in decision-making.[2]

Milton Stewart countered that the environment was more critical than individual characteristics. Most individuals, he argued, had entrepreneurial traits, but the environment determined whether they could act on them. For Stewart, "the entrepreneur is someone who starts a business, starts an enterprise where one did not exist before."[3] Small business, because of its flexibility, is the key. Entrepreneurs cannot exist within the constraints of large organizations. Stewart used a broad definition of small business in defining the necessary environment for entrepreneurs: "Whether the fellow invents a new way of making semi-conductor chips or starts the first new delicatessen in a neighborhood . . . the role he performs is an entrepreneurial role."[4]

The reasons for stressing the environment were developed further by Jack Thorne and Charles James. Thorne insisted that entrepreneurs were extremely committed, independent people who broke "all the rules." Hence, they could not easily operate within the tight structure of a large corporation. (This issue is addressed in the following paper by Freeman.)[5] James, however, differed from Stewart in categorizing the small firms that should be included in a definition of entrepreneurship. He argued that while the person who starts a high tech company and one who starts a filling station or beauty parlor have similar entrepreneurial characteristics, "they're not riding the same horses."[6] The difference is risk. Those who start small, technically-based businesses with new products are faced with a degree of uncertainty that does not exist for those who start more traditional enterprises. To succeed in the former, a much greater commitment and willingness to assume risk are required.

The four small business entrepreneurs, Dorie, Greenspan, Hartmann, and Spencer, voiced similar views of the importance of the small business setting. As with Thorne and James, they stressed the flexibility of small businesses and the element of risk relative to conditions in large firms. Hartmann saw entrepreneurship as "any activity that creates more efficient methods for producing useful products" through a small business setting. A new, small business "allows you to structure the enterprise in a way that is best suited to that particular enterprise." Starting a new business is risky since the entrepreneur must meet a payroll and the cold reality of the market; circumstances that do not exist for innovators within large corporations.[7] Similarly, Spencer argued that there is less risk for an innovator in a large corporation because "there is a big umbrella over the whole operation so that it doesn't really matter if it (the innovation) fails or succeeds."[8]

The insistence on small business as a distinguishing characteristic of entrepreneurs brought a critical reaction from many of the academic participants. Rosenberg cautioned that it entrepreneurship is exclusively identified with the starting of new firms, then older, larger firms are excluded with the implication that they do not engage in entrepreneurial activities, such as the introduction of new technology. Rosenberg held that a small business definition was too limited. Moreover, he pointed out that entrepreneurship involves a very diverse range of activities in different sectors of the economy, and should not be identified with just the introduction of new or high technology.[9] A broader view of entrepreneurship would include organizational changes and the discovery of new raw material supplies. Under such a definition, both individuals and firms of any size could be characterized as entrepreneurs.

Paul Uselding continued by arguing that entrepreneurship goes beyond *new* products and processes to the quiet, cumulative improvement of an existing product or process. Clearly, product improvement can be as important to the economy as a new product.[10] Uselding added that product improvement is typically attempted by large firms and, hence, they should not be excluded in a definition of entrepreneurship. Robert Higgs followed Uselding's point by asking how much technological change is the result of new businesses and products as opposed to product changes within large firms.[11] Given a lack of research on the issue, there was no answer to Higgs' question.

The discussion returned to the business participants. Norm Auerbach commented that the small firm criteria also presented a dilemma. If successful, a small firm will grow; Auerbach asked at what point does an entrepreneur lose the characteristics of being an entrepreneur? Does he cease to be one unless he starts another new business?[12] Stewart responded that at some point in every business the importance of entrepreneurship diminishes and the importance of management increases. More often than not, he continued, entrepreneurs are not good managers. As soon as firm operations become a repetitive activity, the entrepreneur usually becomes bored and either leaves, starts a new business, or hires people to manage the firm.[13]

The wide-ranging discussion of entrepreneurship and the lack of consensus on a definition and an environment demonstrate the need for additional research and understanding of this critical activity. The participants did agree that risk-taking to seize new market opportunities was essential for technological change and economic growth. Hence, entrepreneurship deserves much more attention from academia, business and government. A related issue was addressed which discussed whether business schools should do more to encourage entrepreneurship.

II.   WHAT IS THE ROLE OF BUSINESS SCHOOLS IN TRAINING ENTREPRENEURS?

The dialogue on business schools centered on two related questions: can entrepreneurship be taught, and what curriculum changes are needed to adequately train student entrepreneurs?

The general consensus of the entrepreneurs was that a business school can only provide the tools for implementing ideas, but cannot create entrepreneurs.[14] The characteristics of entrepreneurs described above include self-confidence, independence, and the willingness to take risks; traits unlikely to be significantly molded by academic training. That is, a business school cannot take someone who lacks inherent entrepreneurial interests and motives and recast them into a hard-driving entrepreneur. It is possible, however, to facilitate the progress of students who are interested in entrepreneurship through self-awareness and encouragement.

While there was agreement on the need for more emphasis on entrepreneurship by business schools, there were divergent views how the task should be performed. Hartmann, Stewart, and other small business participants argued that business schools should redirect emphasis from management to more practical problems faced by small businesses. This would require a recognition that small businesses have unique problems which are unlike those commonly encountered by larger corporations. Milton Stewart, for instance, criticized the common academic notion that "whether it's a large company or a small company, we have to teach the same things."[16]

Charles James asked that if we distinguish between managers and entrepreneurs, do we discourage entrepreneurship by focusing business school curricula on management?[17] Ed Frohling responded no, and argued that it is questionable whether entrepreneurial potential can be identified early by individuals. Frohling also pointed out that until a person is exposed to the business world, he does not have the ability to recognize and evaluate opportunities.[18] Accordingly, major curriculum changes are unwarranted and would be premature. Similarly, Paul Uselding questioned whether business schools should teach people how to be a success in business, or whether the direction should be on how to think. He compared the education of engineers and MBAs. The former receive detailed training in specific aspects of technology and a mental outlook to further accumulate technically-relevant knowlege. On the other hand, an MBA student is trained to analyze general market phenomena and to have analytical insight into how business processes work. He concluded that it is not clear that a more narrow, practical focus for MBA students is desirable.[19]

Morton Kamien added that one reason why business schools do not teach the 'nitty-gritty' information needed by an entrepreneur is that in the presence of rapid change, its usefulness evaporates. To illustrate, Kamien described a parable about a Professor of Slide Rule: "And he taught slide rule. He had written books on how to use the slide rule. And that was very nitty-gritty. If you really were an engineer you really had to know how to use a duplex Desitrix, and he was the expert on it. Until Texas Instruments came along."[20]

Ken Smith added that business school curricula were, in part, responses to student and employer demand. To change business schools, Smith argued one must not only create the demand for studies of entrepreneurship or small businesses, but also convince students that such study will advance their career plans. Until recently, at least, student demand has been for training appropriate for fast-rising careers in large corporations.[21] Accordingly, that is where placement has centered and the measure of success of each school's program has been.

John Freeman elaborated on this problem. He noted that in most business schools, the study of entrepreneurship is a 'side-line'; it is never a mainstream subject in the MBA curriculum. The reason for this is that business schools, like all professional schools, have an image of success. The business school image of success is to be a *manager* in a big corporation. In contrast, entrepreneurs are not necessarily good managers. Freeman argued that the difference between entrepreneurial success and failure is frequently an ability to shift from being a creator of new products to being a manager of an on-going concern. Since those activities are quite different, new talents and skills are needed and often embodied in different individuals.[22] Hence, management is the correct focus for business schools.

The dialogue participants agreed that given the importance of entrepreneurship in technological change and economic growth, a reevaluation of business school curricula was in order. A disagreement remained, however, whether the direction should be toward more practical problems in designing courses or whether a more analytical, discipline-based approach to entrepreneurship was required. Libecap noted that programs following both models have been adopted by business schools throughout the country. The University of Arizona has adopted a discipline-based approach which has helped to bring academic acceptance for both the program and the faculty in it. He argued that academic credibility was critical if the programs were to succeed and impact the general college curriculum.

The first session's discussion of a definition of entrepreneurship and appropriate business school curricula brought an important exchange of views from the business and academic participants. While there was a general consensus on the personal characteristics of entrepreneurs, the necessary environment for entrepreneurship continued as a subject of debate. Many participants believed that large corporate settings were not conducive to entrepreneurial activities. John Freeman's paper, which follows, addresses those issues in more detail.

NOTES

1. Rustand, Transcript Eller Center Dialogue, Session I, November 29, 1984, p. 11
2. Rustand, p. 12
3. Stewart, p. 14
4. Stewart, p. 27
5. Thorne, pp. 14, 15
6. James, p. 33
7. Hartmann, p. 36–37
8. Spencer, p. 47
9. Rosenberg, pp. 16–18
10. Uselding, pp. 23–25
11. Higgs, p. 27
12. Auerbach, p. 30
13. Stewart, p. 31
14. Hartmann and Dorie, pp. 40, 41
15. Eller, p. 42
16. Stewart, pp. 52–53; Hartmann, p. 76

17. James, p. 43
18. Frohling, p. 44
19. Uselding, pp. 94–96
20. Kamien, pp. 89–90
21. Smith, pp. 88–90
22. Freeman, pp. 18–19

Chapter 3

ENTREPRENEURS AS ORGANIZATIONAL PRODUCTS:
SEMICONDUCTOR FIRMS AND VENTURE CAPITAL FIRMS

John Freeman

I. INTRODUCTION

This paper examines entrepreneurship in two kinds of organizations: semiconductor electronics firms and venture capital firms. It argues that entrepreneurship can best be understood in terms of the factors impelling individuals to exit the firms that currently employ them, and the environmental circumstances constituting opportunity. The current employer provides individuals with the ability to attract resources and knowledge about where to allocate those resources. He also provides models for organizing new firms (both positive examples to be emulated, and negative examples to be avoided). Finally, the "parent" organization provides knowledge of opportunity: the market niches not being exploited fully, the technical leads not being pursued, the suppliers willing to make particularly attractive deals, and the dissatisfied customers.

Opportunity, then, often appears in an organizational guise. One can see the

Advances in the Study of Entrepreneurship, Innovation,
and Economic Growth, Volume 1, pages 33-52.
Copyright © 1986 by JAI Press Inc.
ISBN: 0-89232-703-0

task facing an entrepreneur as a puzzle whose pieces must first be assembled, and then fitted together. These pieces are outputs of existing organizations. The capital required, the human resources, space, information, permits and licenses are all provided, perhaps grudgingly, by existing organizations. For all these reasons, entrepreneurship is an organizational product.

II.   TECHNICAL AND MARKET CHANGE

Of course, it is true that entrepreneurship is a rather rare practice. Existing firms provide large numbers of employees with access to puzzle parts, but only a few actually assemble them. The opportunity structure that motivates entrepreneurial action is based in the patterns of technical and market change in which existing firms operate. Foundings (and failures) of organizations usually occur in waves. A wave of expansion in the population of venture capital firms has just occurred in the last few years. Most analysts of the microcomputer business expect a wave of bankruptcies and acquisitions in the next few years. Osborn and Atari lead the wave. The frequency of environmental change per unit of time is, probably, just as important as the magnitude of that change (Hannan and Freeman, 1977; Freeman and Hannan, 1983). When environments (markets and technologies in particular) change often, relative to the inertial properties of organizations, opportunity is created.

The frequency of environmental change relative to the level of organizational inertia is the environment's grain, the more frequent the changes, the finer the grain. The grain affects firm behavior. Fine grains are likely to be interpreted by firms as an average, leading organizations to specialize in spite of the uncertainty. They do this because unfavorable states typically do not persist. A set of these states with organizational forms specialized to each is a stable evolutionary outcome. When grain is coarse, riding out such unfavorable states is a less practical firm strategy and organizations are likely to have general responses to change, trying to do tolerably well in each state, rather than optimizing in any one of them.

Such reasoning can help explain why large, dominant organizations with generalist ways of exploiting the environment do not immediately force entrepreneurial firms out of the competitive arena, whenever opportunity appears. Both the venture capital market and the semiconductor industry pose exactly this problem: why did the dominant firms allow young Jacks to climb the bean stalk and make off with geese laying golden eggs? The answer is that the large and relatively inert dominant firms, set up to exploit multiple markets and slowly changing technologies, can not tolerate uncertainty which comes packaged in a fine-grained pattern. Their complicated decision processes and elaborate organizational structures, pervaded by long, multifold links of interdependency, make for slow change. Diversification to deal with uncertainty and risk is an obvious response. Adaptive change, in contrast, requires quicker, orchestrated response.

Ironically, the very organizations which have the longest life expectancies are those that are pervaded by short-run decision structures. An orchestrated but quick response requires planning and vision. Such adaptations imply long-run decision horizons. Venture capitalists, particularly those concerned with start-ups, must have a long time horizon. Their illiquidity absolutely requires it. Entrepreneurs must also take such a long-run view. In both cases, larger more diversified parent firms are pervaded by short-run mentality precisely because orchestrated adaptive change is so rare. Each decision maker operates in a narrow little world created by an elaborate division of labor. Each is judged by how well his little piece of the action is doing, and the whole operation is judged by a capital market driven by short-run evaluation processes (i.e., information emanating from quarterly reports). Finally, we should add, following Williamson (1975), that by developing internal controls and incentive systems designed to minimize opportunistic behavior, large dominant firms lower the willingness of individuals to take risks. When exiting the organization is practicable, entrepreneurship results.

III. ENTREPRENEURSHIP AS AN ORGANIZATIONAL PRODUCT

Why is it that some firms regularly produce entrepreneurs while others rarely do? Anecdotal evidence suggests that there are substantial differences between firms in the same industry. The semiconductor industry provides an obvious example. Texas Instruments (TI) and Fairchild Semiconductor began in the business at about the same time. Both were extremely successful and grew with the exponential rate of the industry. TI, headquartered in Richardson, Texas, produced very few progeny, so far as we can tell. Braun and McDonald (1978) identified forty-one semiconductor firms that are direct or indirect offshoots of Fairchild. Six years later, the number has grown substantially. How can we explain this difference?

When we began our study of the semiconductor industry, the first step was to arrange a series of interviews with high-level executives who had long experience in the industry.[1] The subject of these interviews was why they started their firms, and how they managed the start-up process. Several of these people had worked for Fairchild, and they gave three reasons for leaving to found their own companies. First, they complained that they were not given a sufficiently large financial reward for their efforts. In particular, equity ownership made available in the form of stock options was not adequate to match the contribution they believed they were making, nor did such equity interest approach what they thought they could generate on their own. In short, they talked about economic considerations.

A second set of concerns involved the technology itself, their views about how rapidly it was developing, and in what directions it was changing. Fairchild was not placing priority on developing MOS technology, which was to be the basis of the integrated circuit, and working there was simply less exciting than it might have been.

Third, they mentioned managerial decisions taken by Fairchild's board. In particular, executives from Motorola were hired to manage the company in the wake of Sherman Fairchild's withdrawal as the chief executive officer. This rebuke to the central figures who had started the semiconductor subsidiary led to a political upheaval which shook the company. Political processes, then, constitute a third reason to leave.

These three explanations were, of course, proffered differently by each person we interviewed. Some ignored one or more of them in preference to the others. The historical accuracy of their accounts and relative emphasis on them is less significant for our purposes than the lead they give us for developing general explanations for variations in the entrepreneur-generating tendencies of organizations.

A.   Individuals and Organizations

One of the perplexing problems for organization's researchers, and for most managers, is the inconsistency between rational action defined in terms of individual behavior and the more global rationality often imputed to organizations as a whole. Put simply, individuals making rational (i.e., utility maximizing) decisions for themselves often make choices that are suboptimal from the point of view of the firm (Cyert and March, 1963).

From this perspective, each individual makes a decision to participate or not participate in the organization. This decision involves trading off inducements offered by the organization for contributions of the individual. A "zone of indifference" results. It defines a repertoire of actions which the individual is willing to take on behalf of the organization to which he is relatively indifferent (Barnard, 1938; Simon, 1945; March and Simon, 1958).

This description provides a useful starting point, but suffers from a rather static view of the relationships between organizations and individuals. In fact, both are changing over time and their relationship at any moment involves the intersection of those two processes (Freeman, 1982). Organizations develop through phases which involve, at the very least, an early entrepreneurial phase when someone is planning the organization, seeking resources, making strategic choices about product, market, technology, location and so on. There also is likely to be a start-up phase where the organization suffers from disorganization and resource scarcity. For those that survive the first two, there is a growth phase. And finally, somewhere along the way, a transition occurs from entrepreneurial leadership.

As an organization moves from phase to phase, the degrees of freedom for managers decline and the organization becomes relatively more inert. People who join the organization along the way move through a personal life cycle which involves patterned career changes. Engineers leaving the university with state of the art technical skills find that those skills atrophy and some of them move into management. Others become staff analysts and administrative support people.

As individuals go through these changes, their willingness to take risks probably changes substantially. We can expect this because their domestic responsibilities change and because of aging. In addition, tenure with a particular employer usually brings rights and privileges which would be lost on exit. These include obvious material considerations such as health plan coverage and vesting in retirement and profit-sharing plans. Less obvious perhaps are the social status implications of leaving, particularly to found a new firm. The risk of failure is likely to be a hoary prospect for someone who has risen with an organization successful enough to have survived. Furthermore, such a person has a position in the community where he or she resides (and within his own family) that may be jeopardized by exiting his current employment situation.

All of these arguments seem rather straightforward. Equally straightforward is the recognition that all the arguments apply better to winners than losers in the employing organization. Paradoxically, these winners are the most likely to receive favorable review by outsiders from whom they will have to generate support if they are to become entrepreneurs. Virtually every venture capitalist who cares to have his or her views on the subject published, and all of those we have interviewed, say that they look more closely at the experience of the entrepreneur than at the numbers in his business plan.

This tells us that the current employer provides the potential entrepreneur with much that is required to start a new firm. Furthermore, many of the qualities required to gather resources, attract other people, and make intelligent strategic choices are worth more in the same business as the parent firm than they are in other businesses. Organizations learn by doing. Individuals within these organizations carry some of that organizational knowledge with them. This can be expected to the degree that the skills and knowledge are rooted in a technology or business culture which is difficult for outsiders to fathom.

The point of all this is that entrepreneurs are not likely to be randomly sampled from the human population of any particular parent organization. Even if intelligence and willingness to take risks are randomly distributed or even inversely correlated with level in the hierarchy, we would expect the upper middle ranks of managers to supply the bulk of these prospective entrepreneurs.

B. The Better Part of Valor

Albert Hirschman argues that there is an entropic tendency in organizations, that they are "permanently and randomly subject to decline and decay . . ." (1970:15). This can be expressed as a decline of quality in the goods and services they produce which provokes customers and members to exit or to exercise voice in protest (i.e., to stay with the organization and change its policies so as to reverse the slide). Hirschman is not actually addressing the behavior of employees of firms, but much of what he says makes sense if, like Simon and his colleagues, we consider employees and their participation in the firm as a close analogue to consumers making purchasing decisions.[2]

What Hirschman means by "decline" comes very close to what population ecologists mean by "inertia." His discussion makes it clear that he is concerned with a drop in quality relative to other providers of the product in question. Customers are more likely to exit than exercise voice when there are large numbers of sellers producing at levels of quality bracketing the firm in question. Speaking up to change current managerial practices is an art, and that art must be continuously renewed as protests about the same issues voiced in the same way rapidly lose their effect. Consequently, exit tends to drive out voice (Hirschman, 1970:76). On the other hand, after exit is exercised, voice is no longer an option. For example, a decline in the quality of public schooling often drives parents to transfer their children to private schools. The people most likely to do this are the most quality sensitive, those with the most "consumer surplus," and are most likely to have the political skills necessary to translate protest into remedial action.[3]

Viewed from the perspective of employees, an organization that demands more is likely to lose its most marginal people. When the quality of inducements declines, whether exit or voice results is largely a matter of alternatives and the conditions under which the individual entered the firm. Inducements having to do with the quality of working life, such as the degree of technical challenge in the work or the satisfaction resulting from deep friendships, are most likely to generate voice, rather than exit because gauging the alternatives is difficult. Reductions in relative wage rates are easier to assess and more likely to lead to exit.

From the point of view of management, voice provokes more time-consuming response than exit. "Lazy monopolies," react to the absence of competition by lowering quality. They are managed by officials who prefer some competition to provide alternatives for those who would resort to voice without them. (Hirschman, 1970:58–9). In other words, exit of obstreperous is preferred over voice.

This suggests that firms can expect to lose the employees who have the least to give when they demand higher levels of performance. They are likely to lose key people, those who have the most to give, when they lower the quality of inducements. They can expect to engender the greatest internal dissent from exactly such people, when the least measurable aspects of inducements slide. Top managers in such companies will be tempted to encourage such losses to lower the costs and discomforts associated with voice.

Elite firms, those offering the most challenging work assignments and the richest array of social rewards, face the greatest difficulty in maintaining excellence according to this line of reasoning. But there are some important differences between employees and customers. First, employee exit is not necessarily a binary phenomenon. Employees may withdraw participation in subtle ways. Loss of enthusiasm and initiative may be more severe than actual attrition because such behaviors send out less clear signals than quitting. Second, employees carry assets with them when they leave. In fact, as we will argue below, the knowledge and reputation required for entrepreneurial activity is often only attainable through direct involvement in an organization already in the business. This is most likely when complicated technologies or market structures serve as barriers to entry.

Organizations vary enormously in the kinds of inducements provided for and demanded of employees. For some, the exchange hardly goes beyond pay for labor. For others, being an employee involves deep commitments of a permanent variety. Being a Roman Catholic priest, for example, is not simply a matter of having a job working for the Church. Some scholars have referred to these circumstances as "greedy institutions" or "strong culture" organizations (Coser, 1974). The relevant point here is that such organizations impose a very large overhead cost on themselves and on everyone who works for them. This overhead cost is the price organizations pay to maintain themselves over time. One way to look at this is to consider organizations as subject to daily dissolution.

Each day, when the doors open and employees arrive, all organizations must renew themselves. People have to find their way back into a social structure which has gone temporarily dormant. The more elaborate that structure is, and the deeper its involvement with the people who work in it (or belong to it), the more effort is expended in maintaining the system. Individuals who do not fully accept the worth of such a social system are likely to exit soon after arrival, or as the system elaborates over time. This leads to a form of radicalization. Those whose voices would protest increases in the variety and depth of contributions demanded by the organization are driven out. The remainder are likely to tolerate extreme demands.

Organizations create their own competition by providing the skills and background that provide credibility for the entrepreneur. They provide the knowledge of opportunity by placing that person in a position to know about unserved or badly served markets. And often, as they begin to slide, they provide the motivation for exit as well.

None of this bears directly on the nature of the organization started by someone who exits, or whether that person can be expected to start a new organization. Partly, these issues depend on the environment and its resistance to attempts at organization-building. We turn to this issue next.

C.   Liability of Newness

In any given time interval, new organizations die at higher rates than old organizations; and organizations with a new organizational form die at higher rates than organizations with older forms. Arthur Stinchcombe (1965) is generally regarded as the source of these observations.[4] Why should new organizations, and particularly new organizations of a new kind, be at such higher risk of failure? The answers to this question are of two varieties: internal and external.

One internal reason is that new organizations devote time and human energy toward building role relationships. A division of labor has to be created and inconsistencies must be settled. Roles develop partly in response to the people who fill them. These people are new, and adjusting the structure to them takes time. Furthermore, because the organizational members are new, relationships of trust must be developed, and these too, take time. Finally, this division of labor imposes coordination problems which require the development of control mechanisms. These are also easier to set up if an existing model is followed.

External reasons involve relationships with other organizations and building legitimacy in the broader social system. They also involve costs associated with the labor market. Suppliers of credit and raw materials must be persuaded that the new organization is well managed. Customers must learn of the new organization's existence and they must learn about its products or services.

The person who starts the organization—the business firm entrepreneur—faces these problems at exactly the moment when he or she is most taxed in terms of time, energy and finances. Another way of looking at this is to note that people running existing organizations can devote their full energies to out-competing the new organization.

All of these difficulties are exacerbated when the new organization is unique. A price is paid in these terms for everything about a new organization that is different from the existing ways of organizing. The entrepreneur trades off that price against a competitive edge which some innovation may provide.

Obviously, there are great advantages to keeping innovation to the minimum required to provide such an edge. The more experience one has, the more reluctance to innovate. If one does not know the established ways of doing business, one has little to lose by experimenting. The advantage of experience is bound up in such industry-specific knowledge.

IV.   STRUCTURE OF THE SEMICONDUCTOR INDUSTRY

We have been studying the U.S. merchant market semiconductor industry for two important reasons. First, the industry's markets and pattern of technical change have generated extraordinary volatility in its organizational populations. Foundings and failures abound. Second, the industry is important from a policy perspective. Semiconductor devices are essential ingredients in many other sophisticated products.

To understand the process of entrepreneurship in the semiconductor industry, some historical context is necessary. In the next section, we briefly describe the history of the industry. Along the way, we will identify the major variants which are observable in the technology.

A. History

The industry's history is usually traced to 1947, when the transistor was invented at Bell Laboratories by John Bardeen, Walter Brattain and William Shockly.[5] The Nobel Prize in Physics was awarded to these three in recognition of their achievement. The parent company of Bell Laboratories, American Telephone and Telegraph, settled an antitrust legal action with the federal government. Among its provisions was an agreement to license the transistor and related proprietary technology, an agreement which took effect in 1951. The original licensees of transistor technology included such large, established companies as RCA, General Electric, Raytheon, Motorola, and Sylvania. Texas Instruments (TI), a small company concerned mainly with oil exploration technology, was also one of this original group, which numbered eighteen in 1954.

The early transistor was made of germanium, not silicon. Intolerances of heat variations greatly limited its application. Compared with the vacuum tubes they replaced, early transistors were also about twenty times as expensive.

After the invention of the transistor itself, the next important technical innovation was the development of a commercial process for growing silicon crystals, and the silicon transistor was born. The breakthrough came from tiny Texas Instruments. Between 1954 and 1958 TI had a monopoly on the production of silicon transistors. Its sales grew from $7.6 million in 1950 to $232.7 million ten years later. Earnings rose from $348,000 to $15.5 million during this same period. Transistors directly account for about half that growth. Substantial spillover benefits were generated for TI's other products as well.

In 1960, Fairchild semiconductor announced (and patented) the planar production process. Fairchild had been founded a few years earlier by a group of refugees from William Shockley's unsuccessful attempt at entrepreneurship—Shockley Transistor. Shockley had assembled a group of brilliant technical minds, many of whom were drawn away from Bell Labs. Of the original two hundred employees, none had substantial nontechnical business experience.[6] With venture capital provided by Sherman Fairchild, the CEO of Fairchild Camera, these renegades founded the semiconductor company which, along with TI, was most responsible for the commercial development of much of the early semiconductor technology.[7]

The planar process is noteworthy because it greatly reduced the linkage between product development and production process renovation. Because production was quite capital-intensive, even in those days, weakening this link did much to reduce the uncertainty of the business. At the same time, the planar process was the necessary advance for commercial production of the integrated circuit, which Fairchild and TI had announced the previous year. Through cross-licensing agreements, the two small manufacturers were able to steal a march on the other producers, many of which were much larger and had been conducting active research in the field for several years.

We return now to the question raised in the introduction. Why did the large electronics companies allow these upstarts to run away with this collection of golden egg producers? One answer lies in the organization of their development efforts.[8] The typical pattern in the large, diversified companies was to house the semiconductor development effort in the vacuum tube manufacturing division. This made sense because transistors were, after all, substitutes for vacuum tubes. The problem is that vacuum tube manufacturing is perhaps the epitome of mass production. The confrontation of organizational systems analyzed by Burns and Stalker (1961) was virtually inevitable. From the point of view of the tube division managers, the risk and expense of semiconductor development combined with the loose, fluid form of organization it almost certainly engendered, must have seemed like folly—worse, it must have seemed like subversion.

In mass manufacturing, detailed controls and discipline are essential for efficiency. Long production runs of standardized products make for the good life for managers in such situations. Early transistor manufacturing did not fit these preferences well. They became obsolete quickly, in runs which produced mostly unsalable trash. Early transistor engineers placed little stock in managerial controls. Consequently, these firms strangled their own development efforts and the bean stalk was in place for the entrepreneurs of the semiconductor business to climb.

While most of these companies were small in 1960, by 1970 they had grown into substantial business enterprises. Acquiring them or squeezing them out of the market was not impossible by any means, but either strategy for taking over the business was bound to be expensive and difficult. Furthermore, the technology continued to develop. New firms were started by employees exiting the large businesses. "Thus," Levin notes, "in the well-known geneology of Silicon Valley, Bell Labs begat Shockley Transistor, Shockley begat Fairchild, Fairchild begat Signetics, General Microelectronics, and Intel, among others, and each of these fourth generation firms has numerous progeny of its own" (Levin, 1982:28).

The next major innovation was the microprocessor, introduced by Intel in 1971. The LSI circuit (large scale integrated circuit), development of low-power CMOS technology, and rapid advances in analog devices all provided new avenues for technological and market development. Today, semiconductor foundings occur regularly as do acquisitions and bankruptcies.

Even a short historical sketch should not be concluded without mentioning the advent of foreign competition, principally from Japanese manufacturers. These companies have emerged as serious competitors for United States manufacturers. Although they have been active primarily in production of computer memory chips, the largest-volume branch of the industry, they are also beginning to constitute a challenge in other semiconductor markets. This has led many United States manufacturers to concentrate on proprietary applications of the technology, where designs are intended less for "off the shelf" marketing than for systems integration in at least a semi-custom manner.

B.   Competitive Structure

The U.S. industry has long been divided into two components: the merchant and captive market producers. The former produce and sell semiconductor devices on the open market. The latter produce only for their own use. Examples of captive producers are International Business Machines and Hewlett-Packard. Both are large producers by world standards. These firms are difficult to study because they do not release detailed data on the devices they produce or on the volume of their production. Curiously, all of the large Japanese producers are diversified at least into other branches of the electronics industry. None is a specialist as are most of the American merchant producers. This is due in part to the role semiconductor production plays in the overall planned entrance of Japan into high technology industry. Japan originally invested in semiconductors as a step toward active competition in the computer business (Zysman and Borrus, 1983). So while U.S. computer companies became involved in captive production, undoubtedly to economize on transaction costs, the Japanese did directly the opposite, entering the merchant market to underwrite computer development.

One of the most notable characteristics of the U.S. market is a demand made by customers for second sources of new devices. The second source is required because of the very high development costs often associated with the use of new devices by customers. The second source provides some protection against opportunism. It also provides some protection for the vagaries of the production process. New devices are often difficult to produce in volume and shortages of the most advanced technology have always plagued the industry.

Second sourcing is controversial because it means giving away proprietary technology and shortening leads in development over rivals. The obvious response is to develop a second source that is not a viable competitor. Semiconductor companies have been known to set up sham producers, selling them chips covertly, and allowing them to resell those chips as if they had been manufactured by a second source. More often, as one CEO recently told us, the ploy is to find a low-quality producer to license, one who is good enough to serve as a credible alternative, but not good enough at manufacturing or marketing to provide serious competition. Captive producers do not have to deal with such problems, but they have to be able to fully capitalize the cost of development.

Second sourcing is important for present purposes not only because it is a dominant competitive condition in the U.S. industry, but also because it provides a mechanism for small, new firms to generate business and establish credibility—in short, to avoid the liability of newness. By second sourcing, a new firm can gain cash flow and a place in the market without enduring the cost of research and development and the long time horizons such development efforts require.

C. Competition and Technology

Semiconductor manufacturing decisions are driven by yields, the proportion of a given production run which is salable. Most often, inspection generates three categories of products: military grade, industrial grade, and trash. A new chip still in the development stage may only produce one usable device from more than 400 fabricated on a wafer of silicon.

Commercial production runs begin with yields in the 10 percent range. With repeated runs, marginal costs drop. Each company has its own historical experience to use in estimating the speed with which yields rise with time and volume. Strategic decisions are routinely made on the basis of such experience and management consulting firms do not have to be called to show these engineers how to perform such calculations!

These companies are not immune to the ubiquitous problem of moving new products out of development into production. For semiconductor companies, as in virtually every other manufacturing organization, new designs lower plant efficiency. Conversely, development engineers are often reluctant to let new designs leave their laboratories until they have been cleaned to the point of aesthetic satisfaction. This problem is probably more serious among companies that emphasize being most technically advanced.

Finally, since the subject of this paper is entrepreneurship, we should note the very high turnover rates many of these companies experience. We have been told by high-level Silicon Valley semiconductor executives that the average in the region is about 20 percent per year. Most serious, of course, is the loss of key engineering and management personnel. One obvious way to shortcut a lag in development is to raid one's competition, enticing away key people with attractive bonuses and job assignments. As a result, many of the companies in Silicon Valley do not publish organization charts. Some formally prohibit drawing such charts even in private. Such volatility supports exit as a routine practice and makes entrepreneurial activity a subject of admiration for all but the high-level executives in the companies that lose key people.

D. Strategic Types

Our previous research, and a perusal of the analyses of the industry by management analysts, permits us to discern several strategic types, each of which involves organizational correlates and thereby constitutes a variety of organizational forms.

First, some firms do business by relying upon research acumen to introduce new products before their competitors do. Such companies are sometimes called "first movers" or "first to market strategists." The logic of this approach is to pioneer a market, setting an industry standard in the process. Having to meet such a standard usually slows competitors, who may be hot on the heels of the firm in question. Followers have to adjust their designs and processes to conform to the established standards. Until such time as followers make these adjustments, the focal firm has a monopoly (usually a duopoly with a second source) and can charge the expected inflated margins. Meanwhile, the first mover charges down the learning curve.

Another family of strategies involves concentrating on efficient production and sacrificing quick market entry for eventual efficiency. Such firms often price their version of the device below cost, in effect making believe their yields are higher than they are. In this way, they can spend resources directly on catching up. If their history is to manage their way to quick increases in yield, they can often catch up and seize the lion's share of a market as it reaches commodity production levels. The Japanese producers often follow such a strategy.

Within each of these families, there are specific variants that correspond to applications of the technology. Some of these are rather new. For example, gate array technology involves designing a chip with large numbers of gates which will not be used for most applications, but that can be cheaply modified to yield different performance from the central design. Some firms specialize in gate arrays, while others use them along with other variants of the technology. In all cases, however, the producer is offering a custom-designed chip.

Other firms specialize in custom-designing chips using conventional design and production techniques. The difference between these firms and the others is in organization rather than in technology. To succeed in this business firms must establish close working relationships with their customers. Such relationships usually take long periods of time to nurture. The people who maintain such relationships are typically older and more experienced, and have more technical training than sales people normally do in commodity production manufacturing. Such firms appear to be organized very much like Woodward's (1965) "unit and small batch" manufacturers.

Firms following the efficient producer line of strategy also range across a variety of subtypes. There are, of course, the large, established commodity producers such as TI and National Semiconductor. Recent start-ups have often focused on the manufacturing process itself. Such "silicon foundries," as they are called, do very little research or product development. Their engineering expertise is concentrated on the production process because they produce chips for customers who supply them with the detailed designs for the device. These foundries provide an important service for the industry because they allow new firms, specializing in new product innovation, to enter the business without the large capital investment manufacturing requires, particularly the wafer fabrication processes that lie at its heart.

V. VENTURE CAPITAL

This section argues that there are a variety of organizational forms providing venture capital in the United States. The populations of firms manifesting these forms are volatile. Expansion and contraction of populations reflect the niches they occupy, resource munificence or scarcity, and entrepreneurial behavior of the people who found and manage those organizations. As these populations change, the probability distribution for funding entrepreneurs shifts. So eventually, the population of high technology firms depends on the population of venture capital firms.

A. Organizational Forms

By far the best known vehicles for venture capital funding are organizations that create limited partnerships holding an equity interest in the new firm. Typically, such firms seek investments from limited partners in a fund with a fixed life expectancy, usually about ten years. This fund is then invested in a portfolio of firms with members of the venture capital firm taking an active role in management. These people serve as managing partners of the fund and often occupy positions on the boards of the firms in which they invest.

Observers of this industry generally divide financing activities into types based on a model of the life cycle of the new firm. Typically, these types include:

Seed	financing for concept development and writing a business plan
Start-up	product development and initial marketing, organizational development, have not shipped product yet
First Stage	after companies have expended initial capital, often in developing a prototype
Second Stage	expansion of a company which has expanding accounts receivable and inventories, usually not yet profitable

Mezzanine major expansion for growing sales volume and bor- derline profitable

Bridge company expects to sell stock in a public offering within a year.

Each of these stages of development offer different expected rates of return and risk, require different amounts of funding, and impose different managerial tasks on the venture capital firm. Differences in the level of funding by stage are presented in Table 1.

The majority of funds, about 60 percent of those seeking funding in 1983 by one count, are "balanced funds" (*Venture Capital Journal*, January, 1984). Specialization has been advancing in the industry, however. Many of these funds actually concentrate on second round financing. Seed and start-up specialists constitute 27 percent of the funds counted.

The largest source of funding for these partnerships consists of pension funds (30 percent of 1983 funding). Private individuals and families contributed an- other 21 percent. Foreign investors added 16 percent (up sharply from previous years). The last third of the investments came from corporations, insurance companies, endowments and foundations. Many of these institutional investors manage venture capital investments through venture capital subsidiaries and divi- sions. Many of these firms are providing capital to balanced funds, but others are investing directly, usually in later-round financing.

We can see, then, a variety of organizations providing venture capital. In addi- tion to balanced funds, there are seed money funds, some of which are affiliated with balanced funds, that specialize in second and later round financing. An ex- ample is Onset which seeks to invest its $5 million in new ventures. Nolan Bushnell, the founder of Atari, also runs what might be called an "incubator" firm. Services offered by such seed money specialists involve outright instruc- tion in the nontechnical aspects of running a business, strategy consulting (in-

Table 1. 1983 Venture Capital Disbursements by Stage

	% of Financings	% of Dollars	Average Size ($1000)
Seed	6	3	1,300
Start-up	16	11	2,000
Other Early	21	19	2,700
Second	29	35	3,850
Later	19	20	3,200
Leverage Buy Out/Acquisition/Other	9	12	*
	100	100	

Note: *This row includes leveraged buyouts, acquisitions and a small residual category. Average amount cannot be computed from available data but is somewhere around $4.5 million.
Source: Venture Capital Journal, May, 1984.

cluding advice on how to obtain later round financing), and support in the form of office space and secretarial services, bookkeeping and the like. A similar set of venture capital providers are individuals investing their own money, and money pooled from less formal arrangements than the classic venture capital providers arrange. Such "angels," as they are sometimes called, are separately very small, but in aggregate are major players in the business. What all these seed and start-up specialists have in common is the willingness to provide extensive nonfinancial services. They often act as partners of the entrepreneur.

Finally, we should note two kinds of fund-raising organizations supported by federal government programs. These are SBICs and MESBICs. The Small Business Administration cooperates with private investors in reducing the risk of small business investment. Because federal government money is involved, these organizations operate under somewhat tighter regulatory controls than most of the others. The speed with which they can fund a company is reduced in consequence.

As one shifts attention from early to late round financing, the amount of capital invested in each deal rises. The investment risk declines, as the liability of newness declines, and the return diminishes. The time horizon also moves closer. For many of these investors, the payoff comes when the company "goes public." The investment banking houses, which handle those offerings, enter the venture capital market as they move backward in time. Several venture capital firms have investment banking divisions. Mixing the two activities sometimes raises protests as there is a potential conflict of interest. Venture capitalists serve on the boards of the new firms, and have a fiduciary responsibility to other stockholders which may call for a later public offering, or an offering structured in such a way as to make the deal less lucrative for the investment banker. In general, investment bankers are organized around the one-time sale of stock, while venture capital firms organize funds around long-run commitments.

While there is definitely considerable mixing among the various kinds of deals, and generalism is a viable approach to the business, larger firms tend to appear later in the process. The earlier the involvement, the smaller the venture capital firm tends to be and the smaller its investment is (in absolute dollars).

Venture capital markets are extremely volatile. They respond to overall economic conditions as those conditions affect the supply of capital generally, and as they affect stock prices in particular. The volume of funding available is directly linked to the fortunes of new public offerings. When they do badly, funds dry up quickly. In addition, government tax policy has powerful effects on the market. Most of the vehicles for funding discussed above involve high risk for high returns—40 percent returns compounded annually are common. The logic of these businesses rests heavily on capital gains and the tax rate to which they are subject.

Two of the newer devices, Equity R&D Partnerships and R&D Limited Partnerships, are premised on a change in the Internal Revenue Code, Section 174 which allows investors to write off the entire investment in a limited partnership allocating its money to the development of a particular product or process (rather than simply investing in equity). This means that an individual can invest an amount usually around $100,000 and have the federal government underwrite the deal to the extent of that investor's income tax rate. Typically, people who can afford to put in $100,000 are running at 50 percent tax rates. So the federal government pays half the cost of the investment, reducing the risk substantially. Several firms specialize in these kinds of funds. With such changes in tax policy, the volume of funding available for investment grows and shrinks precipitously. A second dynamic consideration is the flow of requests for funding. Sometimes available money grows much faster than the supply of high quality investment opportunities. If the stock market receives new public offerings well, a wave of request for venture capital funding generally ensues. But of course, this wave is lagged in time.

Finally, the people who manage these funds comprise a rather inelastic supply of labor. Compared with the other resources we have been considering, managerial talent rises and falls slowly because it takes considerable time to build the business contacts. The legal and financial apparatus through which these investments are structured constitutes an elaborate technology which also takes much time to master. But most seriously limiting, according to most published discussions we have seen, is the broad experience required for sound judgment.

What happens when the volume of money to be invested expands rapidly, the number of entrepreneurs seeking funding expands, and the ability of existing firms and managers to process the investments is eclipsed? We expect to see a movement of less well-qualified people into the industry and a wave of entrepreneurial activity by founders of venture capital firms. As the population of firms expands, the number of independent decision-makers expands so each potential entrepreneur, and each seeker of later round financing, has more targets for proposals. The probability of gaining some financing from one of them is, in the aggregate, much higher. So we would expect to see a wave of foundings, particularly high technology foundings, many of which would not otherwise be funded. A subsequent wave of failures is to be expected.

If all of this is true, and it is capable of empirical testing, we see the population of high technology firms (and others that receive venture capital funding) as depending in part on the rate of entrepreneurship which depends on the available money to be invested, and on the number of firms managing the investments. The population of firms expands as a result of an entrepreneurial process based on similar conditions to those which affect the populations of high technology companies—a cyclically expanding market and a complicated technology that changes rapidly.

Activating both processes is a flow of people out of existing organizations into new and smaller organizations. The factors motivating those people to exit or stay with their current employers involve comparisons between current inducements and contributions with those expected in more risky but more flexible new ventures.

VI.   CONCLUSIONS

This paper ends by considering an odd, but well-known phenomenon. A forty-year-old division manager, or managing engineer for a large company is being paid about $80,000 per year, and receives perhaps another $100,000 in direct support. That person leaves to start a firm and, within two years, raises half a million dollars in funding. Two years later, he or she raises eight million more. Why is this person who was worth only $180,000 per year to the previous employer suddenly worth these millions?

Part of the answer, of course, is that the departing employee carries more information than organizational models and awareness of opportunities. He or she also carries proprietory company knowledge. One would think, however, that the parent company would be in far better shape to exploit this knowledge than the individual would. How can one start a new firm, enduring all those inconveniences and difficulties underlying the liability of newness, and not be out-competed by the parent firm? If this were not the case, entrepreneurship would be very uncommon. The parent firm holds all the competitive high cards.

It seems apparent that one of the few advantages held by the entrepreneur is speed. It is simply quicker to start a new firm and move into a new technological or market niche than it is to change the course of an existing (large) firm and move into that same niche.

If this is true, we are confronted by the interesting and complicated question of how it can be that technology transfer within organizations (i.e., across internal boundaries) is slower and probably more costly than the same transfer between organizations (i.e., across external boundaries). Similarly, the capital markets are able to allocate funding to firms with high efficiency, but the reallocation process within them often breaks down. Good ideas do not receive the funds they need to turn into successful projects and funding is often very slow. Venture capitalists trade on these obstructions. From a personal point of view, such characteristics of organizations create frustration, political disputation and lost opportunity. These factors generate entrepreneurs.

ACKNOWLEDGMENTS

This report was written with support from National Science Foundation grant ISI-8218013 and SES-8109382 and from the Institute of Industrial Relations at the University of California, Berkeley. Thanks are due to Martha Reimer for research assistance in the preparation of this paper.

NOTES

1. This research involves statistical analyses of product sales and financial data on the United States merchant market producers and interviews in the Silicon Valley firms in which strategy and structure were the main subjects.

2. We will consider some differences between the circumstances of customers and employees as we consider Hirschman's arguments in detail.

3. This means that they can afford to pay more than the actual price for the product in question. They are not marginal consumers in this sense.

4. See Freeman, Carroll and Hannan (1984) for an empirical analysis of this phenomenon.

5. This historical sketch draws heavily on Brittain and Freeman (1980), Levin (1982), and Wilson et al. (1980). Interested readers should also see Tilton (1971), Webbink (1977), Braun and McDonald (1978).

6. Personal communication from Gordon Moore.

7. This company was eventually managed as a subsidiary of Fairchild Camera and Instrument, but the original relationship was one of venture capital investor and entrepreneur.

8. Much of this line of argument was provided by Lester Hogan in a personal communication.

REFERENCES

Ansoff, I. and Stewart, J. M. (1967), "Strategies for a Technology-Based Business." *Harvard Business Review* 45:71–83.

Barnard, C. I. (1938), *The Functions of the Executive*. Cambridge, MA: Harvard University Press.

Braun, E. and McDonald, S. (1978), *Revolution in Miniature*. Cambridge: Cambridge University Press.

Brittain, J. W. and Freeman, J. H. (1980), "Organizational Proliferation and Density Dependent Selection." In John R. Kimberly and Robert H. Miles (Eds.), *The Organizational Life Cycle*. San Francisco: Jossey-Bass.

Burns, T. and Stalker, G. M. (1961), *The Management of Innovation*. London: Tavistock.

Coser, L. A. (1974), *Greedy Institutions: Patterns of Undivided Commitment*. New York: The Free Press.

Cyert, R. M. and March, J. G. (1963), *A Behavioral Theory of the Firm*. Englewood Cliffs, NJ: Prentice-Hall.

Freeman, J. (1982), "Organizational Life Cycles and Natural Selection Processes." In Barry M. Staw and Lawrence L. Cummings (Eds.), *Research in Organizational Behavior*, Vol. 4. Greenwich, CT: JAI Press.

Freeman, J., Carroll, G. R., and Hannan, M. T. (1983), "The Liability of Newness: Age Dependence in Organizational Death Rates." *American Sociological Review* 48:692–710.

Freeman, J. and Hannan, M. T. (1983), "Niche Width and the Dynamics of Organizational Populations." *American Journal of Sociology* 88:1116–45.

Hannan, M. T. and Freeman, J. (1977), "The Population Econology of Organizations." *American Journal of Sociology* 82:929–64.

Hannan, M. T. and Freeman, J. (1984), "Structural Inertia and Organizational Change." *American Sociological Review* 49:149–64.

Hirschman, A. O. (1970), *Exit, Voice, and Loyalty*. Cambridge, MA: Harvard University Press.

Katz, D. and Kahn, R. L. (1966), *The Social Psychology of Organizations*. New York: John Wiley (Rev. 1978).

Levin, R. C. (1982), "The Semiconductor Industry." In Richard R. Nelson (Ed.), *Government and Technical Progress: A Cross-Industry Analysis*. Elmsford, NY: Pergammon Press.

March, J. G. and Simon, H. A. (1958), *Organizations*. New York: John Wiley.

Simon, H. (1945), *Administrative Behavior*. New York: The Free Press.

Stinchcombe, A. L. (1965), "Social Structure and Organizations." In James G. March (Ed.), *Handbook of Organizations*. Chicago: Rand McNally.

Tilton, J. E. (1971), *International Diffusion of Technology: The Case of Semiconductors*. Washington, DC: The Brookings Institution.

Webbink, D. W. (1977), "The Semiconductor Industry: A Survey of Structure, Conduct, and Performance." Washington, DC: Federal Trade Commission.

Williamson, O. E. (1975), *Markets and Hierarchies: Analysis and Antitrust Implications*. New York: The Free Press.

Wilson, R. W., Ashton, P. K., and Egan, T. P. (1980), *Innovation, Competition, and Government Policy in the Semiconductor Industry*. Lexington, MA: Lexington Books.

Woodward, J. (1965), *Industrial Organization: Theory and Practice*. New York: Oxford University Press.

Zysman, J., Borrus, M., and Millstein, J. (1982), "U.S.-Japanese Competition in the Semiconductor Industry." Institute of International Studies, University of California-Berkeley.

Chapter 4

THE DIALOGUE ON ENTREPRENEURS AND ORGANIZATIONS

In his paper "Entrepreneurs as Organizational Products: Semiconductor Firms and Venture Capital Firms," John Freeman examines the tension that can exist between entrepreneurs and organizations, particularly large corporations. His study investigates semiconductor electronics firms and venture capital firms. He is concerned with the environment that encourages opportunity and innovation and why some firms fail to provide it, forcing would-be entrepreneurs to exit. Freeman points out that when they do leave, they carry with them valuable knowledge, skills and training that make new firms formidable competitors for the parent firm.

These issues raised by Freeman are extremely important for understanding the process of innovation, entrepreneurship, and the organizations in which they can occur. The dialogue discussion of Rosenberg's paper emphasized that a fluid environment was necessary for entrepreneurship, to allow for rapid responses to new market opportunities and to tolerate risky endeavors where products and processes are not well-defined. Under such conditions, the division of labor is limited because new innovations are closely linked to the entrepreneur who must necessarily be involved in most aspects of production and marketing. The payoffs to the entrepreneur for success, despite the risks involved, are high levels of personal satisfaction, prestige and income. As described in Freeman's paper,

Advances in the Study of Entrepreneurship, Innovation,
and Economic Growth, Volume 1, pages 53-58.
Copyright © 1986 by JAI Press Inc.
ISBN: 0-89232-703-0

these conditions are often in conflict with the organizational structure, control systems and management policies of large corporations. In their reaction to Freeman's paper, the dialogue participants identified a number of specific problems and offered some possible solutions. They differed, though, in their perceptions of whether large corporations were receptive to entrepreneurial activities within their organizations.

I. DO LARGE CORPORATIONS PROVIDE AN ENVIRONMENT FOR ENTREPRENEURS?

Milton Stewart had the most pessimistic view. He argued that the layers of committees, review officers and other control mechanisms were formidable barriers to innovation. If an entrepreneur within the corporation has a new idea, he has to make his way through all those layers, and if he does, his only hope is that there is still an entrepreneur at the top to say yes. If there isn't, his idea will go nowhere unless he leaves.[1] Jack Thorne added that the controls placed on projects in their early stages by large firms tend to thwart entrepreneurial activity. Those same controls may be needed in later stages, but imposing them on a new project can impact the project's success significantly.[2] Thorne insisted that entrepreneurship in its early stages requires the kind of environment typically promoted by venture capitalists in working with small, new firms—a flexible organization that allows for learning and rapid, intuitive responses to new market conditions.

Norman Auerbach responded that the differences between large and small firms were a matter of degree and not absolutes. He argued that in large, well-run organizations, executives seek to achieve objectives in terms of established priorities. If entrepreneurs are frustrated because management won't pursue new product development, for example, it may be that management does not view the idea as feasible within the order of priorities, rather than an inflexibility toward change. Auerbach argued that in the long run, management may be contributing just as much or maybe more, if they pursue their objectives for product development and other improvements. He insisted that if the priorities are set, a good management team cannot listen to every new idea because they won't be successful in achieving their plans and goals. Whether or not management has selected the correct priorities, however, is another issue, but it should not be argued that large organizations are a poor environment for entrepreneurs.[3]

Most of the participants thought differently. There was a recurring theme that the culture or management controls, priorities, and compensation schemes of corporations posed important problems for internal entrepreneurship. Morton Kamien observed that even when there is emphasis in large firms on developing new products, managerial controls inevitably emerge so "you spend more time worrying about your mistakes or the problems you create than the possibilities that you may create real value for the company."[4] Normally, he argued, people will stay in a large organization for five or six years, will learn the business, and then, if they're really good, will want to move on and run their own operations.

Both Morton Kamien and Ed Zajac pointed to the problem of providing adequate monetary rewards to successful innovators within traditional corporate compensation plans. Zajac described an experience in Bell Laboratories where it was announced that people would be encouraged to develop innovative proposals to be funded outside the usual budgetary framework. This was to create an entrepreneurial, small company atmosphere within the Labs, but it still required that business plans be submitted for approval to many layers of management. Moreover, there was the issue of how to reward those people within the existing bureaucratic evaluation scheme, and he added, "the monetary incentives were sort of pitiful, really."[5]

Because of these frustrations, many capable employees leave. Jack Thorne commented: "I would propose as a hypothesis that one of the reasons for this is that young entrepreneurial people . . . learn the game very early when they're in their late 20s or early 30s working for a small corporation; they've been in marketing, engineering, production; they've met the financial sources, the bankers, the venture capitalists, and they've been very close as a mentor to the entrepreneur who started the company, so I would say entrepreneurs breed more entrepreneurs . . . "[6]

Large corporations are under competitive pressure to innovate, and the loss of entrepreneurial talent has led to a variety of responses. Firms clearly realize that when entrepreneurs split off to start their own firms, they take company assets with them, ranging from general know-how to actual product designs. Accordingly, large firms are often hostile toward venture capitalists. The latter provide options to entrepreneurs outside the company and encourage them to leave.

One common response is for large firms to spin off separate sub-units, designed solely for research and development, with flexible management policies. For example, Karl Eller noted that Motorola became so concerned about people leaving the corporation and starting their own companies that the firm formed an entrepreneurial division that would examine new products and ideas.[7] Similar examples were described for Lockheed, General Electric, and Westinghouse.

The flexibility of spin-off operations was confirmed by a Westinghouse official in comments related by Jack Thorne. Because of more personal interaction and fewer bureaucratic controls, he was able to "accomplish a great deal ten times faster with one-tenth the money. He has been given almost total freedom, but not the compensation that you would expect if he were an independent entrepreneur."[8] One reason for the lower compensation, noted by Karl Eller was that entrepreneurs within large corporations are not exposed to the same risks as those who are independent, and thus outside the financial support of the corporation. Hence, higher levels of compensation, in part, compensate for higher levels of risk.[9]

Another response to the competitive pressure for innovation is for large firms to acquire smaller firms and their technology. Indeed, Charles James argued that the most common ways for major firms to secure "their window on technology" are through acquisition of or investment in smaller private ventures, rather than "dabbling in internal entrepreneurship."[10] While acquisitions are common, there are problems. John Freeman described the case of a small firm that was acquired by General Electric. Almost immediately, the managerial controls and procedures of the larger organization began to impose constraints upon the more freewheeling activities of the innovative smaller firm. The acquired firm "had the reputation of being . . . a technology leader, a fairly high flier within its specialized part of the industry before GE took it over . . . within two weeks people started asking [each engineer in the company] to justify his time, plan out his time expenditures for months in advance, and it wasn't long before the president . . . split, starting a little company . . . and then went around raiding all the design engineers and key managers . . . [11]

As a result of the problems faced by innovators within large corporate settings, many entrepreneurs seek to avoid acquisition by turning to venture capitalists as an alternative source of funding and expansion. Paul Uselding characterized the venture capitalist in this case as a protector: "He is like the white knight riding in, the firm gets to a certain level of development and instead of finding capital or succor by being clasped to the bosom of a large firm, the venture capitalist . . . says I have an option for you; you can keep control of the key and the sheriff won't get you if you do business with me."[12]

Direct investment in new ventures by large firms is another way of securing technology and avoiding some of the motivation problems described above. Again, General Electric and Citicorp were cited as among the major contributors to venture capital, through holding investments in a large portfolio of small, technically-oriented companies. Their motivation is to receive the benefits derived from the technical innovations of these small companies by acquiring 30 to 40 percent of the equity. In these operations, General Electric and Citicorp normally invest with four or five other venture capitalists.[13]

Louis Pondy and Nathan Rosenberg summarized the problems of large organizations and entrepreneurship, and the roles major corporations play in the process of technological change. Whether they successfully (though perhaps uncommonly) provide incubators through spin offs, drive out entrepreneurs to found new companies, provide seed venture capital, or acquire small, innovative firms, they are essential in the development of new ventures, particularly to bring them to commercial feasibility. Both Pondy and Rosenberg commented that more research was needed on the differential roles of small and large firms in the process of technological change.[14]

II.   AS NEW FIRMS GROW, MUST THEY BE LESS INNOVATIVE? WHAT CAN BE DONE?

The dialogue discussion turned to the life-cycle problems faced by new firms. Morton Kamien led the discussion by noting a paradox. An entrepreneur starts off wanting to be his own boss, to be a success, and ultimately to become part of the establishment. Once the firm grows and is successful, Kamien asked if it is possible to sustain the entrepreneurial environment. Does the success of a venture inevitably lead to a more structured and less innovative environment?[15]

Each of the entrepreneur participants related their experiences and the growing pains encountered in their companies. For example, Dick Spencer described the slow increase in bureaucratic controls within his firm, SLM Industries. One incident involved the hiring of a new comptroller who had previously worked for Chrysler and who brought many of the larger firm's operating procedures: "We've gone to written memos . . . a lot of feedback on controls like purchasing . . . you have to fill out a requisition . . . a day or two later you get notification that the purchase order went through . . . I used to run down to the local electronics store . . . just load up my pockets and tell them to bill the company."[16] Spencer noted that there have been complaints by company engineers about the constraints of the new procedures.

Tom Whitney described Hewlett-Packard's efforts to maintain an entrepreneurial atmosphere by developing a corporate laboratory that was not a research laboratory, but more of "a playground for some of the founders." Out of that laboratory, innovative efforts were pursued that propelled the company into its growth. For instance, the HP35 pocket calculator came from the corporate research laboratories. Whitney, however, pointed out that Hewlett-Packard has had more difficulty in its computer operations, which are "a much more complex business, and require the coordination across multiple functions, software, peripherals, main frames, networks; it has been a very difficult task for Hewlett-Packard to pull together that same innovative spirit that it's been able to develop in the instrumentation business."[17] Similarly, he noted that Apple Computer is still struggling with the problem of how to remain an entrepreneurial company.

Whitney predicted that beyond a certain size, management issues become paramount and an organization starts losing its innovative spirit. Robert Higgs responded that the need for bureaucratic controls and employee monitoring as firm size increased was a recognized problem and that, in this area at least, there was active research by academics on the consequences.[18]

Other remedies were mentioned. Tim Day of Bar-S Foods acknowledged the need for internal controls to maintain efficiency. To insure that management understands the obstacles placed by the corporate structure upon the organization, he assigns each top official with a line responsibility for two weeks each year, so they "can see . . . what we may have created at the corporate level and what it's like living with some of those demands."[19] Karl Eller, Almarin Phillips, and Warren Rustand emphasized the role of the CEO in maintaining an entrepreneurial climate to offset inertia within large organizations. They argued that a major factor in determining a company's success in innovation, regardless of its size, is whether the CEO has a vital interest in pursuing high-risk policies. Moreover, the CEO can decide to maintain an informal communications flow, develop ap-

propriate incentives, such as cash for performance and opportunity for ownership, and can identify and hire people who are creative and use their talents
within the framework of the company. The CEO has to consciously decide to
maintain an entrepreneurial-type organization.[20]

The issues raised by the paper and the dialogue regarding entrepreneurship
within large organizations are serious ones, with important implications for the
direction and nature of technological change in the United States. The participants agreed that more research by business school faculties was needed to
isolate the problems of the organizational structure in large firms and identify
possible solutions for promoting entrepreneurship.

Two other areas requiring attention are venture capital markets and public policy toward entrepreneurship. Both topics are addressed by Willard Carleton in
the following chapter.

NOTES

1. Stewart, Transcript, Eller Center Dialogue, Session II November 29, 1984, pp. 139–140
2. Thorne, p. 145
3. Auerbach, pp. 163–164
4. Kamien, pp. 124–127
5. Zajac, pp. 130–131
6. Thorne, p. 146
7. Eller, pp. 135–136
8. Thorne, pp. 144–145
9. Eller, p. 148
10. James, pp. 142–143
11. Freeman, p. 155
12. Uselding, p. 152
13. Kamien, pp. 128–129
14. Pondy, pp. 170–171
15. Kamien, p. 191
16. Spencer, p. 205
17. Whitney, pp. 212–213
18. Higgs, pp. 235–236
19. Day, p. 226
20. Eller, p. 119; Phillips, p. 151; and Rustand, pp. 206–209, 239–240.

Chapter 5

ISSUES AND QUESTIONS INVOLVING VENTURE CAPITAL

Willard T. Carleton

I. INTRODUCTION

The initial question that arises in an investigation of the venture capital financing process is definitional. What do we mean by "venture capital investment"? For purposes of this paper I mean investment in new, small and risky companies (especially those based on commercial application of technological innovations). It is clear that the supply of capital to finance such investments is critical to the functioning of the United States' economy in terms of capital formation, economic growth, and competitive adaptation in world markets. In this paper, I intend to clarify, from the analytical perspectives of a financial economist, the structure of the venture capital financing decision process. From this structure, it may then be possible (through model manipulation, if you will) to assess the impact of various policies such as alternative tax measures on the venture capital market.

The decision process in venture capital has five critical characteristics. First, the venture capitalist is typically faced with a long-term commitment of funds with little possibility of withdrawal if things go badly, and the likelihood of being called upon to supply more financing if things go well. This leads to a sequential investment problem that can be described as a sequence of "rounds" of

Advances in the Study of Entrepreneurship, Innovation,
and Economic Growth, Volume 1, pages 59-70.
Copyright © 1986 by JAI Press Inc.
ISBN: 0-89232-703-0

financing, with information flows occurring between rounds. Second, in each investment, the venture capitalist enters a continuing sequence of information-gathering and decision-making concerning the project. Initially, he must decide whether the project is worth pursuing in detail; then, whether he should take a financial stake in it; then, whether he should increase his financial commitment, and so on. The common feature of these decisions is that at each decision point, a positive decision involves devoting additional resources to finding out more about the project, and a negative decision essentially involves terminating involvement in the project.

Third, for those projects which are financed, the venture capitalist enters a continuing process of evaluation, aid to the portfolio firm, and further decision-making. The most crucial of these subsequent decisions include termination of involvement in the project, incremental commitment of financing, and the selling of the project. Such decisions occur at least partially in response to events that are not entirely predictable at the start of the investment, such as a major breakthrough in innovations. In this way, the critical decision points, when viewed from the initial decision point of the venture capitalist, are stochastic.

A related, fourth characteristic of venture capital decision-making is that at each decision point, the venture capitalist must weigh the costs of the present and likely future commitments of resources to the project against the likely returns and risk. Ultimately, if the project proves successful, both the venture capitalist and the entrepreneur will be able to realize the returns to their investmments by selling their claims on the firm to other investors. The opportunity to do so arises when the portfolio firm has developed attributes that make it attractive to the regular securities markets as a traded company (either alone or in combination with some existing firm). The characteristics which facilitate this conversion are primarily size and profitability, but other issues such as control, continuing professional management, and legal restrictions may also play a part. Viewed in this way, the role of the venture capitalist is to bring new companies from infancy to early maturity, when they gain access to the regular financial markets.[1]

Finally, the fifth characteristic is that if the above decision problem were not fiendishly complicated already, the necessity for the venture capitalist to work out arrangements with the entrepreneur certainly makes it so. The entrepreneur himself faces a sequential decision problem, and at each point the project will proceed (with the entrepreneur's energy and venture capitalists' funds) only if both parties are in agreement. Thus, the task of financial contracts is to define input and output shares (e.g., earn-outs, warrants) to minimize future disagreements that would jeopardize otherwise promising projects. And in the midst of pervasive uncertainty is the awkward problem that there is information asymmetry between the entrepreneur and the investing public because the entrepreneur knows (or thinks he knows) more about the project's potential.

Frankly, the reason for adopting the format just described is that two other options which might otherwise be appealing cannot be applied. The first, an empirical investigation along the lines of the Federal Reserve's Flow of Funds studies, cannot be executed because available data on the venture capital market are fragmentary and informally gathered. The second, an employment of capitalist contemporary finance theory to describe entrepreneur/venture capitalist interaction fails for a more (professionally) embarrassing reason: by assumption, the theory denies most of the characteristics of venture capital decisions that make them interesting.

What all of the above suggests is that the best we (or at least I) can conclude in regard to the most salient determinants of the supply of venture capital—and whether they can be strongly influenced by public policy decision—is informed conjecture. All that is necessary for a model to be valid is that the people whose behavior is being described act as if they were following the model.

II. GROWTH AND CHANGE IN VENTURE CAPITAL FINANCING

By all reasonable measures, the venture capital business has grown incredibly during the past several years. Private venture capital funds secured $4.1 billion in 1983, compared with $1.7 billion in 1982, and only $39 million in 1977, according to data gathered by *Venture,* June 1984. (The compound growth rate from 1977 to 1983 was 117 percent per year.) At the same time, however, the *Venture* article also predicts that in 1984 only $2.5 billion will be raised by private venture capital funds. These figures represent just the tip of the iceberg. The same issue of *Venture* in June 1984 reported government estimates for fiscal 1983 of more than $20 billion raised under SEC Regulation D (small private offerings exempt from disclosure requirements), more than $2 billion in small public offerings, and $12.8 billion in the new issues market. Similarly, a less formal level, the growth and visibility of the venture capital business, is further attested to by the enthusiasm nowadays of MBA students for careers in the venture capital industry.[2]

The cast of characters in venture capital finance has also undergone a substantial change that has great implications for the future. It has become highly institutionalized as investment banking firms, pension funds and the like have earmarked large sums of money for venture capital investments. One consequence has been the emergence of large (more than $100 million) funds and the public sale of partnerships in venture funds to small investors.

The implications of these changes are profound. Based on informal scanning of the business and financial press (*Inc., Venture, Business Week, Wall Street Journal*) and with only a short intuitive leap, let me suggest a number of possibilities. First, the venture capital business has become more impersonal as a consequence of institutionalization, and portfolio investments may be less well managed as a consequence.

Institutional investors can rearrange their portfolios freely, in a liquid secondary market, and have very little interaction with the managements of the firms whose securities they own. Such an institutional investor mind-set, however, is inappropriate in the case of portfolio investments which are illiquid and in which interactions (including later rounds of financing) with the entrepreneurs are critical to final investment payoffs. Putting the matter in another way, capital market theory and evidence suggest that institutional investors put together portfolios of traded assets (risk/return bundles) for their owners that have zero net present values.

Portfolios of venture capital firms, on the other hand, can generate positive net present values for their owners as a function of (a) how good the venture capitalists are at spotting new opportunities, (b) how well they manage the sequential financing process described earlier, and (c) the quality of their interactions with entrepreneurs, including deal structuring and management advice. It is not obvious that the investment perspectives and skills needed to perform such functions are going to be found in venture capital firms sponsored by large corporations or financial institutions. A portfolio of small, developing enterprises is not the same as a portfolio of blue chip common stocks. My reading of anecdotes reported in the press is that many of the new dollars invested in entrepreneurial undertakings are not being invested wisely or being well controlled. In addition, they are raising venture capital firm/entrepreneur tensions beyond levels inherent in any such relationships.[3]

A recent article provides evidence to support the argument forcefully (*Inc.*, August, 1984, pp. 65–75):

> But venture capital today may well be becoming a victim of its own successes. Once a collection of small firms run by brilliant, if often idiosyncratic, individuals, the venture capital business is developing into a large-scale, highly institutionalized industry. The main impetus has come from pension funds, investment banks, insurance companies, and the like. Lured by annual returns as high as 40 percent to 60 percent, they have poured huge amounts of money into venture capital funds . . .
>
> As the money has flowed in, the game has changed. 'You have to understand this is an industry where people are not used to having a lot of money,' observes Oxford Partner's Stevan Birnbaum, who has been a venture capitalist for 15 years. 'Then somebody gives you $150 million, and you start to feel you can walk on water. You read in the paper that you're a genius, and you believe it. Some of the old constraints tend to get eroded away.'
>
> Exacerbating this situation is the growing involvement of major financial institutions in the venture capital process itself—not just as suppliers of capital, but as direct participants in latter, or 'mezzanine,' round financing. As investment banks, insurance companies, and other large institutions have formed their own venture capital arms, they have added millions of dollars to the already huge pool of money available to companies on the verge of going public. The temptation is to pump these companies full of cash in hopes of increasing the appeal of their initial public offering. It is a temptation that some venture capitalists have found impossible to resist.

There is always the question whether the ultimate constraint on venture capital financing is scarcity of good ideas (the venture capitalist's posture) or scarcity of dollars (the entrepreneur's posture). In 1984, an additional factor, perhaps, is the quality of the dollars. It is difficult to discern what the long term impact of these developments will be. The venture capital business is volatile under the best of circumstances, after all, and 1984 appears to be the hangover year after 1983's binge. To the extent that financial institutions learn to take a long term view of venture capital commitments and develop the management skills to work with portfolio firms, the 1984 phenomenon will be temporary.

The shift to large, institutional sources of venture capital dollars can also shape the quality of entrepreneurial projects undertaken if institutional portfolio objectives are different from those of more traditional, small private firms. These can include insistence on a larger piece of the pie and short-term payoffs. It would seem that the financing deals made under such criteria and, hence, the kinds of business projects undertaken in the United States, could well be affected. The issue here is really one of time horizons in investment decisions. In recent years, some public discussion has wondered if the managements of large corporations have been put under pressure to achieve short-term performance at the expense of long-term performance. This pressure is coming from the financial institutions which increasingly own their common stock. I know of no evidence on this matter other than the sort which appears in letters to the *Wall Street Journal*. To the extent that this phenomenon does exist, however, institutional venture capital dollars will tend to finance quick payoff projects, rather than longer-term business activities. The kinds of innovations financed and the qualitative pattern of economic growth will also be logically affected.

Finally, success can be its own enemy in an increasingly institutionalized environment. Maintenance of the flow of venture capital at high levels presupposes some combinations of both new dollars and recycled funds from liquidated profitable investments. I would guess that these two sources go hand in hand and are sensitive to the same capital market conditions: when the glamour of the new issues market fades (as it has this year), not only does the recycling of "old" dollars get thwarted, but the availability of "new" dollars managed under short term investment horizons also is cut back.[4] Evidence suggests that this is indeed happening. The June 1984 issue of *Venture* describes recent initial public offerings and declines in valuations in second and third round financings. The proportion of institutional investment dollars dedicated to venture capital activities is small, but its impact is very large. A minor cyclical retrenchment by major financial institutions constitutes a major shift in dollars of venture capital availability. The interesting question is whether, with the passage of time, institutional sources of venture capital will become less volatile.

III. FACTORS THAT COULD DETERMINE VENTURE CAPITAL AVAILABILITY

It takes no great imagination to concoct a list of the factors that could determine the availability of venture capital to finance entrepreneurial undertakings over time and in different regions of the country. On the other hand, if we are to be honest about the matter, given the great growth and visibility of venture capital financing in recent years, we have to be careful not to fall into the *post hoc ergo propter hoc* trap of assuming that the political and economic changes of the mid to late 1970s necessarily had to bear a causal relationship to growth of the venture capital market.

With this caveat, my favorite list of factors would include interest rates and capital market conditions. Conjectures in the mode of the financial economist on the role of this variable are a bit sneaky, but they go as follows. First, conventional risk/return investment packages are always available in the secondary market for debt and equity securities. Consequently, the better the opportunities available in that market with all other factors being equal, the higher the hurdle rate and hence smaller the flow of dollars into venture capital investments. At first blush, this reasoning would appear to be contradicted by the facts. After all, the flowering of the venture capital market in recent years occurred simultaneously with the highest interest rates in U.S. history. Once we peel away the impact of expected inflation rates, however, the contradiction may disappear. There is some evidence to suggest that during the late 1960s to late 1970s *nominal* interest rates were reaching new peaks, venture capital financing was growing rapidly, and average *real* interest rates were extremely low. For example, from 1967 to 1978, the average difference between yields on Treasury bills and rate of change of the consumer price index (proxy for short-term expected rate of inflation) averaged only 1.19 percent per year. The implication is that investment dollars were looking for higher real rates of return than were available (at any risk level) in traded securities, and they spilled over into the financing of new ventures. There is a corollary, though, with more negative implications for the future. There is evidence that during the past few years, real interest rates have been quite high, averaging around five percent in recent months. Those high rates may explain references in the business press that the bloom is off the rose in 1984 for venture capital funding. (The joint impact of real interest rates, which are pre-tax, and the income tax structure, may be more complex.)

A second factor is the income and wealth distribution. This is an obvious influence, given that wealthy investors probably provide most of the venture capital dollars. But let's consider the matter in greater detail. Under fairly reasonable assumptions, a person's aversion to investment risks (including those of illiquidity) decrease as their income and wealth increase. Additionally, their savings to income ratios rise. These forces jointly increase the likelihood that high risk venture capital assets will be found in their investment portfolios. Whether this effect has been present in political decisions in recent administrations (Carter's and Reagan's) is unknown. Unfortunately, the evidence of income and wealth distribution tends to be assembled and asserted more in the spirit of partisan politics than that of economic inquiry.

A third factor is taxes. This factor is blatant: prospective venture capital returns are overwhelmingly in the form of long-term capital gains. Increase the after-tax return possibilities for venture capital investments, and you should see more money transferred into long-term, risky investments. Economists may quibble over the distinction between correlation and causation, but not the most knowledgeable students of the venture capital industry, such as Stanley Pratt: "The dramatic expansion of the venture capital industry which began in 1978 under the impetus of the 1978 capital gains tax reduction continues today."[5]

Fourth is the panoply of government regulations and subsidies. It is difficult to determine systematically the role of government, but obviously, when government provides direct grants or interest rate subsidies or loosens SEC rules, the flow of venture capital dollars should increase. A good example is the National Science Foundation's (NSF) Small Business Innovation Research (SBIR) program, which awarded $3.5 million to fund 100 new projects early in 1983 (at an average amount of $35,000). In this program, the most promising projects get larger developmental funding in phase two, averaging around $200,000 each. Phase three involves only private funding to pursue potential commercial applications.

The first SBIR solicitations (1977 and 1979) ultimately resulted in more than a $50 million investment by private sources at phase three. The NSF program, in a spillover effect, was the model for P.L. 97–219 (signed into law in 1982) that required Federal agencies (who fund 99 percent of government research and development) to set aside a small percentage of their budgets for similar SBIR programs. We don't know, unfortunately, the separate impact (or social benefits) of each of the diverse actions by government for purposes of comparison to their cost.

Finally, the cultural environment affects the availability of venture funding. I grew up near Boston, but from 1974 to 1984, I lived in North Carolina. Governor Luther Hodges tried to stimulate a Route 128 phenomenon in establishing the Research Triangle Park in North Carolina many years ago. It has been my impression that, at least until fairly recently, economic growth in the Triangle area was mostly based on large firms coming in with very little spin-off development in the form of new, small, high risk ventures. It is a cliche that the cultural environments of New England, Texas and California have been conducive to venture capital financing of small high technology firms. Fast and Pratt (1983), for example, estimate that in 1980, 56.2 percent, and in 1981, 64.4 percent of all venture capital investment dollars were invested in these states.[6] Having lived for many years in New England and North Carolina, I am almost persuaded that social attitudes toward business and financial risk-taking are the dominant forces that explain regional differences in venture capital markets. The interesting question is whether pro-entrepreneurial attitudes have spread more rapidly in recent years, given advances in communications, mass media and population mobility. This is dangerous ground for the financial economist, but my hunch is that the country as a whole is becoming more fertile for entrepreneurial risk taking.

The brew made up of the above ingredients may or may not be fragile, but it is volatile. Milton Stewart argues that the venture capital business goes through seven-year cycles. If he is correct in this Biblical-like pronouncement, then it may be time to batten down the hatches, given the retrenchment of 1984. Whether correct or not, his view of the cyclical nature of venture capital finance conjures up a more interesting speculation: Is its recent growth, much of which has involved ventures built around technological innovations, simply a supply response to demand generated by an underlying Kondratieff-like wave of innovations? In other words, when the flow of venture capital dollars expands and contracts, is this merely a response to the underlying innovative process's consequences, or do shifts in capital availability themselves constrain or encourage innovation? If the answer is yes, then there is a most important social question which needs answering, namely whether public policy choices influencing venture capital availability can significantly constrain or encourage this engine for economic growth and development.

IV.   A FRAMEWORK FOR ANALYZING ENTERPRENEUR VENTURE CAPITALIST INTERACTIONS

At the outset of this paper I suggested that data limitations on the informal and fragmented nature of the venture capital market presently create difficulty in executing an empirical investigation of the questions just raised. The dodge of the economist in such conditions is to restate the obvious characteristics of the venture capital financing decision in a model, then see whether the model's qualitative predictions conform to the fragmented and informally gathered facts that we do observe. A doctoral student, Ian Cooper, and I carried out such an investigation in 1976–77 under the sponsorship of the National Science Foundation. What follows is a greatly condensed (and nonmathematical) rendering of Cooper's doctoral dissertation (1977) and two published papers which resulted.

A.   What the Venture Capital Decision Process Entails That Distinguishes It From the More Conventional Capital Budgeting and Financing Decisions

The essential property of venture capital decision-making is a process of sequential decisions conducted under uncertainty. These decisions involve the entrepreneur and the venture capitalist. The problems that arise in analyzing (or modeling) venture capital investment are four-fold. First, the diffuse nature of the information available for an external investor to evaluate the company means that investors may be in an inferior position to judge the true value of the investment in relation to entrepreneurs who are seeking financing. This asymmetric information induces investment behavior that is not proportionally present in large, marketable companies. It makes the venture capitalists' claims on the portfolio companies, whose securities they hold, difficult to market. Venture capitalists must take the returns to their investments as cash flows from the portfolio firms (or wait until they have proven their worth) so the asymmetric information disappears and financial claims on the portfolio firms become marketable.

Information asymmetry's effects are especially pronounced in new high technology firms. Loosely speaking, equity claims on an enterprise cannot be sold to the public until there is information available on the enterprise's management. Of particular concern is whether the firm's return possibilities are positive and largely independent or whether the entrepreneur continues with the firm. Until such a time, there is an equivalency between firm, project and entrepreneur. And although the firm may quickly develop proprietary information bearing an ultimate return possibility, premature disclosure could destroy the competitive advantage that is the basis of the project's value.

The development of publicly-traded venture capital firms as specialized financial intermediaries may be considered a response to this problem. That is, such firms can acquire funds from investors directly in the capital market on the basis of being privy to information not available to the public. Such a reputation can be fleeting. But Martin and Petty (1983), in a comparison of firms with maximum-growth oriented mutual funds and the S&P 500 index, did find that, while such firms are riskier, this risk "did not preclude even risk-averse investors from preferring the one or more venture capital firms over some of the mutual funds on the stock index."[7]

The second special feature of venture capital investment is the long time-horizon investment must be held before it can be liquidated. The time period is usually a minimum of five years. Of course, many portfolio firms will never reach the stage where they can be sold, but the anticipated returns for venture capitalists rest largely on the expectation that some of their investments will reach that stage. Given the volatility of the new issue market, the riskiness of a venture capital investment due to its profit-making uncertainty is magnified by uncertainty of the capital market's receptiveness when the project matures.

Third, the investment required to carry the portfolio firm through this long holding period takes place in several stages. This is a further complication to the evaluation of venture capital projects. The initial investment is made, not with the purpose of carrying the project through, but to purchase more information concerning ultimate payoffs. In light of this new information, the project will either be continued through its next stage or be abandoned. One can visualize a decision tree with several future decision points where new dollars will be required or the project be abandoned. An initial funding decision is optimally made only if all future contingent decisions are also expected to be made optimally. Since no market values for the project can exist until the firm goes public, conventional options pricing theory (which presupposes market prices at all stages of the contingent decision sequences) cannot be invoked to evaluate the decisions. This multi-period contingent decision process makes venture capital investment intractable for the conventional, single-period tools of modern finance theory.

Last, entrepreneur/venture capitalist contractual arrangements are made in an environment where a special hazard exists: the entrepreneur needs financing, and the venture capitalist needs the entrepreneur's contribution (at least to a certain stage of development) to bring the profit possibilities to fruition. It is unclear what kinds of financial contracts will induce the entrepreneur to make optimal business decisions (including staying with the enterprise). Generally speaking, each round of financing requires a contractual arrangement specifying relative input shares (including implicit acknowledgment of the entrepreneur's "sweat capital") and output or payoff shares. Because there may be future conditions where the venture capitalist and the entrepreneur will differ on whether to continue, interaction between the two parties necessarily involves some losses relative to an "ideal" policy which would maximize the value of the undertaking. This is a familiar problem in the agency cost literature, one that is solved by devising efficient contracts that minimize the divergence between actual and ideal behavior. The complexity of the problem is increased in the venture capital environment because several (contingent) contracts and decisions are involved.

B.   Some Basic Assumptions of the Model

We assumed that both entrepreneur and venture capitalist wish to maximize the value of the project at each stage of financing. Conceptually, at each stage a decision must be made whether to continue or to abandon the project. And if they decide to continue, they must decide what kind of financial package (debt, equity, warrants, etc.) is optimal for the two parties. At time zero, then, the model is a sequence of contingent decisions maximizing value under a final payoff sharing rule. Formally, the model is solved using the mathematics of dynamic programming.

C.   Implications and Predictions of the Model

There are many implications that conform to informal observations of the venture capital financing process. The first is that venture capitalists generally will prefer not to provide financing until they reach a stage where the entrepreneur has already invested substantial amounts of his own financial and human capital. Second, venture capitalists tend to specialize in the types of ventures they invest in (microelectronics, biotechnology, etc.). Third, venture capitalists express a desire for risky projects. Interpreted in terms of the model, they think they can take projects with initially very diffuse payoffs, truncate the worst outcomes by a willingness to abandon in the future if the information development is adverse, and hence, create a managed final payoff distribution that is skewed in the direction of high returns. Fourth, on the basis of number three, one expects to observe realized venture capital project payoffs characterized by modest to average returns, but where there are many low or negative returns and few substantial returns. Finally, the optimal financial packages tend to be complex, involving debt, convertible securities, warrants and equity.

More generally, manipulation of our model leads to the conjecture that some public policy proposals, such as improving venture capital firm liquidity by making it easier to take newer firms public or reducing capital gains taxes, should unambiguously increase the supply of venture capital finance. On the other hand, properties of a specific project—expected time and number of financing rounds to maturity, initial uncertainty and its prospective rate of resolution, prospective growth of dollars required at each stage—dictated what kind of public policy stimulus would be most effective in bringing project financing. These policies include either subsidizing financial inputs or outputs. The NSF's SBIR program is a clear example of subsidizing inputs, while capital gains tax reductions are the most obvious example of subsidizing outputs. The social costs of such policies are, in principle, measurable. Nothing, however, in our model or available data makes possible the measurement of their social benefits.

Virtually all of our model's predictions assured Dr. Cooper and I that we had captured some of the most important features of the venture capital financing process. Note, however, that this is a long way from proving the matter. Because the process lies beyond the domain of contemporary finance theory at this time, and data useful for empirical research are basically unavailable, one cannot be sure. Note also that understanding the venture capital market is very important societally, and that our model provided only limited qualitative insights into what makes the venture capital market tick. Clearly the cliché appearing at the close of many papers in finance and economics is once again appropriate: We need to do more research on the topic.

V. CONCLUDING REMARKS

At the outset of this paper, I suggested that the best I could come up with, as to the determinants of the supply of venture capital and the responsiveness to public policy decisions, would be informed conjectures. At the risk of redundancy, let me draw some implications from the principal conjectures. First, the long term value of institutionalizing the venture capital market will be enhanced to the extent that growth in the number of capable trained venture capitalists who deploy the institutions' dollars keeps pace. Volatility in the market, however, will not disappear. Second, the publicly traded venture capital firm is a very useful device for mitigating the effects of information asymmetry which otherwise raises cost and/or restricts capital flows to new projects. Third, from the standpoint of an entrepreneur seeking government decisions which improve his lot, SBIR types of programs are most attractive: they are cheap in tax dollars, hence cheap politically, relative to income tax changes. They don't dilute owner shares in project payoffs. Additionally, they build the investment made prior to contracting with a venture capitalist and therefore improve the entrepreneur's bargaining position in partitioning final project payoffs. Finally, we need more research in this field not only for its direct benefits in understanding what makes the American economy grow and adapt, but also to improve the conceptual understanding of financial markets and financial decision-making in general.

NOTES

1. The above description is adopted from Cooper, (1977).

2. In 1968, while on the Tuck School faculty, I advised Ed Glassmeyer (who has since had a distinguished career as a venture capitalist) that he would have more fun working for Citibank's newly formed SBIC than in editing red herrings for Morgan Stanley. During most of the 1970s there was a drought however, as most of my best students with career interests in finance opted for commercial banking or corporate treasury jobs. Now once again student enthusiasm for careers in venture capital is riding high. (Needless to say, enthusiasm for careers on the demand side of the market is also running high, among students whose preferences are entrepreneurial rather than organizational).

3. See, for example, "Venture Funds Stop to Catch Their Breath," *Venture*, June 1984, pp. 54–58; also, "It's the Morning After for Venture Capitalists," *Business Week*, September 24, 1984, pp. 118–119.

4. Slumping Market in Initial Stock Offerings Squeezes Some Investment Banking Firms," *Wall Street Journal*, October 16, 1984, p. 10.

5. *Guide to Venture Capital Sources*, Sixth edition, by Stanley E. Pratt. Wellesley Hills, Mass: Capital Publishing Corporation, (1982, p. 7).

6. See Fast and Pratt, (1983).

7. Martin and Petty, (1983).

REFERENCES

Carleton, W. T. and I. A. Cooper (1982), "Venture Capital Investment." In Roy T. Crum and Frans G. Derkinderen (Eds.), *Strategies of Corporate Investment*. Toronto, Canada: Pitman Publishing Co.

Cooper, I. A. (1977), *A Model of Venture Capital Investment*. Unpublished Ph.D. dissertation, University of North Carolina.

Cooper, I. A. and W. T. Carleton (1979), "Dynamics of Borrower-Lender Interaction: Partitioning Final Pay-offs in Venture Capital Finance." *Journal of Finance* 34(2):517–29.

Fast, N. D. and S. E. Pratt (1983), "Regional Patterns of Venture Capital Investment." *Small Business Research Summary* (August).

"It's The Morning After for Venture Capitalists." *Business Week* September 24, 1984, pp. 118–9.

Martin, J. D. and J. W. Petty (1983), "An Analysis of the Performance of Publicly Traded Venture Capital Companies." *Journal of Financial and Quantitative Analysis* 18(3):401–10.

Pratt, S. E. (1982), *Guide to Venture Capital Sources*. Wellesley Hills, MA: Capital Publishing Corporation.

"Venture Funds Stop To Catch Their Breath." *Venture*, June 1984, pp. 54–8.

"Why Smart Companies are Saying No to Venture Capital." *Inc.*, August 1984, pp. 65–75.

Chapter 6

THE DIALOGUE ON VENTURE CAPITAL MARKETS

In his paper "Issues and Questions Involving Venture Capital," Willard Carleton raised a number of issues that were of concern to the dialogue participants, including the nature of the venture capital decision process, its relation to more conventional financing, recent changes in venture capital markets, the impact of government policies on the supply of venture capital, and the ability of entrepreneurs to successfully compete in international markets.

I. WHAT IS THE NATURE OF THE VENTURE CAPITAL DECISION PROCESS? HOW DOES IT DIFFER FROM MORE CONVENTIONAL FINANCING? HOW HAS THE MARKET CHANGED IN THE PAST FIVE YEARS?

Carleton pointed out that venture capital markets differ from other financial markets because of the importance of information problems and the associated high level of risk that are inherent in entrepreneurial activities. There is general uncertainty about new products and processes, management's capabilities, and long-term market conditions that affect contracts between venture capitalists and entrepreneurs. Additionally, in negotiations for funding, the entrepreneur has an information advantage because he knows more about the new product or process

Advances in the Study of Entrepreneurship, Innovation,
and Economic Growth, Volume 1, pages 71-78.
Copyright © 1986 by JAI Press Inc.
ISBN: 0-89232-703-0

than does the venture capitalist. In response to these risk and asymmetrical information problems, venture capital financing is typically a sequential process, involving contingent contracts and several levels of funding. This procedure benefits both parties. It allows the venture capitalist to limit his investment until more information is gained, and it allows the entrepreneur to renegotiate on more favorable terms if the venture becomes a success.

The first level of funding discussed in the dialogue was seed financing. Seed financing is funding for a new venture that is being organized around the plans and dreams of the entrepreneur. This is the most risky period for financing, and the stage where most entrepreneurs fail to secure outside funding. Accordingly, start-up funding typically starts with the entrepreneur, his family, friends, or others who know and trust the individual. At this point, the new venture is embodied in the entrepreneur and the prospects for the venture are hard to predict.

Beyond some initial development, the entrepreneur can secure additional seed funding of $500,000 or less from small venture capital firms. These firms invest for local business persons, lawyers, physicians, and others who want to invest a portion of their assets in risky ventures with high expected rates of return.

Unfortunately, there is little statistical record of how much is provided nationally by such firms in the support of new operations. For example, small seed capital firms exist in Boston and the San Francisco Bay areas, and their focus is local where their knowledge is best. Tom Whitney pointed out that his firm confines its investment activities to a 30-mile region within Santa Clara County, California.[1] Charles James added that approximately 90 percent of the new companies in the Santa Clara area were financed by Northern California venture capital firms.[2] Moreover, Whitney argued that because of the risks involved, his firm specializes in particular types of new ventures to better evaluate investment potentials and to provide managerial support: "We occasionally invest in situations where the management is not yet in place, and it is our function to help bring management to the company."[3] Both James and Whitney commented that initial financing for new ventures requires a significant time commitment from the venture capitalist. The necessary close relationship between entrepreneurs and venture capitalists is assisted through the use of limited partners. In local financing, many partners are retired and are able to serve on boards of directors and become involved with the venture's daily operation. All participants agreed that seed financing was an important area for academic research. Much more must be learned regarding the amount of funding provided and the contractual relationship between the venture capitalist and the entrepreneur in the venture's early stages.

The next level of contingent financing occurs after the new product or process is more clearly developed and its market potential better established. Tom Whitney noted that such funding typically ranges from $500,000 to $5,000,000 and is usually organized by the seed capital firm which brings other investors into the venture. Again, the question was raised about the magnitude of such support. But this is also an informal market of local firms and no national data exist. Jack Thorne estimated, however, that the investment from local sources for new ventures probably equals the total supplied nationwide by larger institutional venture capital investors at later stages of development.[4]

As the venture becomes more firmly established and requires greater funding, it can appeal to the major national venture capital firms. Larry Campbell estimated that there are approximately 50 large venture capital firms in the United States, many of which are headquartered in New York.[5] Most of the larger venture capitalists who provide financing of $5,000,000 and above are not as intimately involved in firm management as are the smaller venture capital firms. Such involvement is generally no longer necessary, and large investors have diversified portfolios of investments throughout the country to reduce risk. Diversification is promoted by interaction among the major funds. For instance, Larry Campbell described the network as follows: [Rather than going over a detailed prospectus for each new venture] "you typically will have a discussion with somebody you trust . . . and you'll get a summary of two, three, four pages, and then if it looks interesting, you will begin your due diligence just as you would for merger and acquisition or registration statement or anything else."[6] He noted, though, that a difficulty remains in all venture capital transactions, since judgments must be made without the benefit of credit ratings or other established parameters. Through diversification, the institutional venture funds can blunt the riskiness of new venture financing.

At all levels of venture funding, a major contracting issue is deciding the input and output shares for the entrepreneur and venture capitalist. The input shares involve specifying the managerial roles of both the entrepreneur and the venture capitalist. As described by Whitney, the managerial assistance from venture capital is most critical in early stages of product development when the new firm is being organized and before a tested managerial team with business training has been assembled. The output shares involve equity. Milton Stewart insisted that the entrepreneur must be left sufficient equity in a new firm to maintain incentives and to encourage the intense investment of energy necessary to bring a new firm on line. Typically, the maximum a venture capitalist would require in such cases is 40 percent of the company, leaving the entrepreneur with at least 60 percent of the equity.[7] The entrepreneur requires that much because he generally has to give equity to scientists, engineers or other people critical to the success of the new enterprise in lieu of high salaries. At early stages, few firms can pay such salaries and, moreover, equity shares link all parties to the anticipated growth of the company. As the firm becomes more developed, venture capitalists can require less equity because the enterprise is now less risky.

Tom Whitney provided additional insight into the contingent nature of venture capital contracts described by Carleton. He outlined the decision points where the firm's progress must be evaluated before additional funds are committed: "Generally, there is a business plan that has been proposed by the entrepreneur. If that plan is not met, then some hard questions have to be asked. One of the hardest things for a venture capitalist is to decide that this management team isn't going to make it and if we're going to invest more money, it's going to be with some other people in charge."[8]

Stewart noted that the longer a venture capital group is in the business, the more prepared they are to change management and withhold further investment until fundamental changes in business policies and organization are made.[9] Gerrit Wolf questioned whether the venture capitalist can distinguish between managerial failure and unforeseen market changes. Whitney, Phillips and Campbell responded that they expect the management to correctly forecast and respond to market changes. If the entrepreneur does not adequately plan, the venture capitalist must employ his option to change management. Campbell argued that in this way, venture capitalists assist the process of technical change in the economy by making shrewd market judgments and installing more efficient management teams.[10] .

A new and increasingly common financing practice is a leveraged buy-out. Under leveraged buy-outs, the venture capitalist helps an entrepreneur purchase the company he is managing from a parent company. As a result, instead of being a manager, the entrepreneur becomes an owner. Leveraged buy-outs are attractive for venture capital firms because they involve less risk than in other types of new venture financing. With a buy-out, the venture capitalist is investing in an existing, on-going business rather than a new concern. Milton Stewart emphasized these advantages: "What you're doing really is removing the element of risk . . . you're backing someone who is in place, running the assets, clearly knows what he's doing, and you are, in effect, lending him the money he doesn't have to take over the business, using the earning power of the business to finance the transaction."[11]

Karl Eller added that leveraged buy-outs often involve a company that was public, but is now going private. In those circumstances, the company may want to sell one of their divisions. The manager can then purchase the division through a leveraged buy-out. To finance the transaction, the venture capitalist will obtain senior financing from banks or insurance companies and secure equity financing from other investors and venture capitalist firms. Eller noted that the latter is called mezzanine or equity financing.[12]

The dialogue turned from the contingent nature of venture capital contracting to recent changes in the venture capital market. In this paper, Carleton pointed out that in the last seven years there has been a rapid growth in institutional lenders with the emergence of mega funds of more than $100 million. Charles James added that in the last three years there was, perhaps, a ten-fold increase in the amount of money available and five times as many people involved in new ven ture financing. He conjectured that the average fund size is now $20 million, with much of the institutional financing from foreign investors[13].

Associated with the expansion in the number and size of venture capital firms is an increased specialization in particular industries, such as communications. As noted earlier, such specialization is necessary because of limited information and the high risks involved in new enterprises. In emphasizing this specialization, Lawrence Campbell and Warren Rustand disagreed with Carleton's assertion that large institutional lenders were likely to manage their investments less efficiently than smaller firms. For example, Rustand argued that institutional lenders "tend to be more sophisticated, more knowledgeable and do a better job of due diligence perhaps than we've seen in recent years . . . "[14]

While there is a trend toward specialization in particular industries, venture capital firms still must diversify their portfolios. In diversifying, Campbell and Whitney noted that firms often have a policy that if they do not have reasonable expertise in a given field, the venture will not be funded unless a consultant who is trusted by the firm can offer that expertise. They added that in portfolio diversification most venture capitalists limit their investment in any project to 10 percent of their total investment. Moreover, they avoid investing in competing firms.[15]

In final assessment of the current market, Campbell and James offered a note of caution. They argued that five years ago the market was tight because of losses from earlier investments. At that time, there was little recycling of funds. Now, the market appears to be in a new cycle with rapid increases in the supply of venture capital. They predicted, though, that the cycle was likely to enter a down-swing, since many venture funds have poorly performing assets. Additional liquidity will be needed for existing investments so that less will be available for new activities.[16]

II. HOW DO GOVERNMENT POLICIES AFFECT THE SUPPLY OF VENTURE CAPITAL AND THE ABILITY OF ENTREPRENEURS TO SUCCESSFULLY COMPETE IN NATIONAL AND INTERNATIONAL MARKETS?

Of all government actions, the participants agreed that tax policies, particularly capital gains taxes, had the greatest potential impact on the supply of venture capital and the ability of entrepreneurs to finance new enterprises. Morton Kamien outlined why capital gains taxes were so critical. Because of the inherent lack of information on the likely success of new products and firms, venture capital is riskier than other types of investment. Kamien argued, however, that all investments at the margin must give equal rates of return adjusted for risk. Accordingly, venture capital investments require larger expected returns to compensate for risk.[17] These returns are usually capital gains from the sale of the investor's portion of the new firm once it has become established and marketable.

Hence, changes in capital gains taxes can importantly affect expected returns from investments in risky new enterprises. Similarly, a stock option is critically important in drawing talent away from major companies because small companies cannot pay large salaries, but can provide stock options. Capital gains on those options are a significant incentive for joining a new enterprise, but they are vulnerable to tax policies.

Tom Brown argued that to encourage innovation, the government should not be taxing income, but instead expenditures. Indeed, given the increased competitiveness of international markets, the United States must reevaluate the incentive effects of its tax policies.[18] Robert Higgs added that the problem was broader than merely the level of capital gains taxes. He asserted that the more ominous threat was the scale of government and the associated increase in the government's command of economic resources. Higgs argued that regulatory policies constrain private decision-making authority and ability to respond to changing market conditions. Moreover, he predicted that increases in government spending, relative to total national income and the corresponding federal deficit, would either crowd out private investment or bring renewed inflation as the debt became monitized.[19] Higgs asserted that entrepreneurs and venture capitalists must lobby for more fundamental changes in government policy, rather than focus on capital gains taxes.

Carleton offered an additional dimension to the problem. He noted that innovation and new enterprise can be stimulated by various government subsidies, such as tax cuts, and direct investment funds, such as those provided by the National Science Foundation's Small Business Innovation Research (SBIR) program. In making policy decisions regarding subsidies, the relative efficiency of the sources and the amount of money must be evaluated. Given the lack of research on the supply of venture capital in the United States and the social returns of the new enterprises supported, Carleton asserted that it is not clear what the optimal amount of new venture funding should be. There may be too little or too much, and the question of the optimal amount must be addressed before deciding the source of the subsidy.[20]

Another public policy issue discussed was property rights. The security of ownership of intellectual knowledge determines whether an entrepreneur can obtain financing for his venture. If the entrepreneur cannot "stake a claim" to an idea, he may not be able to attract funding, since without secure property rights to new ideas, they are quickly copied by others and any expected returns are competed away. The participants noted that this problem has long been recognized, and patents have been provided by the government as a source of property rights. Unfortunately, patents appear to be an incomplete solution.

Two problems with patents are the mobility of employees who can take company secrets with them to competitors despite patent protection, the high marginal costs to small firms for defending patents, and a low probability of success. Charles James commented: "But in patents one wonders if you can possibly create a Xerox today, given the Court's attitude."[21] Milton Stewart added: "The better patent lawyers often will ask a client, 'Are you sure you would not be better off without a patent, simply relying on lead time in the market place? How long can you maintain your position against competition if you don't disclose, through the patent process, what you have?' And that is a proper entrepreneurial question.''[22]

Because of the ease in which many new processes can be copied with minor modifications to confound any infringement litigation by the source company, Dick Spencer argued that patents were irrelevant for his small medical technology firm: "We have a number of patents and quite frankly, I doubt if we're going to be able to enforce them.''[23] He noted that his firm spends from $20,000 to $50,000 just paying patent fees, and that $80,000 is an estimation of the costs of bringing court action against an infringer. With unlimited ways of evading patents, such investments are unprofitable for his firm.

A third public policy issue addressed in the conference was the impact of federal export licensing restrictions. Again, there was agreement that the existing arrangements were costly to American firms and were ineffective in controlling the flow of technology to other countries, particularly the Soviet Union. A common complaint was that export licensing controls significantly reduced the competitiveness of United States' firms vis-à-vis their foreign competitors. For instance, Curtis Hartmann commented: "Our experience with export controls shows a very onerous problem. We sell over half of our output to Japan, Hong Kong, Taiwan and Korea. We are taking jobs away from those areas and bringing them here because of our technology, and we're ahead. And for a while we're going to be able to remain ahead . . . the biggest problem we see in trying to serve certain markets is our ability to be responsive to our customers.''[24] Because of licensing restrictions, Hartmann noted that it typically takes four months to ship new technology-based products to Japan, while local and other foreign competitors can often respond in three weeks. The U.S. technology advantage is unlikely to continue to provide a cushion to offset those delays. Tom Brown and Dick Spencer voiced similar concerns about the high costs imposed on their firms from export controls and the resulting long run viability of their firms on foreign markets.[25]

Throughout the dialogue on venture capital markets, entrepreneurship and public policy, the participants emphasized the need for credible research. Much of the debate stemmed from a basic lack of knowledge and analysis of these important issues. Accordingly, a rich research agenda is waiting for academic attention. In the following chapter, Almarin Phillips discusses the relevance of current theoretical models for research on entrepreneurship.

NOTES

1.   Whitney, Transcript, Eller Dialogue, Session III, November 30, 1984 p. 261
2.   James, p. 259
3.   Whitney, p. 262
4.   Thorne, p. 284

5. Campbell, p. 244
6. Campbell, p. 245
7. Stewart, p. 247
8. Whitney, p. 270
9. Stewart, p. 270
10. Wolf, Whitney, Phillips, Rosenberg, Stewart and Campbell discussions, pp. 272–274
11. Stewart, pp. 256–257
12. Karl Eller described a case where his venture capital firm was involved in a leverage buy-out of a San Antonio radio station.
13. James, p. 253
14. Rustand, p. 266
15. Campbell and Whitney, pp. 275–277
16. Campbell and James, pp. 248–250
17. Kamien, pp. 309, 327
18. Brown, pp. 316, 320
19. Higgs, p. 336; see also Higgs, 1985
20. Carleton, p. 318
21. James, p. 359
22. Stewart, p. 360
23. Spencer, p. 360
24. Hartmann, p. 348
25. Spencer, p. 362; Brown, p. 347. Other public policy issues briefly discussed included SEC regulations, state Blue Sky laws, and interest rate controls.

REFERENCES

Higgs, R. (ed.), (1985), *The Emergence of the Modern Political Economy*, Suppl. 4 to *Research in Economic History*. Greenwich, CT: JAI Press.

Chapter 7

THEORETICAL AND RESEARCH ISSUES REGARDING ENTREPRENEURSHIP, VENTURE CAPITAL AND INNOVATION

Almarin Phillips

I. INTRODUCTION

The role and operation of financial intermediaries in a market economy are familiar topics of economic discourse and inquiry. Focal institutional groups include commercial banks, the thrift institutions (savings and loan associations, mutual savings banks, credit unions, postal savings), investment banking, reserve life insurance, mutual funds (of many sorts), pension and related funds, the commercial paper market and the Eurodollar market. Strangely, most economists have paid little attention to venture capital markets and the financing of high risk, innovative economic activities.

Accordingly, the dialogue was as unstructured as the subject matter. The participants had hitherto demonstrated, through their own research, a willingness to tread unfamiliar (and often unpopular) grounds. Had even a small group of high skilled, mathematically-oriented, static modelers of markets been present, a different and less productive session would surely have transpired. This leads to my point that existing theoretical models require important revision if they are to be used fruitfully for analyzing venture capital markets and entrepreneurship.

Advances in the Study of Entrepreneurship, Innovation, and Economic Growth, Volume 1, pages 79-82.
Copyright © 1986 by JAI Press Inc.
ISBN: 0-89232-703-0

II. THEORY AND THE ANALYSIS OF FINANCIAL MARKETS

To assert the inappropriateness of the theories of mainstream economists is not to denigrate either them or their theories. The point is rather that the markets to which those theories are applicable have little in common with the markets in which venture capitalists operate. This requires more emphasis. The neoclassical models—from Ricardo to the present—concern markets in which price is a "sufficient statistic" for transactions. That is, suppliers and buyers only need knowledge of market price to determine the quantities of a good or service they are willing to sell or to buy. The quantity of the good or service is fully and uniquely defined with no ambiguity about what the sellers are offering or the buyers are procuring.

Schumpeter, a leading student of entrepreneurs, admired Ricardo's ability and success as an actual market trader, but deplored his "analytic engine." It was, Schumpeter said, "[A]n excellent theory that can never be refuted and lacks nothing save sense." The Ricardian engine "spelled decisive advance" in theorizing. But, of course, if a defective engine meets with success, that advance may easily prove to be a detour. And, Schumpeter continued, "let me state at once: *a detour Ricardian analysis was.*"[1]

There is a stream of modern theory—maybe it is something of a resurrection and clarification of a few early writers—that is quite pertinent, nonetheless.[2] The most complete articulation is by Williamson, with attention to concepts such as "bounded rationality," "information impactedness," "small number bargaining," "idiosyncratic (human and physical) capital" and "opportunistic behavior."[3] With attention to these concepts and to the notion of "transactions cost" that flows along with them, one can better appreciate why particular market functions are organized as they are. Let me define some terms and concepts.

Bounded rationality means that actors in the market place are unable to obtain accurate information fully and certainly, even with expenditures of time and money, and are dealing in complex circumstances such that, even with more complete data, optimizing behavior is difficult either to define or, if defined, still difficult to achieve. Under those circumstances, transactions, if they occur, occur with incomplete and possibly inaccurate information. Further, repeated transactions yield learning—learning about what is relevant and what is not, which actions to avoid and which to repeat, and so forth.

Information impactedness relates to the fact that different actors have different information. The information available to the buyer is different from that of the seller, and different people within the selling firm have different skills and knowledge. Information transfer designed to reduce the degree of impactedness or information asymmetry is again costly and imperfect. Further, there is a "paradox of information" that limits the efficiency of market exchanges of information: buyers become more willing to pay for information as they better realize what they are to buy, but then they have it and need not pay! And sellers, after conveying information to one buyer, are no less able to sell the same thing to another.

If there are but few sellers, a buyer has limited alternatives to turn to in the event that transactions with any one fail to be satisfactory. The converse is true for buyers. But even if the number of buyers and sellers is larger, problems still arise if the buyer or seller or both must invest in human or physical capital that is fully useful in *only* a particular transaction.

All of these factors—bounded rationality, information impactedness, and a small number of bargainers—lead to the potential for opportunistic behavior by the trading partners. Opportunistic behavior is self-interest practiced in a strategic manner and perhaps with guile, and fear of it limits market transactions.

With these notions in mind, Williamson argues that spot markets work well when many buyers and many sellers transact for an easily defined commodity. Since conditions are not complex, price conveys complete information for the exchange, rules for transacting are easily established and understood, and they can be enforced at low costs. In this case, idiosyncratic capital is unnecessary for traders because, should a transaction with any one party break down, it costs little to shift the transaction to another.

With some exaggeration, this characterizes the market for commercial bank credit. At a step removed, it is somewhat similar to investment banking and new issues underwriting, since each issue has peculiarities that do not repeat and for which there are "front end costs" that can be recovered only if the particular transaction materializes.

Under more complicated market conditions, however, when idiosyncratic capital is necessary for repeated and frequent transactions, vertical integration becomes attractive. As such, market mediation is replaced by managerial controls. This occurs for at least two reasons. First, market-based contingent claims contracts will necessarily be incomplete, costly to amend and difficult to enforce. Second, opportunistic behavior is encouraged in the post-contractual period as either or both parties perceive that the other has no good alternative to continued performance—even with radically less attractive terms than those considered when the agreement was initially reached. Under these circumstances contracting and market exchanges are more difficult than commonly viewed.

These conditions are descriptive of venture capital markets. Venture capital involves some highly idiosyncratic transactions. For example, prior to commitment of funds, the venture capitalist typically must learn a great deal that is relevant to that transaction *alone*. In some cases, expertise gained in one transaction might reduce the learning costs for subsequent transactions. Where this is true, specialization emerges *within* venture capital firms. There is, however, reluctance to rely heavily on *outside* experts for information. Information asymmetries are not easy to correct through purchasing, and there is added exposure to opportunistic behavior.

Opportunism (and other aspects of failures to adhere to contracts) on the part of those demanding venture capital funds are often constrained by controls established, operated and monitored by the venture capitalist. In particular, active management of the enterprise (or options to replace management) often follows with the financial transaction. An ownership interest—for control and for potential monetary gain—usually runs with venture capital funds. The dialogue suggested that financing is so structured that minimal reliance on litigation or on costly third-party arbitration or mediation is necessary. That is, while there is not the classically defined vertical integration between the venture capitalist and the firm being financed, means for expeditious and fiat-like resolutions of conflicts are incorporated in the relationships.

Among the participants there was also concern about opportunism arising in the "markets" in which venture capitalists raise funds. A few unscrupulous operators, by fraudulently or carelessly behaving so that some investors needlessly lose substantial assets, cause the intermediation of venture capital to be less efficient. To reduce that problem, close "relational" contracts are employed between venture capitalists and those relying on them for profitable investments.

Accordingly, the effective markets between entrepreneurs and venture capitalists are not those characterized by the impersonal trading in so-called perfect markets as commonly portrayed in economics. Rather, the venture capital markets are more complex when the parties rely on one another through sets of sequential and satisfactory transactions.

III. CONCLUSION

One conclusion is clear. There is room for research on the topics covered. The fruitful approaches, however, are likely to be those using unorthodox conceptual approaches to explain market phenomena. The Ricardian influence, carried now into such sophisticated formalisms in equilibrium analysis, may not be a costly detour for all financial analysis, but it's usefulness is surely questionable in matters of entrepreneurship, venture capital and innovation.

NOTES

1. See Schumpeter (1954, pp. 473, 474). Emphasis in original.
2. In addition to Schumpeter, Saint Simon, St. Antonine of Florence, Cantillon, J. B. Say, Adam Smith (reading a bit into *Wealth of Nations*), and Antonio Serra, for example.
3. See Williamson (1975).

REFERENCES

Schumpeter, J. A. (1954), *History of Economic Analysis*. New York: Oxford University Press.
Williamson, O. E. (1975), *Markets and Hierarchies*. New York: The Free Press.

PART II

RESEARCH IN ENTREPRENEURSHIP AND INNOVATION

INTRODUCTION: RESEARCH ON ENTREPRENEURSHIP AND INNOVATION

Gary D. Libecap

The four papers in Part II of the volume are examples of important new research on the broad topics of innovation and entrepreneurship. In each case, they introduce a new emphasis, bring additional data, and offer fresh techniques for analyzing technical and economic change.

The first paper, by David Mowery, examines the translation of scientific and technical knowledge into productivity-enhancing innovations at the firm level. He begins with a critical survey of the existing literature on the interaction among innovation, organizational and market structures, market demand, entry barriers, and R&D investment. Mowery concludes the survey by arguing that too much attention has been focused on the supply of R&D and too little attention on R&D utilization, and in particular on the organizational issues involved in the adoption of new technology. He stresses that in most cases there is limited transferability of R&D results across firms because of a lack of in-house knowledge for adopting the new technology. Those factors, according to Mowery, are critical to innovation diffusion. Mowery calls for more research on the characteristics of organizations which are successful in responding to innovation, as well as on the characteristics of organizations which are less innovative.

To develop his arguments, Mowery examines the semiconductor industry. In that industry, he finds that smaller firms tend to be the most innovative, but that market shares change dramatically following shocks from the infusion of new technology and entry by other firms. Among semiconductor firms, there appears

---

Advances in the Study of Entrepreneurship, Innovation, and Economic Growth, Volume 1, pages 85-87.

to be little proprietary, firmspecific technology. The limits on inter-firm transfer of technology come not from the characteristics of the technology, but from the internal organizational capital or expertise needed to adopt innovations. Mowery goes on to examine the diffusion process within the semiconductor industry to show how organizational issues affect the rate of adoption.

The impact of organization structure and individual decisions on innovation are examined from another direction by David Tansik and Gerrit Wolf in Chapter 9. They are concerned with the incentives of decision-makers to adopt new technology and, once adopted, how the technology is spread through the firm. Two critical individuals are identified as entrepreneurs: the producer entrepreneur who investigates commercial possibilities of an invention or new technology, and the product champion within the adopting firm who promotes the technology by developing multiple applications. In contrast to the general literature, they argue that there are many inventions, but that the more difficult task is to refine ideas into usable products or processes.

In developing their argument, Tansik and Wolf outline stages of innovation and how the two entrepreneurial types enter in the transitions between invention, production, adoption, and routine utilization of new technology. In each stage, they identify the decision-makers and the criteria considered for adoption. Because the innovation process within firms is complex, examination of the details involved is essential for understanding how technology is acquired or rejected.

The importance of organizations and institutional structures is also examined in the paper by Mark Isaac and Stanley Reynolds in Chapter 10. Using the unique techniques of experimental economics, Isaac and Reynolds ask how various property rights arrangements affect the incentives for R&D investment. They investigate three hypotheses: (1) if new ideas cannot be fully appropriated, there will be underinvestment in R&D; (2) where there is full appropriability (property rights are complete), there will be aggregate overinvestment in R&D by the industry because of the common property nature of undiscovered ideas; and (3) as the number of firms in the industry rises, the aggregate industry investment in R&D increases.

Isaac and Reynolds survey the literature and point out that these three hypotheses have been subject to debate with no clear resolution because of a lack of empirical data. Fortunately, these questions lend themselves to experimental examination. Using undergraduate students, Isaac and Reynolds ran 12 four-person experiments to test the hypotheses. Each student was given $3.00 to invest in R&D under strictly controlled conditions. Investment decisions involved the purchase of draws at $.10 per draw, with a successful innovation represented by a type A draw and an unsuccessful innovation by a type B draw.

A monetary prize was fixed for a successful innovation, representing the future stream of profits. Under conditions of full appropriability, the prize was given to the individual with a type A draw. Experiments were run also with partial appropriability where the type A individual (firm) received the largest share of the prize, but the unsuccessful type B individuals (firms) received smaller shares. The latter experiments represented the cases where property rights to new technology were not well defined or enforced, so that all firms benefited from the R&D investments of the successful firm. In the experiments, the aim for each student was to maximize profits; additional income depended upon type A draws, while additional costs depended upon the number of draws chosen at a cost of $.10 per draw. Based on the experimental results, Isaac and Reynolds find support for all three hypotheses and, as such, provide tangible evidence for improved understanding of the importance of property rights arrangements in the R&D process. Their paper also shows how experimental techniques can be used to address significant policy issues.

Chapter 11, by Arne Kalleberg, shifts attention from organizational questions to the entrepreneur. To begin, he addresses the debate over the definition of entrepreneurship by examining the importance of individual characteristics, the role of innovation, the contribution of risk, and the nature of the environment (small firms versus large organizations). Kalleberg concludes that entrepreneurship refers to both activities and individuals, and he defines it as a continuum where certain activities and individuals are more entrepreneurial than others. Among the entrepreneurial characteristics examined by Kalleberg, innovation, risk, and control in decision-making are emphasized as important in any definition of entrepreneurship. For his survey of entrepreneurs, Kalleberg focuses on small firm owner-operators.

His survey of 411 Indiana owner-operators investigates the determinants of innovation in three industries: health related services, eating and drinking, and computer hardware and software service. Several questions are asked, including: What makes some individuals more entrepreneurial than others? What are their characteristics? What social and market contexts make it easier or more difficult for innovative behavior? What are the determinants of business performance? In addressing each of the questions, Kalleberg systematically reports and analyzes the data collected from the survey. His study is one of the most ambitious efforts to collect data on entrepreneurs, and represents a major advance in the literature.

The final chapter of the volume is a research bibliography on entrepreneurship. It is divided into four sections: the Economics of Technological Change; Finance and Venture Capital; Entrepreneurship and Intrapreneurship; and Small Business. While not complete, the bibliography reveals the richness of the existing literature and provides sources for future research.

Chapter 8

MARKET STRUCTURE AND INNOVATION:
A CRITICAL SURVEY

David C. Mowery

I. INTRODUCTION

As a key contributor to the economic growth and wealth of nations, technological change has long received considerable attention in economics. Indeed, the work of Karl Marx and Joseph Schumpeter portrayed technological change as a central engine of economic growth and social change. More recently, the economics of technological change has spawned a vast theoretical and empirical literature. This paper briefly reviews this literature, dealing primarily with its empirical component, in an effort to reach some conclusions about the interactions among innovation, organizational and market structures of interest to an audience of academics, managers, and policymakers.

Despite its size, this vast body of scholarship has yielded a modest intellectual payoff for either the formulation of sectoral policy or the management of innovation within organizations. While the analysis of the contribution of innovation to the long-term economic growth of nations has been advanced significantly by the efforts of Abramovitz, Kuznets, Denison, and Solow, our understanding of the

Advances in the Study of Entrepreneurship, Innovation,
and Economic Growth, Volume 1, pages 89-113.
Copyright © 1986 by JAI Press Inc.
ISBN: 0-89232-703-0

mechanisms underpinning the translation of scientific and technical knowledge into productivity-enhancing innovation at the level of the industry or firm remains remarkably thin.

Immediately below, I discuss the intellectual foundations of the theoretical and empirical work carried out by economists on market structure and innovation. Due to the large volume of this literature, I simply summarize its general conclusions, rather than discussing individual papers in detail.[1] Following this, is a brief consideration of the theoretical literature on government policy and innovation. A critique and discussion of the relevance and applicability of this work to the microelectronics industry follow.

II. MARKET STRUCTURE AND INNOVATION: SCHUMPETER AND AFTER

The empirical study of market structure and innovation was greatly influenced by Schumpeter (1954). The Schumpeterian "hypothesis" was largely a response to the sea change in the structure of the innovation process that took place within the industrial world during this century. Invention and innovation shifted during the late 19th and early 20th centuries from processes dominated largely by individuals to a far more formalized structure, in which corporate sources of invention played the central role.[2] The emergence of industrial research within the firm was a response to significant structural changes within manufacturing firms, the scientific advances in physics and chemistry that sparked the so-called "Second Industrial Revolution," and the development of scientific research within higher education within the U.S. during this period.[3] Schumpeter argued that "innovation is being reduced to routine. Technological progress is increasingly becoming the business of teams of trained specialists who turn out what is required and make it work in predictable ways" (1954, p. 132).

The perceived dominance of the innovation process by the largest firms in the industrial nations[4] led Schumpeter to modify his earlier emphasis on the individual innovator as the key actor in spurring the "gale of creative destruction" (1934), arguing instead for the importance of large, monopolistic firms as innovators:

> there are superior methods available to the monopolist which either are not available at all to a crowd of competitors or are not available to them so readily; for there are advantages which, though not strictly unattainable on the competitive level of enterprise, are as a matter of fact secured only on the monopoly level . . . There cannot be any reasonable doubt that under the conditions of our epoch such superiority is as a matter of fact the outstanding feature of the typical large-scale unit of control, though mere size is neither necessary nor sufficient for it. These units not only arise in the process of creative destruction and function in a way entirely different from the static schema, but in many cases of decisive importance they provide the necessary form for the achievement. They largely create what they exploit (pp. 100–101).

The Schumpeterian hypothesis is hardly a model of precision, yet it has exerted a hold over the empirical study of the economics of technological change matched by few other intellectual constructs. A central reason for this fascination, of course, is the importance of technological change as an engine of economic growth. Schumpeter also posed a significant challenge to the prevailing theory of market organization, in arguing that the perfectly competitive conditions viewed as essential to the achievement of static efficiency conflicted directly with the structural conditions necessary for the attainment of high levels of dynamic performance and growth.

Empirical tests of the Schumpeterian hypothesis have tested two variants of the original statement. A number of investigations of the relationship between market structure (primarily industry concentration) and R&D investment have explored the link between imperfect competition and innovative performance that was stressed by Schumpeter. A second group of empirical studies has analyzed the relationship between firm size and R&D investment, focusing on Schumpeter's statements concerning the role of the large firm as an agent of technical change. While the results of these analyses have frequently been interpreted as either supporting or demolishing the hypotheses of Schumpeter, in fact they do not support such conclusions, as Fisher and Temin (1973) have noted. Observations of the relationship between innovative inputs and firm or market structure say nothing about the efficiency with which such inputs are translated into economically significant innovations. This question of innovative efficiency or productivity is at the heart of the Schumpeterian hypothesis. Without very strong and essentially tautological assumptions about the nature of the innovation production function within the firm, most of the existing "tests" of these Schumpeterian hypotheses test nothing of the sort.

The basis for the hypothesized relationship between producer concentration and innovative performance was not clearly spelled out by Schumpeter. His successors have also failed to provide straightforward theoretical explanations for this relationship. Firms in more concentrated industries may be better able to appropriate the returns from innovation, but other theorists (notably Arrow, 1962) have argued that perfectly competitive firms face greater incentives to pursue innovation than do monopolists (Arrow's conclusions have been disputed by Demsetz, 1969). High industry concentration may lead to monopoly profits, enabling firms in such industries to finance the risky activities of R&D and innovation more easily, avoiding reliance on imperfect capital markets. Other authors (notably Blair, 1972) have employed anecdotal and historical evidence in arguing that concentrated industries are associated with poor innovative performance. The theoretical basis for any relationship between either R&D investment or innovative performance, and market concentration, on the other hand, thus remains unclear.

The theoretical ambiguity concerning this relationship is reinforced by the results of empirical analyses of R&D investment.[5] Most recent studies (Scherer,

1967; Scott, 1984; Levin, Cohen, and Mowery, 1985) have found an "inverted-U" relationship between an industry's four-firm concentration ratio (i.e., the share of industry shipments accounted for by the four largest producers) and research intensity in cross-sectional analyses of industry data. According to these studies, R&D intensity is maximized at a four-firm concentration ratio of roughly .50–.55; at higher levels of concentration, R&D intensity declines. While seemingly undercutting the Schumpeterian hypothesis, these results are suspect on methodological grounds. Specifically, when variables are inserted to measure the effects of unmeasured industry conditions, as in Scott (1984), the statistical significance of concentration vanishes. Moreover, Levin et al. (1985) find that concentration and R&D investment may in fact be jointly determined, rather than R&D investment being caused unidirectionally by concentration.

Of greater interest and significance, however, is the finding, first noted by Scherer (1965, 1967) and supported by Levin et al. (1985), that the apparent statistical significance of producer concentration in explaining research intensity is spurious; concentration in fact proxies for industry conditions of technological appropriability and opportunity. In this interpretation, highly concentrated, R&D-intensive industries are those in which the fertility of the underlying knowledge base ("technological opportunity"), as well as the ability of firms to appropriate the returns from such investment through a wide range of mechanisms ("ease of appropriability"), are relatively high. Rather than suggesting that concentration causes high levels of R&D intensity, Levin et al. (1985) suggest that industry-specific conditions of technological opportunity and appropriability may support a certain level of both R&D investment and producer concentration. Such joint determination of R&D investment and market structure is consistent with Schumpeter's original work, which stressed the dynamic impact of R&D investment and innovation on market structure.

A second body of work has focused on the relationship between firm size and R&D investment, testing another variant of the Schumpeterian hypothesis. Once again, the theoretical rationales for the linkage between firm size and innovative performance are numerous and ambiguous.[6] Imperfect capital markets may support higher R&D investment within large firms, or firms operating in concentrated markets, due to the possibility that large firms, or firms earning monopoly profits, are more liquid, and thus better able to finance R&D than are smaller entities. Since R&D is a fixed cost, the higher sales associated with giant firms allow these costs to be spread across a greater volume of output, increasing the returns to R&D investment. The risks of R&D may also be lower for larger firms reflecting greater diversification across product markets and/or R&D projects. If larger firms possess higher market shares within their product lines, their ability to appropriate the fruits of R&D investment may be enhanced. Finally, the productivity of R&D investment may be increased by interactions between the R&D and other nonmanufacturing functions within the firm, e.g., marketing and financial management. These functions are typically less highly developed within smaller firms. Rebuttals to these arguments invoke the supposedly bu-reaucratic, less creative atmosphere of the large research laboratory and/or firm (see Mueller, 1962; Hamberg, 1963); the incentives of monopolists, as opposed to perfectly competitive firms, to pursue innovation; and the ready availability via contract of the nonmanufacturing services held to be lacking within smaller firms.

In addition to the imprecise character of the arguments for and against large firm size as a factor supporting innovation, theoretical and empirical investiga-tions of the firm size-R&D investment relationship have been limited by the as-sumption, explicit or implicit, that firms are single-product entities. As a result, no distinction has been made between the effects of large firm size and large size within a given product market (e.g., the size of a specific business unit within the firm)—yet these two measures of size clearly capture very different structural attributes in a world of diversified manufacturing firms. Some of the factors af-fecting the innovative performance of large firms operate only at the level of the individual business unit. These factors include market share and sales volume within a specific market. On the other hand, corporate liquidity, product diversification, and in-house nonmanufacturing services are corporate attributes. Considerable refinement of these arguments and their empirical tests is required.

Until recently, an empirical consensus of sorts had been reached on the influence of firm size on corporate R&D investment. Although size was associa-ted with increasing R&D intensity up to some size threshold (near the lower end of the 500 largest U.S. firms), R&D intensity (defined as the share of total sales devoted to R&D) did not increase, and in many industries declined above this threshold, with the occasional exception of the chemicals industry. Similar to analyses of industry concentration and R&D intensity, these studies included a limited number of explanatory variables. Due in part to the limited set of explan-atory variables in these empirical specifications, considerable inter-industry vari-ation in the relationship between firm size and R&D intensity remained unexplained. Throughout this work, firms were treated as single-product entities; that is, a given firm was "assigned" to a primary industry, and assumed to face conditions in all of its product markets that were identical to those of the primary industry.

Two recent studies have obtained results that differ from this consensus. Scherer (1984a) employed data from the Federal Trade Commission's Line of Business program on business unit size and R&D intensity, where a business unit is defined as a single product-line entity of a larger corporation, operating in a specific three- or four-digit S.I.C. Thus, Scherer's study was one of the first to penetrate beneath the corporate unit of analysis, although he did not explicitly compare the relative importance of corporate and business unit size. Scherer found "mild support" (p. 233) for the "Schumpeterian" position that business unit R&D intensity increased with business unit size. The Line of Business data analyzed by Scherer are restricted to large U.S. firms, as is true of the data analyzed in most previous studies. The study by Bound, Cummins, Griliches, and Hall (1984) utilized a much broader sample of firms in its analysis of the relationship between corporate size and corporate R&D intensity. Bound et al. also found some support for the Schumpeterian position, concluding that there exists "significant nonlinearity in the relationship {between firm size and R&D intensity}, implying that both very small and very large firms are more R&D intensive than average-size firms" (pp. 48–50). This study was once again restricted to treating firms as single-product entities, but it suggests that significant empirical work remains to be done in establishing more definitively the relationship between corporate and business unit size, on the one hand, and R&D intensity on the other. The empirical and theoretical work on the firm size-R&D investment relationship resembles that on the relationship between market structure and R&D, in that firm size is a proxy for a number of other influences, ranging from liquidity to product diversification.

The studies reviewed above are concerned almost exclusively with R&D inputs, as was noted; yet the Schumpeterian hypotheses are really concerned with the relationship between R&D inputs and outputs. Empirical studies of this relationship are handicapped by the lack of reliable and accessible data measuring innovative output. Nonetheless, several studies have examined the relationship between input measures, such as R&D investment or employment, and patents, an imperfect but accessible measure of innovative output, as a function of firm size. Both Scherer (1965) and Bound et al. (1984) found that patent output per dollar of R&D investment declined above a modest firm size, although within the upper reaches of the firm size distribution, this productivity measure remained constant. Scherer (1984a) considered patents as well as R&D expenditures in analyzing Line of Business data. Noting that the largest firms in the Line of Business data accounted for a share of total patents that was lower than these firms' share of R&D investment, Scherer concluded that patent output relative to business unit size declined slightly as business units grew in size. The evidence thus is surprisingly unanimous in suggesting that firm or business unit size is not strongly correlated with this measure of innovative performance—a more fundamental issue, however, concerns the appropriateness of patents as measures of innovative (as opposed to inventive) output.

If a deeper understanding of the relationship between firm or market structure and R&D investment or output is to be achieved, the influence on R&D investment of the underlying influences, rather than the size or producer concentration proxies for these influences, must be analyzed directly. A modest body of work has examined the influence on R&D investment of several dimensions of firm structure that may be correlated with increasing corporate size, with mixed results. Grabowski (1968) considered the role of liquidity, arguing that higher levels of cash flow enabled (presumably larger) firms to finance R&D investment more easily. Grabowski's hypothesis was supported by the finding that corporate cash flow was associated with higher levels of corporate R&D intensity in the chemicals, pharmaceuticals, and petroleum industries. An alternative interpretation of the significance of cash flow has been set forth in Mueller (1967) and Elliott (1971), who argue that high levels of profits or cash flow may proxy for expected future profits, attracting higher levels of R&D investment. One means for resolving this dispute relies on the distinction between the corporate and business unit levels of analysis. If liquidity is the primary reason for the significance of cash flow in explaining R&D investment, then corporate cash flow should be highly significant in explaining R&D investment within a given line of business within the firm. On the other hand, if cash flow proxies for future profits, then business unit cash flow should be the only significant cash flow measure in explaining business unit R&D investment.

Another dimension of firm structure that may have been confounded with firm size in the theoretical and empirical analyses discussion is product diversification. First hypothesized to be a positive influence on basic research investment by Nelson (1959), the influence of diversification on overall R&D investment, as well as basic research investment at the corporate level, has received some empirical scrutiny in recent work. The results have been mixed; while Grabowski (1968) found weak support for the hypothesis that diversification was associated with higher levels of corporate R&D intensity, other scholars (e.g., Comanor, 1965) have found that product diversification is associated with lower levels of corporate R&D output (measured in this case as the proportion of sales of pharmaceuticals firms attributable to new products). Link and Long (1981) found that higher levels of product diversification were weakly associated with higher levels of corporate investment in basic research, supporting the original Nelson hypothesis. Scherer (1984a) presented results suggesting that diversification has a modest positive influence on patenting. Still another dimension of corporate structure that has received some empirical scrutiny is vertical integration, primarily in Armour and Teece (1981). Their results were weak and pertained to a single industry (petroleum), but provided some support for the hypothesis that vertical integration is positively correlated with corporate R&D intensity.

Several studies have examined aspects of market structure that may be associated with industry concentration. Among these factors is market demand, which plays a complex role. While firms holding large market shares may face a higher return to investment in R&D,[7] changes in overall industry demand could also affect innovative activity, due to the effects of increased demand on either entry or return to R&D investment. The role of demand in innovation was investigated in considerable detail by Schmookler (1966). Schmookler used patenting activity as a measure of innovation in capital goods industries. Changing industry demand conditions were measured by investment in the industries employing those capital goods. Finding that investment exerted a statistically significant influence on this measure of inventive output, Schmookler concluded that "invention is largely an economic activity which, like other economic activities, is pursued for gain; [and] expected gain varies with expected sales of goods embodying the invention . . ." (p. 206). In other words, market demand "pulls" and affects the direction of innovative activity, due to the fact that, according to Schmookler, "mankind today possesses, and for some time has possessed, a *multipurpose knowledge base*. We are, and evidently for some time have been, able to extend the technological frontier perceptibly at virtually all points" (p. 210; emphasis in original). Schmookler's results, which applied to a limited number of capital goods industries, were qualified, but not overturned in Scherer's study (1984b) of patenting activity in a wider sample of manufacturing industries.

Entry plays an important yet unspecified role in Schmookler's conceptual framework. The influence of barriers to entry on industry R&D intensity has been examined by several scholars. Clearly, ease of entry and producer concentration are likely to be inversely correlated in a cross-sectional analysis. Nonetheless, identification of the nature of any entry barriers that affect R&D investment, as well as some delineation of their impact, are important potential advances in understanding the interaction between market structure and R&D activity. Comanor (1967) examined the role of entry barriers indirectly, finding that concentrated industries exhibiting high levels of product differentiation, a factor that typically operates as an entry barrier, were less research intensive, ceteris paribus. In other words, entry barriers may operate jointly with industry concentration to affect the level of R&D investment, a finding that modifies the hypotheses of Schumpeter. Broadly similar results were obtained by Shrieves (1978), who found that concentrated industries in which imitation was difficult and product differentiation was common were less research intensive.

A final dimension of industry structure that is associated with, but should be distinguished from, industry concentration relies on the notion of industry lifecycles, arguing that mature industries are less research-intensive. Abernathy (1978) asserted that as industries age, the relative importance of process innovation increases substantially, reflecting slowing rates of growth in market demand and a strong tendency toward product standardization. Both the level of R&D intensity and the productivity of R&D investment decline as industries mature in this theory, which is largely based on case studies of the automobile and other metalworking industries.

While Schumpeter was concerned primarily with long-run processes of economic change and dynamics, the empirical analyses of the hypotheses based on his work have been largely ahistorical and static in their orientation. As was noted, Schumpeter's speculations on the changing structure of the innovation process were written following a fifty-year period of upheaval in the organization of research and innovation. Indeed, several of the advantages of large firm size discussed by Schumpeter and others may well change as a result of the introduction of new technologies for the processing, storage, and transmission of information. Nonetheless, the analysis of the Schumpeterian hypotheses has proceeded on the assumption that the relationships between market structure, firm size, and innovative performance are invariant. Rather than focusing solely on the strength of these relationships, it may prove more fruitful to analyze the conditions that underpin, and thus may alter, the relative innovative performance of large and small firms.

III. MARKET STRUCTURE AND INNOVATION: A CRITIQUE OF THE EMPIRICAL AND CONCEPTUAL FOUNDATIONS

The large body of work on the relationship between firm and market structure on the one hand, and R&D investment or output on the other, has failed to reach strong conclusions concerning these relationships at the level of either the industry or the individual firm. Moreover, this empirical research has not provided guidelines for management and policy at the sectoral or firm levels. Concern over the innovative impact of firm and market structure, for example, has played a very modest historical role at best in antitrust policy and litigation within the United States.[8]

The empirical literature on market structure and innovation occupies an awkward position within economics—not only are the empirical phenomena poorly understood, the techniques employed in the exploration of these phenomena are not solidly grounded in a theoretical model. As a result, theoretical explanations for many of the empirically established relationships between market structure and R&D investment are lacking.[9]

While the empirical analysis of innovation and market structure has not had a great impact on government policy within the United States, the same cannot be said about the policy impact of economic theory. The dominant theoretical model of R&D investment developed in papers by Nelson (1959) and Arrow (1962), has exerted a major influence on U.S. science and technology policy. These papers, which predated the bulk of the empirical literature, portrayed research and development as an activity resulting from investment decisions made by profit-maximizing firms, consistent with the general tenets of neoclassical economic theory.[10] The critical element in understanding the research investment decision of the firm was the nature of the returns to such an investment. Nelson and Arrow argued that the social returns to research investment exceeded the private returns faced by the individual firm, a condition leading to underinvestment by the firm (from the social point of view) in research.

The reasons adduced for the existence of this market failure are of considerable importance in understanding the implications of these theories for both research and policy. Arrow in particular argued that while the firm's costs of investment in knowledge production were substantial, the costs of transferring the knowledge once discovered were zero. Reflecting its "public good" character, the widest possible diffusion of this knowledge was socially optimal. However, the price necessary to achieve this end, i.e., one equal to the costs of transfer, was so low as to bankrupt the discoverer. Thus, the supply of socially beneficial research in civilian technologies in particular was likely to be too low, due to the disjunction between the privately and socially optimal prices for the results of such research. These analyses provided the intellectual basis for government subsidies during the 1960s and 1970s for civilian basic and fundamental applied research.

Despite its great elegance and influence, this neoclassical analysis of the economics of R&D is incomplete. Appropriability of research results, while perhaps necessary for the encouragement of R&D investment, is certainly not sufficient to explain the success and failure of various organizational structures for the performance of R&D. In many cases, the central element influencing both the structure of such organizations and their innovative success or failure is the fact that the transfer of technological knowledge is itself a resource—a knowledge-intensive process.[11] An equally serious deficiency for policy purposes is the exclusive focus of this analysis on the supply of research and development, rather than on the utilization, diffusion, and adoption of the results of R&D. It is the adoption of new technologies, rather than their development within the laboratory, that is the key dimension of innovation for economic growth.

The diffusion and adoption of new technologies are neglected within this analytic framework; yet these are the critical channels through which R&D exerts its impact on productivity and income growth within the economy. U.S. government policy in particular has focused almost exclusively on supporting the supply of R&D (a significant and important exception is U.S. agricultural research). Many of the stated goals of this policy framework, however, might be pursued more effectively through a systematic effort to support the diffusion of innovations.[12] Indeed, a striking characteristic of Japanese industrial policy in such sectors as robotics and computers is the support provided for the adoption and diffusion of new technologies.[13] The lack of a well-developed theoretical analysis of diffusion undercuts the relevance of the economic theory of innovation for policy purposes.

In addition to their inattention to the diffusion of innovations, economic theories of innovation typically ignore the organization of R&D within the firm and the economy, overlooking both the ways in which the underlying technology influences this organizational structure, the effects of this structure on the outcomes of the innovation process. The received theory of R&D investment, for example, is hard-pressed to explain the obvious fact that the overwhelming majority of industrial research performed within the U.S. economy is organized on an intrafirm basis.[14] Nor does this theoretical framework provide insights into the basis for recent changes in the organization of industrial research, as joint ventures and other forms of multifirm research consortia have proliferated.[15]

The neoclassical analysis also overlooks the fact that a great deal of R&D investment produces intermediate inputs for the firm's products and processes. While R&D clearly generates transferable and often marketable knowledge and know-how, it also produces nontransferable know-how, components of the firm's "organizational capital" (Prescott and Visscher, 1980; Gort and Klepper, 1982). In conceptualizing the results of R&D as solely marketable final goods (a term that includes process innovations), and assuming that knowledge transfer is essentially costless, the neoclassical analysis of R&D has been emptied of useful implications for the analysis of the organization of R&D. As such, the resulting analytic framework cannot address a great many issues of importance for public policy and private management.

The acquisition and accumulation by firms of intangible organization capital was cited by Penrose (1958) as a key influence on growth and diversification, as firms expanded or reorganized in a continual effort to utilize these assets fully. More recently, the role of such firm-specific assets has been emphasized by Hymer (1961), Kindleberger (1967), and Caves (1982) in explaining the growth of multinational firms. Significantly, much of the empirical work on the determinants of direct foreign investment has focused on R&D activity as a critical determinant, due to the contribution of research and development to growth in the firm's stock of such intangible assets.[16]

Intrafirm exploitation of such technological assets was responsible for firm growth and diversification, as well as foreign investment, in the analysis of these scholars. Such intrafirm exploitation reflected the difficulties of sufficiently separating a given intangible asset from the rest of the firm and assessing and establishing its value, activities that are necessary to support the exploitation of such assets through arms-length sale or licensing agreements. More recently, as the costs of intrafirm exploitation (e.g., rapidly rising development costs) of such assets have increased, while those of information transfer, storage and analysis have fallen, domestic and international cooperative ventures have become more attractive alternatives to intrafirm exploitation of components of the firm's organization capital. As numerous analysts have noted, such joint ventures, especially those involving development of, as well as research on, new products, exploit complementarities between the intangible assets of partner firms,[17] while at the same time somewhat ameliorating the difficulties of valuation and moral hazard that attend licensing and other arms-length transfers.[18]

The preoccupation with the salable outputs of R&D is reflected in the "demand-pull" work of Schmookler and subsequent scholars, and is critically reviewed in Rosenberg (1976) and Mowery and Rosenberg (1979).[19] All too often in this work, market demand is confused with the far wider and more amorphous notion of consumer "needs."[20] One consequence of such confusion is the failure in case studies and elsewhere to empirically distinguish between influences on innovation that arise from "within" the economic unit, such as increases in output or changes in production technology, which are a result of factors that are external to the firm and are in fact mediated by the market. Moreover, the nature of the "demand shifts" to which such studies refer is ambiguous. Is an innovation introduced because the demand for a products has increased, suggesting an outward shift in the demand curve, or because process improvements make it possible to sell a given product at a lower price, constituting a movement along the demand curve? Presumably, the first example is a true case of "demand-pull," but the information necessary to distinguish between the cases is not provided in most empirical studies.

The key issue in understanding the origins of an innovation is rarely that of whether a demand for the product existed; it is instead why a given innovation did not appear before or after the date at which it was introduced. Changes in supply or demand conditions, rather than the existence and character of these influences for this purpose are critical. Establishing the causal primacy of demand-side forces for a specific innovation requires proof that demand conditions in a given market change in ways that were more significant than changes in supply conditions. In the final analysis, there is no good a priori reason for the dominance of innovative activity by demand-side forces. In a world populated by profit-seeking firms, any change presenting a profitable opportunity for innovation presumably will be acted on, be this a change in demand, process technology, or conditions of supply.

This focus on the generation of organization capital through R&D investment, as well as the distribution and utilization of the results of R&D among the firms within an industry, yields some policy implications that differ from those of the neoclassical framework.[21] The recurrent proposals for cooperative industrial research activities as substitutes for in-house R&D (for example, the National Science Foundation's experiment in university-industry research cooperation, or the Stevenson-Wydler Act of 1980) reflect a belief that the critical factor contributing to poor innovative performance by an industry is insufficient in-house R&D, which in turn stems from the limited appropriability of the results of such R&B. While limited appropriability may well contribute to insufficient R&D investment, the limited transferability of R&D outputs, as well as the requirements for an in-house knowledge base sufficient to support such absorption, may undermine the capacity of firms to fully absorb the output of cooperative R&D. Cooperative research functions most effectively as a complement to, rather than as a substitute for, the in-house research activities of firms. This relationship is overlooked entirely by an exclusive focus on the appropriability of the output of R&D.

Emphasis on the "intermediate good" character of the results of much R&D also suggests that a government role in supporting the development of an industry-wide knowledge base, be this role effected through publicly financed cooperative research or contracts with individual firms (an alternative less likely to yield an easily accessible generic knowledge base within an industry) as a complement to in-house research, may have a great impact on industry structure. Government funding, by broadening the industry-wide knowledge base, may encourage entry, and thereby support a more competitive environment. Evidence from the civilian aircraft industry prior to 1960 (see Phillips, 1971; Mowery &

Rosenberg, 1982) semiconductors (see below), pharmaceuticals (see Grabowski & Vernon, 1982), and agriculture (see Evenson, 1982) within the U.S. all suggest that such public support of R&D in civilian industries indeed can encourage entry and a more dynamic, fluid market structure.

The potentially procompetitive impact of policies designed to enhance an industry's generic knowledge base has important implications for antitrust policy, among other things. In particular, a permissive attitude toward joint research ventures among erstwhile competitor firms may aid, rather than retard, the operation of competitive forces within an industry. In order that such joint R&D activity may yield industry-wide knowledge spillovers, rather than inhibiting competition, joint research must be confined to the basic and fundamental phases of R&D, and disclosure to nonparticipants may be necessary. Nonetheless, in conjunction with vigorous intrafirm R&D activity, joint research may enhance competition within a given industry, as technological leaders' positions are undermined by wider diffusion of technological capabilities. Japanese industrial policy in many high-technology sectors follows such a model. Cooperation among firms is encouraged (or required) in certain phases of precommercial research (see Peck and Goto, 1982; Mowery and Rosenberg, 1985). Competition among these firms in production remains intense, however, and supports a high level of international competitiveness. Thus the supposed conflict between the preservation of international competitiveness and the enforcement of interfirm competition may be illusory once R&D is conceptualized as an activity yielding intangible assets that may be highly firm-specific. The degree to which the results of R&D reinforce or undercut market power in turn depends on the structure of the research system, which itself can be influenced by public policy.

IV. MARKET STRUCTURE AND INNOVATION IN SEMICONDUCTORS

The empirical literature discussed in this paper is concerned primarily with cross-sectional comparisons of a number of industries, rather than the intensive longitudinal study of one or two sectors. Moreover, most empirical studies have found considerable inter-industry variation, particularly in the relationships between firm size and research intensity. Nonetheless, if the general insights provided by that body of work are valid, they should apply to the development of a specific industry over time. This section discusses the evolution of the semiconductor industry, in an effort to determine the utility of this large body of empirical work for analyzing or predicting innovative performance and the evolution of market structure within a single industry.

In general, the behavior of firms within the semiconductor industry is not strongly supportive of either variant of the Schumpeterian hypothlesis. While the industry is an extremely research-intensive one, it is also highly competitive. In particular, monopoly profits are exceedingly short-lived and are growing even more fleeting, as the duration of significant technological leads has become shorter. Moreover, while the largest merchant producers in the industry are highly research-intensive by almost any comparative measure (Intel, for example, spends roughly 10–12% of annual revenues on R&D, as compared with an average for all U.S. manufacturing of approximately 3–5%), smaller firms are generally even more research-intensive, spending as much as 20% of annual sales on new product development. Neither the prediction concerning the role of monopolistic market structure, nor that concerned with the role of large firm size in supporting innovation, are borne out by the R&D investment behavior of firms in this industry.

While the Schumpeterian predictions concerning market structure and R&D investment do not receive great support from the semiconductor industry's record, the non-Schumpeterian conclusions of analyses of innovative output receive considerable support from the experience of this industry. Small, new firms, rather than the largest, highly research-intensive enterprises, have produced many of the major innovations within this industry. Paradoxically, given the fact that the conclusions concerning innovative output were based largely on analyses of patents, the semiconductor industry is one in which that particular measure of innovative output is almost certainly worthless. Patents are either ignored and widely infringed, not sought for new devices, or widely licensed at very low fees. The behavior of this industry is not encouraging to those scholars who would rely heavily on patent statistics as measures of innovative behavior.

Despite the rather poor predictive performance of these Schumpeterian hypotheses, the broader Schumpeterian vision of the evolution of industries, in which innovation causes recurrent upheavals in market structure, is illustrated very effectively by the semiconductor industry. Indeed, a key aspect of this industry is precisely the unstable nature of individual firms' market shares and the important role of entry.[22] New entrants from outside the industry, and firms not committed financially or technologically to the previous receiving tube technology, played a major role during the 1950s and early 1960s as innovators in transistors and integrated circuits, especially the latter.[23] Similarly, new entrants led the semiconductor industry into the era of microprocessor and VLSI technology. Thus, entry and the associated infusion of radical new technologies into the industry, rather than large-scale R&D, have been critical forces affecting the innovative performance of this industry, once again in some contrast to the Schumpeterian predictions.[24] In this regard, the U.S. and European semiconductor industries have followed very different evolutionary paths. Malerba (1985) has argued that the low rate of entry into the European by new or "outside" firms, and the industry's resulting dominance by established, vertically integrated producers of tubes and consumer electronic products, led to lower rates of innovation.

The persistence of high rates of entry by new firms into the semiconductor industry is also at variance with the predictions of the lifecycle models of industry evolution and innovative performance. Entry rates have declined in recent years below the high levels of the early 1970s; however, this trend is not well-established.[25] Moreover, neither the predicted dramatic shift in the relative importance of product and process innovation, nor the hypothesized decline in the overall rate of innovation, have occurred within the industry.

Semiconductors have long been characterized by a very high degree of "process sensitivity," i.e., the large-scale production of new devices is critically dependent on process technology.[26] Among other things, as Mowery (1983d) has noted, this aspect of semiconductor technology has meant that throughout the life of the industry, product innovation has required process innovation—at no point in the commercial life of semiconductor devices have these two dimensions of the innovation process been separable, and in many cases, significant new products have been spurred by or dependent on process innovation.[27] In addition, as Levin (1982b) and others have noted, there has been no perceptible decline in the rate of innovation or the level of R&D productivity in recent years.[28] Therefore, the central predictions of the lifecycle analysis are not borne out by the recent history of the semiconductor industry.

The semiconductor industry has throughout its history been characterized by a complex pattern of interaction between established and newly founded firms. The primary mechanism for such interaction, of course, is the movement of people, particularly scientists and engineers. The high level of personnel turnover that is characteristic of the industry operates as a powerful device for the rapid diffusion of technical knowledge. This mechanism for the diffusion of technology is arguably more powerful than publication of scientific results in the open literature, due to the importance within this industry of less easily codified "knowhow," and the effectiveness with which such knowhow is diffused via personnel flows.[29] Such interfirm flows of people and technical knowledge operate to undermine technological leads very rapidly. The research installations of such major firms as IBM and Xerox, as well as Western Electric and Bell Labs have played an important role as "incubators" and sources of technical personnel for the foundation of new firms, since they provide many of the personnel for new firms in the electronics industry.

The important role played by institutions such as Bell Labs in the early development of the semiconductor industry was facilitated by, and contributed to, the development of an industry structure characterized by a widely diffused knowledge base. A critical influence on the early development of the semiconductor industry was the licensing policy followed by Bell Labs. Licensing fees for transistor product and process patents were very low, and Bell Labs actively worked to transfer transistor knowhow to other firms through the famous symposia and other channels.[30] While this liberal licensing policy predated the 1956 consent decree settling the Justice Department's antitrust suit against the Bell System, the liberal nature of the policy was undoubtedly influenced by the ongoing litigation. Of even greater importance, however, is the fact that the 1956 decree prohibited

Western Electric or AT&T from activities outside of telecommunications, thus preventing Bell System domination of this rapidly growing industry. The interfirm diffusion of knowledge was further aided by the requirements of the Department of Defense, the major purchaser of discrete components and integrated circuits during the 1950s and early 1960s, for liberal licensing and second sourcing of new devices.

Another form of interaction among the firms within this industry involves the tendency for larger semiconductor producers, such as Motorola, Texas Instruments, or National Semiconductor, to follow, rather than lead, smaller firms in marketing new devices. As Finan (1975) noted,

> Some firms deliberately let smaller firms have the early lead into new markets. This allows the larger firm to focus its resources on established, profitable markets, while the smaller firms attempt to develop markets for new technology. Once the direction of the market is ascertainable and the type of technology most likely to succeed in it is well defined, the larger firms turn their resources to new technology (p. 10).

In other words, an informal division of labor in the innovation process between small and large firms exists within this industry. Such a division of labor is similar to that observed elsewhere within the U.S. economy, as smaller firms or individuals often invent, and larger enterprises develop and market on a large scale (see Mueller, 1962). In addition, smaller innovative firms still often seek to have their devices "second-sourced" by a larger firm, in order to guarantee availability and quality (see Finan, 1975, pp. 31–34). The practice of second sourcing underlines the limited importance of proprietary, firm-specific product technology within this industry.

The role of demand in the innovative performance of the semiconductor industry raises some complex issues. On the one hand, a detailed examination of the histories of a number of the major innovations within this industry does not support a naive demand-pull interpretation of their origins.[31] In many cases, the key innovations were driven by process improvements, or were responses of one sort or another to changes in some other aspect of the product technology.

Nonetheless, the role of military procurement demand was clearly critical for the development of the U.S. semiconductor industry, primarily as a vehicle for supporting entry into the industry by firms that historically had not been producers of electronic devices or components. In the terminology of Teubal, Amon, and Trachtenberg (1976), the military market was characterized by a high level of "market determinateness," i.e., uncertainty about the demand for performance and other device characteristics was low. Particularly during the period in which discrete devices formed the bulk of the industry's output, government procurement standards were very specific, spelling out comprehensive standards for individual devices. The military design specification or the prime systems contractor bore a large share of the overall component design and engineering costs, specifying the requirements for descrete devices in great detail. Indeed, during this period, Pentagon R&D funding played a very minor role in encouraging entry, inasmuch as such funding was channelled almost entirely toward established producers of tubes and military systems.[32]

With the advent of integrated circuits, however, component producers had to shoulder more of the burden of systems design and integration. The risks and fixed costs of pursuing military contracts increased, due to the decline in device standardization for this market. The military market declined in importance as an avenue for entry into the semiconductor industry by smaller firms.

The role of the military market in the postwar semiconductor industry contrasts sharply with the situation in another high-technology industry, commercial aircraft, during this period. The postwar military aircraft market provided no channel for entry by small firms into commercial aircraft production, in contrast to the military market for electronic components. The different roles of the military market in these two industries reflect the fact that the fixed costs of design, testing, and development for new commercial aircrafts vastly exceeded those for new discrete semiconductor devices during the 1950s. Despite clear performance specifications for new aircrafts, reimbursement of development expenses for successful prototypes (especially during the 1950s), and substantial technological spillovers from military to civilian designs, these fixed costs represented an important barrier to the entry of new firms into production of military aircrafts and reduced somewhat the impact of military-civilian spillovers as a mechanism lowering entry barriers.

Clearly, the military semiconductor device market would have been largely irrelevant to commercial production of these components in the absence of substantial technological commonality between military and civilian devices. In the first 15 years of the industry's history, such commonalities were substantial, and military-civilian technological spillovers played an important role in the development of the commercial semiconductor industry. Military contracts and production funding enabled firms to acquire production experience, reducing production costs sufficiently to make semiconductor devices price-competitive with tubes for many applications. High profits from military contracts also supported rapid growth in the size of producers of military devices, many of which were relatively young firms. Over time, however, the technological overlap between military and commercial semiconductors declined greatly, to the point at which most contemporary observers argue that civilian semiconductor technologies are well ahead of military ones. There are several reasons for this shift, which dates back to the integrated circuit era. ICs are less generic in their application (as, indeed, are VLSI circuits, by comparison with ICs) than were discrete components; greater application-specificity in the design of devices thus became necessary. The rapid growth of commercial demand, as well as the proliferation of applications, drew the two areas of technological development further apart. The recent VHSIC (Very High-Speed Integrated Circuit) program is an effort to dramatically shrink the military technological lag behind civilian applications; its ultimate success remains uncertain.[33]

The critical discussion of the empirical literature on market structure and innovation proposed several elements of an alternative intellectual framework for the analysis of R&D investment and behavior. How well does this framework perform in explaining the semiconductor industry's evolution and behavior? This alternative view shifts the focus away from an exclusive preoccupation with the marketed output of the innovation process, output that is measured poorly in this industry by patents. The importance of "organization capital", however, as well as its high degree of firm-specificity, both seem undeniable in understanding competitive dynamics in this industry. As was noted, process technology, rather than product technology, historically has been central to the competitive process within this industry and is a central component of firms' organization capital. Such process expertise is acquired over time, in a cumulative fashion, and is largely firm-specific, rather than industry-wide, in character. This is the basis for the role of production experience and learning curves within the industry. Interestingly, the liberal licensing and widespread interfirm diffusion of product technology are not characteristic of process technology. Finan (1975) notes the absence of process technology transfers in second-sourcing agreements, as well as the extreme reluctance of semiconductor firms to license their process technology.[34]

The role of firm-specific organizational capital is also important in explaining the performance of established U.S. and European producers of tubes in the semiconductor industry. In effect, the existing stock of organization capital was not easily transferred to the new "technological trajectory" (Nelson and Winter, 1982) represented by semiconductor devices. This transferability appears to have been particularly limited in the case of integrated circuits. In order to rapidly exploit the new technology of semiconductors, therefore, new entrants were necessary. In Europe, the vertically integrated structure of the major potential consumers of devices, as well as the limited size of the market in most nations, operated to discourage such entry. In the United States, however, the vast requirements of military procurement, coupled with the willingness of policymakers to place major contracts with young firms, facilitated a massive infusion of new talent and supported the commercial exploitation of semiconductor technologies.

Entry, as well as the rapid technological development of this industry, were also aided substantially by the development of a relatively accessible industry-wide knowledge base. As was noted, the peculiar circumstances of Bell Labs and the Justice Department's antitrust suit meant that critical elements of Bell Labs' process and product knowhow were widely diffused throughout the industry. Moreover, the actions of the Defense Department in requiring liberal licensing of product technologies and second sourcing further accelerated the development of an industry knowledge base that was not under the proprietary control of any single firm. These forces were critically important in promoting a high level of interfirm competition, entry barriers, and rapid technological progress.

V. CONCLUSION

Despite its great importance, the economics of innovation still lacks a solid theoretical or empirical foundation. Empirical analyses of the Schumpeterian hypotheses have been hampered by data limitations and the absence of a tighter theoretical framework. As a result, the conclusions of this extensive literature remain ambiguous and fragmentary at best. Moreover, they provide very few clear guidelines for either policymakers concerned with the innovative performance of sectors or private managers concerned with the innovative performance of a firm or business unit. A more explicit acknowledgement that most major research performers in the U.S. economy are multiproduct firms, and greater attention to the internal structure and boundaries of the firm are needed for the empirical work to yield clearer results.[35] Modelling and analysis firms as multiproduct entities, however, dramatically increase the data requirements of empirical research. In light of this need for more disaggregated data, the decision of the Federal Trade Commission to cease collection of line of business data from firms is unfortunate.

The theoretical analysis of innovation also remains incomplete, by virtue of its view of R&D as an activity that generates saleable outputs, rather than an investment that produces a firm-specific intermediate good. Among other things, this narrow view of the role of R&D investment and the nature of its output has contributed to a misconception of the role and significance of market demand in innovation. The focus on the appropriability of the results of R&D that is characteristic of this conceptualization also does not provide a great deal of useful insight for policy purposes. While important, appropriability is an insufficient guide for the formulation of science and technology policy. Greater attention must be devoted to the requirements for transfer and utilization of the results of R&D, which requires that the importance of the intangible firm-specific assets created by R&D be acknowledged. This conceptualization of the function of R&D also yields a policy prescription that contrasts with that of the existing theory. Finally, this alternative view of R&D more explicitly acknowledges the importance of changes in the organization of the innovation process.

Applied to a single industry, the alternative analysis of R&D investment and innovation performs reasonably well in explaining structural evolution and innovative behavior. In addition, recent changes in the structure of the manufacturing firm (e.g., the development of multinational enterprise) and the R&D process itself (e.g., the growth of joint R&D ventures) can be illuminated with the aid of this analysis of R&D investment. Indeed, the growth of the semiconductor industry, and the diffusion of its products throughout U.S. manufacturing, are key factors in the decline in the costs of information transfer and storage that is driving much of the current reorganization of the firm and its R&D activities.

The increased resort to external sources of research, be this through joint ventures, research consortia, or university-industry cooperation, contains considerable potential for established firms to widen the range of sources from which they accumulate intangible assets. Properly managed, such joint ventures and other cooperative approaches allow firms to monitor technological developments in a much wider range of technologies at a far lower cost than is characteristic of in-house research. Thus, such techniques may enable firms to renew their stock of technological knowhow through a more regular and less wrenching mechanism than that provided by the competitive threat of new entrants or import penetration of domestic markets. In undertaking such a strategy, however, it must be remembered that the absorption and utilization of new technologies are themselves knowledge- and resource-intensive undertakings. In-house research activity must be sustained, if external sources of expertise are to be tapped successfully.

ACKNOWLEDGMENTS

A previous version of this paper was presented at the conference on ''New Technology as Organizational Innovation,'' Netherlands Institute for Advanced Studies in Humanities, Wassenaar, Netherlands, May 21–22, 1985. Preparation of this paper was aided by research support from the National Science Foundation and the Center for Economic Policy Research at Stanford University. I am grateful to the conference participants for their comments on the paper and to Pamela Reyner for secretarial assistance.

NOTES

1. An excellent and thorough survey of this literature may be found in Kamien and Schwarts (1982).

2. See Schmookler (1957) for a discussion of the shifting sources of patenting activity during this period. Rosenberg (1983) also argues that this change in the structure of the innovation process may have made progress in basic scientific knowledge a more endogenous process.

3. See Mowery (1983a, 1985) for a brief discussion of some of the factors underpinning the development of industrial research in the U.S. and Great Britain during this period; Landes (1969) provides a useful discussion of the ''Second Industrial Revolution.''

4. A ''dominance'' that is not revealed within a sample of the available data for U.S. manufacturing industry in the 1920–46 period; see Mowery (1983a).

5. This discussion draws on that in Levin, Cohen and Mowery (1985).

6. The following paragraphs draw on Cohen, Levin, and Mowery (1985).

7. J. B. Rosenberg (1976) empirically investigated the impact of market share and concentration on research investment. However, his data were extremely crude and his results rather inconclusive.

8. A brief review of the antitrust impact of the Schumpeterian hypothesis and the empirical studies spawned by it is in the National Academy of Engineering (1980).

9. In addition to the studies examined above, the basis for the observed complementarity between federal contract funds and privately financed R&D investment within individual firms (see Levy and Terleckyj), 1983; Scott 1985; Link, 1981) has not been satisfactorily explained, making very difficult the translation of this finding into a basis for firm-level or sectoral policy decisions. Similarly, the empirical finding that basic research significantly improves productivity growth within firms (Mansfield, 1980) has no explanatory model illuminating the channels of influence of basic research on productivity growth.

10. The arguments in these paragraphs are based on Mowery (1983c).

11. See Cohen and Levinthal (1985) for an analysis of investment in "absorptive capacity" by firms.

12. See David (1985).

13. These arguments are developed further in my testimony before the Science Policy Task Force, Committee on Science and Technology, U.S. House of Representatives, April 24, 1985.

14. See Stigler (1956), who argued that "with the growth of research, new firms will emerge to provide specialized facilities for small firms. It is only to be expected that, when a new kind of research develops, at first it will be conducted chiefly as an ancillary activity by existing firms . . . We may expect the rapid expansion of the specialized research laboratory, selling its services generally. The specialized laboratories need not be in the least inferior to 'captive' laboratories" (p. 281). One attempt to examine aspects of the historical organization of U.S. industrial research is Mowery (1983b).

15. During the 1960s, data cited by Harrigan (1985) on domestic U.S. joint ventures indicated that such ventures were concentrated in the chemicals, primary metals, paper, and stone, clay and glass industries. Since that time, the number of such ventures has increased substantially, and they now appear with greater frequency in a much wider range of industries.

16. Caves (1982) notes that "as indicators of these [firm-specific] assets, economists have seized on the outlays for advertising and research and development (R&D) undertaken by firms classified to an industry. That the share of foreign subsidiary assets in the total assets of U.S. corporations increases significantly with the importance of advertising and R&D outlays in the industry has been confirmed in many studies . . ." (p. 9).

17. "Generally, complementarity is found in many JVs, encompassing not only functional complementarity . . . but also technological complementarity, e.g., the development of a new product that requires technical knowhow not available in a single company" (Gullander, 1976, p. 105).

18. Brodley (1982) summarizes the advantages of joint ventures, defined as newly created corporate entities in which all partners hold equity shares, over mergers or market transactions as follows: "By providing for shared profits and managerial control, joint ventures tend to protect the participants from opportunism and information imbalance. The problem of valuing the respective contributions for the participants is mitigated, because they can await an actual market judgment. The temptation to exploit a favored bargaining position by threatening to withhold infusions of capital or other contributions is reduced by the need for continuous cooperation if the joint venture is to be effective. Moreover, a firm supplying capital to the joint venture can closely monitor the use of its contributed capital and thereby reduce its risk of loss. Common ownership also provides a means of spreading the costs of producing valuable information that could otherwise be protected from appropriation only by difficult-to-enforce contractual undertakings. Finally, joint ventures can effect economies of scale in research not achievable through single-firm action. Because of these advantages, joint ventures are especially likely to provide an optimal enterprise form in undertakings involving high risks, technological innovations, or high information costs" (pp. 1528–1529).

19. Much of the following argument is drawn from Mowery and Rosenberg (1979).

20. Prominent examples of this work include Gilpin (1975), Utterback (1974), and Myers and Marquis (1969); a more complete listing may be found in Mowery and Rosenberg (1979).

21. The following arguments are discussed in greater detail in Cohen and Mowery (1984).

22. Levin (1982a) notes the "remarkable rate of turnover among market leaders . . . only one (Texas Instruments) of the top five U.S. producers of integrated circuits in 1955 is among the top ten producers of integrated circuits today. Five of the top ten integrated circuit producers were not among the top ten semiconductor firms a decade earlier, and four of these firms were established after 1960" (p. 29).

23. Many established tube firms (e.g., Philco) were important producers of discrete devices throughout the 1950s—it was only with the rise of integrated circuits that these firms were eclipsed.

24. Nonetheless, as is discussed below, large-scale R&D programs have played an important role as facilities within which personnel and ideas for new firms could be "incubated."

25. While entry remains substantial, Levin (1982a) and others have noted that new firms now increasingly are highly specialized producers, rather than participants in a wide range of product markets.

26. Quantity production of transistors by Western Electric was infeasible prior to Teal's pioneering (and initially unsupported) research into the technology of "pulling" pure crystals of silicon. Teal's move from Bell Labs to Texas Instruments was directly responsible for TI's entry as the sole merchant producer of silicon transistors in the 1950s.

27. Indeed, the real source of firm-specific technological advantages within this industry, discussed below, is process technology, protected from disclosure by trade secret regulations, rather than the more widely disclosed product technology.

28. See Levin (1982b) for a discussion of "R&D productivity" within this industry.

29. The low level of such interfirm labor mobility within the Japanese electronics industry has been hypothesized to be a major reason for the reliance by MITI on interfirm joint ventures, in order to facilitate more rapid diffusion of knowledge (see Okimoto, 1983).

30. As Jack Morton, a Bell Labs engineer involved in the development of the transistor, noted, "There was nothing new about licensing our patents to anyone who wanted them. But it was a departure to tell our licensees everything we knew" (cited in Tilton, 1971).

31. See Mowery (1983d).

32. See Tilton (1971) and Utterback and Murray (1977).

33. See Levin (1982a) and Brueckner and Borrus (1984) for discussions of the VHSIC program.

34. "American companies are also unwilling, as a general policy, to let other firms have access to their advanced process technology" (p. 49).

35. Teece and Winter's more general critique of the applicability of the neoclassical theory of the firm contains a similar criticism:

> If multiproduct firms exist, then {in the neoclassical theory} they are flukes in that they have not distinct efficiency dimensions . . .
> The boundaries of the firm—the appropriate degree of vertical, lateral, or horizontal integration—thus lie outside the domain of the traditional textbook analysis . . . the firm is an entity which barely exists within received neoclassical theory (1984, pp. 118–119).

REFERENCES

Abernathy, W. J. (1978), *The Productivity Dilemma*. Baltimore, MD: Johns Hopkins University Press.

Abramovitz, M. (1956), "Resource and Output Trends in the United States Since 1870." *American Economic Review* 46:5–23.

Allen, T. J. (1978), *Managing the Flow of Technology*. Cambridge, MA: M.I.T. Press.

Armour, H. O. and Teece, D. J. (1981), "Vertical Integration and Technological Innovation." *Review of Economics and Statistics* 62:470–474.

Arrow, K. J. (1962), "Economic Welfare and the Allocation of Resources for Innovative Activity." In *The Rate and Direction of Inventive Activity*. Princeton, NJ: Princeton University Press for the National Bureau of Economic Research.

Blair, J. M. (1972), *Economic Concentration: Structure, Behavior, and Public Policy*. New York: Harcourt Brace Jovanovich.

Brodley, J. F. (1982), "Joint Ventures and Antitrust Policy." *Harvard Law Review* 95:1523–1590.

Bound, J., Cummins, C., Griliches, Z., and Hall, B. (1984), "Who Does R&D and Who Patents?" In Z. Griliches (Ed.), *R&D, Patents, and Productivity*. Chicago: University of Chicago Press for the National Bureau of Economic Research.

Brueckner, L. and Borrus, M. (1984), "Assessing the Commercial Impact of the VHSIC (Very High Speed Integrated Circuit) Program." Working paper, Berkeley Roundtable on the International Economy.

Caves, R. E. (1982), *Multinational Enterprise and Economic Analysis*. Cambridge, England: Cambridge University Press.

Cohen, W. M. and Mowery, D. C. (1984), "Firm Heterogeneity and R&D: An Agenda for Research." In B. Bozeman, M. Crow, and A. Link (Eds.), *Strategic Management of Industrial R&D*. Lexington, MA: D. C. Heath.

Cohen, W. M., Levin, R. C., Mowery, D. C. (1985), "Firm Size and R&D Intensity: A Re-Examination of the Stylized Facts." Working paper, Carnegie-Mellon University.

Cohen, W. M. and Levinthal, D. C. (1985), "The Endogeneity of Appropriability and R&D Investment." Working paper, Carnegie-Mellon University.

Comanor, W. S. (1965), "Research and Technical Change in the Pharmaceutical Industry." *Review of Economics and Statistics* 47:182–190.

Comanor, W. S. (1967), "Market Structure, Product Differentiation, and Industrial Research." *Quarterly Journal of Economics* 81:639–657.

David, P. A. (1969), "A Contribution to the Theory of Diffusion." Center for Research in Economic Growth Memorandum 71, Stanford University.

David, P. A. (1985), "New Technology Diffusion, Public Policy, and Industrial Competitiveness." Presented at the Symposium on Economics and Technology, Stanford University, March 18–19.

Demsetz, H. (1969), "Information and Efficiency: Another Viewpoint." *Journal of Law and Economics* 12:1–22.

Elliott, J. W. (1971), "Funds Flow vs. Expectational Theories of Research and Development Expenditures in the Firm." *Southern Economic Journal* 37:409–422.

Evenson, R. E. (1982), "Agriculture." In R. R. Nelson (Ed.), *Government and Technical Progress: A Cross-Industry Analysis*. New York: Pergamon Press.

Finan, W. F. (1975), "The International Transfer of Semiconductor Technology Through U.S.-Based Firms." National Bureau of Economic Research working paper.

Fisher, F. and Temin, P. (1973), "Returns to Scale in Research and Development: What Does the Schumpeterian Hypothesis Imply?" *Journal of Political Economy* 81:56–70.

Gilpin, R. (1975), *Technology, International Growth, and Competitiveness*. Prepared for the Joint Economic Committee, U. S. Congress. Washington, DC: U. S. Government Printing Office.

Gort, M. and Klepper, S. (1982), "Time Paths in the Diffusion of Innovations." *Economic Journal* 92:630–653.

Grabowski, H. G. (1968), "The Determinants of Industrial Research and Development: A Study of the Chemical, Drug, and Petroleum Industries." *Journal of Political Economy* 76:292–306.

Grabowski, H. G. and Vernon, J. M. (1982), "The Pharmaceutical Industry." In R. R. Nelson (Ed.), *Government and Technical Progress: A Cross-Industry Analysis*. New York: Pergamon Press.

Gullander, S. (1976), "Joint Ventures and Corporate Strategy." *Columbia Journal of World Business*, pp. 104–114.

Hamberg, D. (1963), "Invention in the Industrial Research Laboratory." *Journal of Political Economy* 71:95–115.

Harrigan, K. R. (1985), *Strategies for Joint Ventures*. Lexington, MA: D. C. Heath.

Hymer, S. H. (1961), *The International Operations of National Firms: A Study of Direct Foreign Investment*. Ph.D. dissertation, Massachusetts Institute of Technology.

Kamien, M. and Schwartz, N. (1982), *Market Structure and Innovation*. Cambridge: Cambridge University Press.

Kindleberger, C. P. (1969), *American Business Abroad: Six Lectures on Direct Investment*. New Haven, CT: Yale University Press.

Landes, D. S. (1969), *The Unbound Prometheus*. Cambridge: Cambridge University Press.

Levin, R. C. (1982a), "The Semiconductor Industry." In *Government and Technical Progress: A Cross-Industry Analysis*. New York: Pergamon Press.

Levin, R. C. (1982b), "R&D Productivity in the Semiconductor Industry: Is a Slowdown Imminent?" In H. I. Fusfeld and R. N. Langlois (Eds.), *Understanding R&D Productivity*. New York: Pergamon Press.

Levin, R. C., Cohen, W. M., and Mowery, D. C. (1985), "R&D Appropriability, Opportunity, and market Structure: New Evidence on Some Schumpeterian Hypotheses." *American Economic Review* 75:20–24.

Levy, D. M. and Terleckyj, N. E. (1983), "The Effects of Government R&D on Private R&D Investment and Productivity: A Macroeconomic Analysis." *Bell Journal of Economics* 14:551–561.

Link, A. N. (1981), *Research and Development Activity in American Manufacturing*. New York: Praeger.

Link, A. N. and Long, J. E. (1981), "The Simple Economics of Basic Scientific Research: A Test of Nelson's Diversification Hypothesis." *Journal of Industrial Economics* 29:105–109.

Malerba, F. (1985), *The Semiconductor Business*. Madison: University of Wisconsin Press.

Mansfield, E. (1980), "Basic Research and Productivity Increase in Manufacturing." *American Economic Review* 70:863–873.

Mowery, D. C. (1983a), "Industrial Research and Firm Size, Survival and Growth in American Manufacturing, 1921–46: An Assessment." *Journal of Economic History* 43:953–980.

Mowery, D. C. (1983b), "The Relationship Between the Contractual and Intrafirm Forms of Industrial Research in American Manufacturing, 1900–1940." *Explorations in Economic History* 20: 351–374.

Mowery, D. C. (1983c), "Economic Theory and Government Technology Policy." *Policy Sciences* 16:27–43.

Mowery, D. C. (1983d), "Innovation, Market Structure, and Government Policy in the American Semiconductor Electronics Industry: A Survey." *Research Policy* 12:193–197.

Mowery, D. C. (1985) "Firm Structure, Government Policy, and the Organization of Industrial Research: Great Britain and the United States, 1900–1950." *Business History Review* 58:504–531.

Mowery, D. C. and Rosenberg, N. (1979), "The Influence of Market Demand Upon Innovation: A Critical Review of Some Recent Empirical Studies." *Research Policy* 8:102–153.

Mowery, D. C., and Rosenberg, N. (1982), "Government Policy and Innovation in the Commercial Aircraft Industry, 1925–75." In *Government and Technical Progress: A Cross-Industry Analysis*. New York: Pergamon Press.

Mowery, D. C. and Rosenberg, N. (1985), "Commercial Aircraft: Cooperation and Competition Between the United States and Japan." *California Management Review* 27:70–92.

Mueller, D. C. (1967), "The Firm's Decision Process: An Econometric Investigation." *Quarterly Journal of Economics* 81:58–87.

Mueller, W. F. (1962), "The Origins of the Basic Inventions Underlying DuPont's Major Product and Process Innovations, 1920–1950." In *The Rate and Direction of Inventive Activity*. Princeton, NJ: Princeton University Press for the National Bureau of Economic Research.

Myers, S., and Marquis, D. G. (1969), *Successful Industrial Innovation*. Washington, DC: National Science Foundation.

National Academy of Engineering (1980), *Antitrust, Uncertainty, and Technological Innovation*. Washington, DC: National Academy of Sciences.

Nelson, R. R. (1959), "The Simple Economics of Basic Scientific Research." *Journal of Political Economy* 67:297–306.

Nelson, R. R., and Winter, S. (1982), *An Evolutionary Theory of Economic Change*. Cambridge, MA: Harvard University Press.

Okimoto, D. I. (1983) *Pioneer and Pursuer: The Role of the State in the Evolution of the Japanese and American Semiconductor Industries*. Occasional Paper, Northeast Asia-U.S. Forum on International Policy, Stanford University.

Peck, M. J. and Goto, A. (1982), "Technology and Economic Growth: The Case of Japan." *Research Policy* 10:222–243.

Penrose, E. (1958), *The Theory of the Growth of the Firm.* Cambridge, England: Blackwell.

Phillips, A. (1971), *Technology and Market Structure.* Lexington, MA: D. C. Heath.

Prescott, E. C. and Visscher, M. (1980), "Organization Capital." *Journal of Political Economy* 88:446–461.

Rosenberg, J. B. (1976), "Research and Market Share: A Reappraisal of the Schumpeterian Hypothesis." *Journal of Industrial Economics* 25:110–122.

Rosenberg, N. (1976), *Perspectives on Technology.* Cambridge: Cambridge University Press.

Rosenberg, N. (1983), *Inside the Black Box: Technology and Economics.* Cambridge: Cambridge University Press.

Scherer, F. M. (1965), "Firm Size, Market Structure, Opportunity, and the Output of Patented Inventions." *American Economic Review* 55:1097–1125.

Scherer, F. M. (1967), "Market Structure and the Employment of Scientists and Engineers." *American Economic Review* 57:524–531.

Scherer, F. M. (1984a), "Corporate Size, Diversification, and Innovative Activity." In *idem., Innovation and Growth,* Cambridge, MA: M.I.T. Press.

Scherer, F. M. (1984b), "Demand-Pull and Technological Invention: Schmookler Revisited." *Journal of Industrial Economics* 30:225–237.

Schmookler, J. (1957), "Inventors Past and Present." *Review of Economics and Statistics* 39:321–333.

Schmookler, J. (1966), *Invention and Economic Growth.* Cambridge, MA: Harvard University Press.

Schumpeter, J. (1934), *The Theory of Economic Development* (trans. b y R. Opie). Cambridge, MA: Harvard University Press.

Schumpeter, J. (1954), *Capitalism, Socialism, and Democracy,* 3rd ed. New York: Harper & Row.

Scott, J. T. (1984), "Firm versus Industry Variability in R&D Intensity." In Z. Griliches (Ed.), *R&D, Patents, and Productivity.* Chicago: University of Chicago Press for the National Bureau of Economic Research.

Shrieves, R. (1976), "Firm Size and Innovation: Further Evidence." *Industrial Organization Review* 4:26–33.

Steinmueller, W. E. (1985), "Industry Structure and Government Policies in the U.S. and Japanese Integrated Circuit Industries." Presented at Stanford University, April 15.

Stigler, G. J. (1956), "Industrial Organization and Economic Progress." In L. D. White (Ed.), *The State of the Social Sciences.* Chicago: University of Chicago Press.

Teece, D. J. and Winter, S. G. (1984), "The Limits of Neoclassical Theory in Management Education." *American Economic Review, Papers and Proceedings* 74(2):116–121.

Teubal, M. Arnon, N., and Trachtenberg, M. (1976), "Performance in Innovation in the Israeli Electronics Industry: A Case Study of Biomedical Electronics Instrumentation." *Research Policy* 5:354–379.

Tilton, J. E. (1971), *International Diffusion of Technology: The Case of Semiconductors.* Washington, DC: Brookings Institution.

U.S. Department of Commerce (1979), *A Report on the U.S. Semiconductor Industry.* Washington, DC: U.S. Government Printing Office.

Utterback, J. W. (1974), "Innovation in Industry and the Diffusion of Technology." *Science* 183:620–626.

Utterback, J. W. and Murray, A. E. (1977), "The Influence of Defense Procurement and Sponsorship of Research and Development on the Development of the Civilian Electronics Industry." Working paper CP–77–5, Center for Policy Alternatives.

Wilson, R. W., Ashton, P. K., and Egan, T. P. (1980), *Innovation, Competition, and Government Policy in the Semiconductor Industry.* Lexington, MA: D. C. Heath.

Chapter 9

ENTREPRENEURIAL ROLES IN THE PROCESS OF TECHNOLOGICAL INNOVATION

David A. Tansik and Gerrit Wolf

I. INTRODUCTION

This paper is concerned with an understanding of the role of the entrepreneur, as contrasted to the roles of the inventor, adopter or manager, in the process of technological innovation in organizations.

We make an important distinction between scientific *inventions* and technological *innovations*. Many people believe that inventions are relatively rare events, but that once they have occurred innovation can proceed in a rapid and straightforward manner. We, however, take the opposite view; inventions are many, while successful innovations are rare.

"*Invention* is the process by which a new idea is discovered or created . . . ." (Rogers, 1983, p. 176). An invention is simply the new idea. It is the application of this new idea that leads to an innovation. Mansfield (1968) makes the point that "An invention, when applied for the first time, is called an innovation" (p. 99). Martin (1984) makes a similar statement contending that an "*invention* only becomes an *innovation* when it is transformed into a socially usable product" (p. 2).

Advances in the Study of Entrepreneurship, Innovation,
and Economic Growth, Volume 1, pages 115-127.
Copyright © 1986 by JAI Press Inc.
ISBN: 0-89232-703-0

The refinement of an idea into a usable product, i.e., an innovation, is a crucial and often difficult task in organizations. The innovation process is strongly influenced by the ability of certain individuals to foresee applications of new ideas and their willingness to take the social and economic risks inherent in developing these new applications. These individuals, entrepreneurs, are important but often overlooked actors in the technological innovation literature.

Our focus is on *technological* innovations. Schon (1967) has a conception of technology as tools or techniques, physical equipment or other methods of doing or making things, by which human abilities or capabilities are extended. Perrow (1967) likewise takes a broad view of technology by simply viewing it as work done in organizations. Thus, we are studying the application of new ideas (i.e., of inventions) that extend human capabilities in organizations. Innovations, in this conception, are defined in terms of their newness to a particular organization; not in terms of their absolute newness. Thus, although microcomputers have been produced and marketed for some years, they would still be considered to be an innovation if/when they are introduced into an organization such as a small business that had heretofore never had office equipment more advanced than, say, manual typewriters and adding machines.

Previous work on the process of diffusion of innovations or of technology transfer has focused heavily on both the inventor and the adopter of new technologies. It is our contention that a focus on just these two actors fails to consider the key roles played by the entrepreneur who is the individual who creates the innovation from an inventor's idea or who develops applications for new technologies within organizations.

The sections that follow discuss the various stages in the innovation process and show the key roles played by the entrepreneur in the transition points between invention and production, and between adoption and routine utilization of new technologies in organizations.

II.   STAGES OF INNOVATION

Research on innovation in organizations has generally been categorized according to two main premises. First, innovation can be viewed as a *process* involving many discrete decisions that occur, often slowly, over time. Secondly, innovation involves *social* units or actors at all levels of aggregation (individual, group, and organization) acting alone or in combination.

The concept of stages in the innovation process gives us a basis for organizing the decisions inherent in the innovation process and for determining the role(s) of the various social actors at the various points of the process. Stages of innovation have typically been analyzed from two points of view—that of the producer of new technologies and that of the user. In general, these two viewpoints can lead to different types of research emphases because they focus on dissimilar types of decisions and actions. The producer point of view focuses on the stages inherent in the development of a new technology from an idea to a specific product. The user point of view focuses on the stages spanning an awareness of the new product to routinized use of the product in the organization. Often it is assumed that producers and users are in separate organizations, however this need not be the case; technologies can be produced and used in the same organization.

Figure 1 illustrates the commonly discussed stages in both the producer and user arenas. Within the producer segment of the model, the stages progress as an innovation goes from an idea to a well-developed product. For users, the stages progress from product awareness to routinized use within the organization.

Figure 1. Producer and user stages in the innovation process.

While the segregation of the producer and user models may highlight various aspects of the innovation decision process, there is no sound reason to assume that, in practice, the two models are separate. For example, it is probably true, in general, that the producer stages take place before the user stages. However, von Hipple (1976) has shown that for particular technologies, there are crucial interactions between producers and users that occur during various of the producer stages. Specifically, von Hipple showed that for sophisticated scientific innovations, potential users were often involved in identifying possible areas of research and in helping guide product development for producers. Moreover, as noted above, organizations may produce and then use within their own organization both process and product innovations (e.g., a manufacturing firm developing and then using a new production process or a new piece of equipment).

In addition, many innovations have to be "custom fit" into the user organization. Thus, some aspects of development can take place as apart of the implementation process. Custom computer systems are illustrative of this process.

And, finally, the logical flow from the last stage of the producer model (marketing) to the first stage of the user model (awareness) cannot be overlooked. Adding further complexity here is the tendency of some producers to make *pre-release* announcements of new technologies still in development or testing. This can serve to both prepare the user for the upcoming marketing stage by developing an early awareness, and to also generate potential user inputs (à la von Hipple) into the developmental process.

Clearly, then, the two stage models are not definitive representations of the decisions made in the innovation process. However, they do serve to point out the reality of the innovation process more effectively than would a static model that focuses only on discrete decisions (i.e., on components of the process).

III. ACTORS IN THE PROCESS

The central dependent variable in most research on innovations in organizations involves *adoption* by the user of the new technology. Without adoption, technologies would not be used and their social and economic value would be negligible. A key factor is, then, the adopter; the person in the user organization who makes the decision to adopt or acquire the new technology. While an elegant concept, defining the adopter and the point of adoption is often difficult.

Adoption is usually considered to be that point in time which divides an organization's not having a technology from its having it. Some researchers simply denote a dichotomous adopt/not adopt variable and classify the unit being observed as to whether the technology is or is not present at a particular point in time. Others prefer to view the adoption decision in a longitudinal manner and view adoption as the point at which an ''authoritative commitment'' was made to acquire the technology (Lambright, 1980). Thus, we must often distinguish between the symbolic act of *deciding* and the behavioral act of *acquiring*. The actors doing each of these may well be different. The ultimate routine user of the technology in the organization may well be someone other than the original decider or acquirer. In addition, the decider/acquirer may well have been made aware of the technology by some other organizational actor; e.g., a ''technological gatekeeper.''

Within the producer portion of the model, numerous actors may also be involved. The inventor of the new technology or idea may not develop an application. And the person designing the application may not take the technology through the testing, manufacturing, and marketing stages.

Previous research has mostly focused on the invention and adoption phases of the models. Hence, it is focused upon the actors most closely associated with these; the inventor and the adopter. Recent work has identified another actor, the product champion, who must also play a crucial role in the process. Some individual must take the responsibility for moving an invention from an idea to a tangible product in a producer organization. And, someone must take a newly acquired technological tool and integrate it into the routine operations of a user organization.

Schumpeter (1961, 1964) has discussed the central role of the entrepreneur in technological innovation: ''the person who creates new combinations—the one who sees how to fulfill currently unsatisfied needs or perceives a more efficient means of doing what is already being done'' (Kamien and Schwartz, 1982, p. 8).

Schumpeter differentiates between the acts of invention and entrepreneurship. Inventers can, but need not, be entrepreneurs. It is, however, entrepreneurship that brings an invention to the point of being a usable product. While Schumpeter's main argument is that entrepreneurship should be rewarded with extraordinary profits, even if perfect competition must be hindered in the process, he nonetheless makes an important and useful differentiation between the invention and entrepreneurial acts.

IV. AN INTEGRATIVE MODEL: PROCESS AND ACTORS

Realizing that the producer and user stages can be interrelated, as shown, for example, by von Hipple (1976), we present the combined stage model shown in Figure 2, Part A, as a sequential process. Imposed on these decision stages are the major relevant actors, including the entrepreneur. We believe that the entrepreneurial role has been neglected in much previous research on the innovation process, and further, the entrepreneurial role is an important one in the *transitions* between invention and sales, and between adoption and routine use.

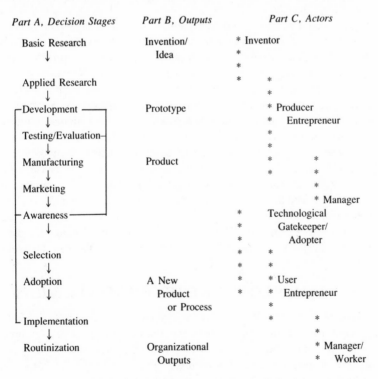

Figure 2.   Combined stage model.

There are two types of entrepreneurial roles that are relevant to our stage model. First is the producer entrepreneur. This person is the one upon whom Schumpeter focused in terms of receiving extraordinary profits. This entrepreneur is the one who is able to take an invention or concept and see ahead to commercial possibilities. These persons are often characterized as product champions within organizations. These entrepreneurs play several important transitional roles. First, as already noted, they perceive the product opportunity inherent in an idea or invention and bridge the applied research/development gap. Then, after showing the product's feasibility, the entrepreneur must pass the new technology on to management for manufacture and marketing.

Clearly one person can perform all three roles (inventor, entrepreneur, manager), but need not. These roles would seem to call for different skills and to involve different administrative concerns. For example, basic researchers would have different qualifications and job evaluation criteria than would manufacturing or marketing executives. The transitional role of the entrepreneur is most complex and demanding. The entrepreneur must be creative in sensing the technological opportunity and administratively adept at dealing with both scientists/inventors and managers.

There is also another type of entrepreneur or product champion operating in user organizations. This entrepreneur serves in a transition role between the adopter and routine user of a new technology and also plays a product champion role, but here the focus is on applications rather than development. An example of such a user entrepreneur would be the person who champions the use of microcomputer decision support systems throughout an organization. Or, it could be the person who promotes new communications systems for the organization once the decision is made to lease a satellite channel.

These user entrepreneurs often act in ways resembling missionaries as they attempt to "convert" managers into the routine use of the technology (Tansik and Radnor, 1971; Hollmann and Tansik, 1977). Clearly, this user entrepreneur role could, but need not, be played by either the adopter or the end user. The lack of a user entrepreneur leads to a low use rate or elimination of the new technology from the organization. Without the "championing" behavior, managers would not likely become aware of, or risk the use of, the new technology.

V. DIMENSIONS OF ENTREPRENEURIAL WORK

The disciplines of economics, psychology, sociology, and engineering have presented concepts and information about the innovation process and entrepreneurship. These contributions can be interpreted and integrated in the combined producer-user model presented in Figure 2. The model suggests that the important variables surrounding the entrepreneurial role are the entrepreneur's job compared to other jobs in the organization, the incentives for the entrepreneur compared to the other actors, the transactions between the entrepreneur and the other actors in the innovation process, and the organizational context of the producer-user innovation process.

A. The Job

The scope of the entrepreneur's job varies from large to small. A large scope job extends the job backward in the producer part of the innovation process toward invention and awareness, and forward to manufacturing and sales. In the user part, the job expands backward toward adoption and forward to implementation. The larger the scope, the more diverse are the talents required of the entrepreneur. If the entrepreneur starts a business, then initially all jobs will be performed by the entrepreneur. As the business grows, the entrepreneur needs to relenquish the inventor and marketing roles (in the producer portion of the model) and the adopter and routine user roles (in the user portion of the model).

In the small scope entrepreneurial job, the inventor and adopter roles are well-defined in the initial portion of the process and the manager's job is well-defined in the later portion. The entrepreneurial job becomes focused on the tasks the entrepreneur usually does well; developing the product for the market or getting the process adopted and used by the user. In this job, the entrepreneur needs to be able to talk to, influence, and listen to the actors both up and downstream as well as direct feedback from the user's process to the producer's process. For the producer part, the entrepreneur needs to be aware of the differences found in research and development between basic and applied research, and in engineering between process and product innovation. For the adopter part, the entrepreneur needs to understand the power position and forces acting on the adopter and the needs of the user.

The entrepreneur's job, whether large or small in scope, calls for the articulation of the concept or idea, the development of a plan to implement the idea, and finally the execution and test of the plan. Each of these three parts has prescriptive and descriptive behavioral components.

The entrepreneur connects a user's need to an inventor's solution by building a concept. This creative act requires a different kind of ingenuity from that of the inventor. The entrepreneur usually knows the users and defines the innovative concept so that it is somewhat different from other concepts and informally considers costs and returns. With enough knowledge of inventions, often obtained through the experience of working in large organizations (Freeman, 1986), and knowledge of the user, the entrepreneur considers an implicit pairing of inventions and user needs. Creativity occurs because the user may not understand the need until the entrepreneur invents the concept; a process which may require combining together multiple inventions to build a solution (Koestler, 1964).

After forming the concept, the entrepreneur designs a project and thus needs to understand project management. As a project manager, the entrepreneur plans for expected cost and revenue streams along with the associated activities of funds and supplies acquisition, design of operations activities, and marketing and distribution activities. There are often manual and computer based tools to aid in this process (Chase and Aquilano, 1985). The behavioral involvement in the plan and its critique by others typically sharpens the concept and commits the entrepreneur to the project. This commitment helps carry the entrepreneur where others would not go. The behavioral effect of the plan may be more important than the plan itself. Peters (1983) has noted that many successful ventures have little detailed planning. A few pages of notes about concepts and a substantial amount of "elbow grease" for implementation is often enough; costs and revenue plans can be largely guess work.

After the project is underway with some costs expended, but most (or all) revenues yet to come, the entrepreneur may fall prey to inadequate reactions to cost overruns or revenue shortfalls (Northcraft and Wolf, 1984). This can happen because of the entrepreneur's heavy involvement in the project, the absolute uncertainty of future revenues and costs, and the magnitude of the costs already incurred. It may take outside financial interests such as venture capitalists or lenders, or the review process of a bureaucracy to control the entrepreneur. The entrepreneur's willingness to persist in the face of long odds often brings about the big success (as well as many failures).

These three components of the entrepreneur's job—concept, plan, and implementation—indicate that the entrepreneur is an experimenter (Peterson, 1981) and that the job may either be specialized or be a part of every employee's job. Organizations (Staw, 1977), managers (Staw and Ross, 1980), and workers (Northcraft, 1985) have been described as experimenting under certain conditions which are similar to these three components. The experimenting job is more detached than the entrepreneur's job and builds in systematic tests and evaluations. The entrepreneur's job may produce commitment that limits detachment and evaluation, and the success of the entrepreneur may depend on the marginal improvement in the concept through experimentation and testing.

B.   Incentives

Economists and psychologists have been concerned with incentives and rewards for the entrepreneurial job. Because the job is risky and has less apparent intrinsic rewards than are found in the inventor's job, pay-offs must be contingent on the entrepreneur's performance and be (relatively) large (Schumpeter, 1961), much like the incentive for a salesperson in the private sector. The economist approaches the problem by focusing on the rules and regulations of an economy where the costs (in terms of taxes and regulated actions) should not inhibit the entrepreneur from receiving the "extraordinary" profits he or she deserves for the "extraordinary" risks incurred. Psychologists focus on the motivation of persons who are driven toward goal achievement, personal responsibility, and feedback. Called achievement motivation (McClelland, 1961), persons who exhibit this tendency are not usually interested in the power or trappings of a bureaucracy and would tend to be frustrated by excessive rules and regulations in the private economic system or government. Young (1983) has argued that there are different kinds of entrepreneurs in the not-for-profit sector. These persons are motivated by many factors, among which income is but one. Their motivations are similar to those of the artist who is motivated by pride of work, of the professional who seeks recognition from peers, or of the true believer who is simply in pursuit of a cause. In public sector organizations, entrepreneurs can be highly motivated by power needs (McClelland, 1961), the fulfillment of which can come about through the design and implementation of social policies and programs that effect large segments of the population.

Both the economist and psychologist might recommend having the entrepreneur personally invest financially or psychologically in the venture. A commitment of his or her own funds may cause an increase in the amount of effort expended by the entrepreneur to accomplish objectives. However, this investment may entrap the entrepreneur into being unwilling to terminate a project that is going badly. The large organization may have some difficulty in accommodating the entrepreneur, given the perspectives developed by the economist and psychologist. To obtain the freedom and personal investment necessary to be maximally motivated, the entrepreneur may best function in a small organization less subject to market regulations or bureaucratic rules. The incentives approach, also, assumes that the job of the entrepreneur is well-understood and nonproblematic. From the producer-user model, though, we see that the essence of the entrepreneur's job does not include inventing or managing. In large organizations, the job of the entrepreneur is more clearly defined in that specialized individuals typically perform the invention and management functions; however there is a problem in developing an incentives package for the entrepreneur. In the large organization, the entrepreneur may well be subject to rigorous compensation and promotion policies and not be able to receive the "extraordinary" rewards (or to incur the possible losses) usually associated with entrepreneurship. In small organizations, the incentives package is more easily developed, however the entrepreneur's job is less rigorously defined and will probably involve elements (e.g., aspects of invention or management) that the entrepreneur finds less appealing.

C. Transactions Among Actors

Carleton (1986) has described the bargaining process between the entrepreneur and the venture capitalist. Here, the entrepreneur's job is usually of large scope as part of a start up venture. Alternatively, in a small scope entrepreneurial job, the entrepreneur needs to interact with an inventor and the managers of marketing and manufacturing in the producer organization, and with the technological gatekeeper and manager in the user organization.

Economists are concerned with conditions under which the inventor is or is not brought into a firm with an entrepreneur and managers who will attempt to exploit the new technology in the market. Williamson (1975) contends that the decision should be made on the basis of the cost of carrying on the transaction. These costs would be both economic and behavioral and would include such factors as the price that must be paid to the inventor for rights to the invention, the expected profits the inventor would receive if he or she is brought into the firm as a part owner, the perceived "difficulties" the entrepreneur would have in dealing with the inventor as a partner or employee, and the like. Thus, the entrepreneur may purchase rights to the invention, or may hire the inventor along with giving part ownership in the firm. The option that is chosen should be based upon the entrepreneur's perception of the behavioral and economic costs involved in each alternative; clearly the entrepreneur should opt for the low cost decision.

The process of bringing the inventor into the firm or of buying rights to the invention requires negotiation skills on behalf of the entrepreneur. Entrepreneurs are believed to be individuals who enjoy "making deals" (Peterson, 1981). Working on, for example, a make or buy decision has an analytical component, but this seems to be less exciting to an entrepreneur than experiencing the behavioral stimuli surrounding the activities involved in putting a "deal" together. Executing a new venture plan is a series of "deals" with financial supporters, customers, users, and suppliers (Carleton, 1986); activities that are clearly stimulating to the entrepreneur.

D.   Organizational Contexts

Entrepreneurial work can be viewed from the context of the organization in which it takes place. Sociologists identify four different kinds of firms: specialist first-movers, specialist second-movers, generalist first-movers, and generalist second-movers (Hannan & Freeman, 1977). These types of firms are differentiated on the basis of the width of their product lines and on the timing of their entry into the market. Specialist first-movers are restricted to a particular sector of an industry and strive to be first in the market with new products. At the other extreme, generalist second-movers produce a variety of products in a variety of industrial sectors and are not first producers of new products. Rather, they compete by producing products at lower cost through more efficient manufacturing, often capitalizing on the mistakes of first-movers.

Firms have life cycles in which we can see them evolve from a young specialist first-mover into a mature generalist second-mover. The mature firms usually wait until market shakeouts occur among first-movers and then acquire surviving organizations in order to remain innovative. Entrepreneurs who start the acquired firms typically leave their organizations after acquisition and go off to start another. Some large organizations have tried to develop methods for keeping an independent entrepreneur in the firm while recognizing the problems inherent in the reward and regulatory systems under which entrepreneurs are willing to operate. Peters and Waterman (1982) describe mechanisms such as skunk works that provide the illusion of working in a small firm while being a part of a large organization as one such method.

In the combined stage model of Figure 2, we showed the sequence of decisions that are involved in the innovation process, the outputs that result from the various stages, and the organizational roles that are enacted at each stage. An important aspect of Figure 2 is the degree to which the roles of the various actors overlap various stages and the degree to which the entrepreneur occupies key transition points in both the producer and user portions of the model.

Referring back to Figure 2 allows us to note the different contexts in which entrepreneurial work can occur in an organization, and the degree to which entrepreneurial activities can transcend their original intentions. As an example, we pose the development of the personal computer. Various inventors by the late 1970s had developed electronic equipment that two (producer) entrepreneurs creatively combined to produce the Apple Computer. Jobs and Wozniak later moved out of their Silicon Valley garage into a production facility and created an organization, complete with managers, accountants, marketers, etc., to produce and sell their product.

In a given organization far from Silicon Valley, there resided an individual who liked to read about and work with new "gadgets"; it was his hobby, so to speak. This "technological gatekeeper" soon was talking about the new computers and not long after had a demonstration machine in his office. A manager saw the new product and noted that among other things, it did word processing. This manager, having problems with a small secretarial staff not being able to keep up with the demand for typing, entrepreneurially "created" a solution. Managers would be given PCs and would produce rough drafts of their own reports which the secretarial staff would then edit and print. ("Just give me your floppy" became a common phrase.) Soon the process was further improved upon by the staff as people became more familiar with the technology. They searched out continuous form letterhead paper for form letters and began keeping various personnel records on the computer, improving office efficiencies in many ways. Not long after, other managers heard about, investigated, and implemented an electronic mail system to send messages to each other. This, of course, changed many operating practices in the organization since some people could work at home and communicate with colleagues electronically. Future developments are expected.

This example illustrates that the eventual *process* used by an adopting organization may be far different from the purposes of the original *product* acquisition, and that there are numerous points in both the producer and user system where entrepreneurial actions are relevant. The not-for-profit sector shows an equally complex picture of innovation. "Think tanks", government research and development labs, and universities often produce inventions that may be spun off to the private sector or developed by related not-for-profit firms. The motivations in these contexts are not just economic (Young, 1983), but also deal with status and prestige. Also, service organizations in the not-for-profit and public sector may be heavy users of inventions. Young (1985) documents cases of innovations in this sector where perceptions of quality and trust by the customer are important. The entrepreneur innovates a service in these sectors for other than profit reasons and is "rewarded" through witnessing the accomplishment of something of value. Young (1983) argues that entrepreneurship is as common in the not-for-profit sector as in profit seeking firms because of these varied intrinsic motivations acting upon individuals.

VI. CONCLUSION

Our premise in this paper is that the entrepreneur is a key actor in the technological innovation process; an actor that has been largely ignored in previous research that has focused primarily on the invention and adoption process. The creativity of the entrepreneur is a critical part of the innovation process both in producer and user organizations. Entrepreneurship has been clearly identified in producer organizations; entrepreneurs are closely identified with new innovations that they bring to the market. Entrepreneurs in user organizations are less visible, but are critical to the effective adoption of new technologies. We differentiate between the technological gatekeeper who simply identifies a new technology and the user entrepreneur who creates the applications and uses of the technology. The model in Figure 2 illustrates the similarity of these two types of entrepreneurial behaviors. Inventors and technological gatekeepers play similar roles; each "discovers" new technologies. Similarly, managers in producer organizations and mangers/workers in user organizations simply deal with technologies that have been delivered to them.

The central focus in both organizations is the role in the middle; that of the entrepreneur who creates a new product from an invention or who creates a new use for a product. The entrepreneur must develop effective interpersonal skills in order to facilitate the transitions required, and must be adequately rewarded in order to promote the risk taking behavior required of persons in these roles. Clearly the "care and feeding" of entrepreneurs, given their personalities, seems to be different from other actors in organizations. Entrepreneurs may be different, but they are also very important.

REFERENCES

Carleton, W., (1986), "Issues and Questions Involving Venture Capital." In G. D. Libecap, (Ed.), *Advances in the Study of Entrepreneurship: Innovation and Economic Growth*, Greenwich, CT:JAI Press.

Chase, R. B. and N. J. Aquilano, (1985), *Production and Operations Management*, 4th ed. Homewood, IL: Richard D. Irwin.

Freeman, J., (1986), "Entrepreneurs as Organizational Products: Semi-conductor Firms and Venture Capital Firms." In G. D. Libecap, (Ed.), *Advances in the Study of Entrepreneurship: Innovation and Economic Growth*. Greenwich, CT:JAI Press.

Hannan, M. and Freeman, J. (1977), "The Population Ecology of Organizations." *American Journal of Sociology*, 82:929–964.

Hollmann, R. and Tansik, D. A. (1977), "A Life-Cycle Approach to Management by Objectives." *Academy of Management Review* 2:678–683.

Kamien, M. I. and Schwartz, N. L. (1982) *Market Structure and Innovation*, New York: Cambridge University Press.

Koestler, A., (1964), *The Act of Creation*. New York: Macmillan.

Lambright, W. H., (1980), *Technology Transfer to Cities*. Boulder, CO: Westview Press.

McClelland, D. C., (1961), *The Achieving Society*, New York: Free Press.

Mansfield, E., (1968), *Industrial Research and Technological Innovation: An Econometric Analysis*. New York: W. W. Norton and Company.

Martin, M. J. C., (1984), *Managing Technological Innovation and Entrepreneurship*, Reston, VA: Reston Publishing Co.

Northcraft, G. (1985), "The Effective Employee: The Importance of Feedback." Working Paper, College of Business and Public Administration, University of Arizona.

Northcraft, G. and G. Wolf, (1984), "The Dollars and Sense of Sunk Costs." *Academy of Management Review* 10:223–231.

Perrow, C. B., (1967), "A Framework for the Comparative Analysis of Organizations." *American Sociological Review* 32:194–208.

Peters, T., (1983), "The Mythology of Innovation." *The Stanford Magazine* (Summer):13–21.

Peters, T. J. and Waterman, R. H. (1982), *In Search of Excellence*. New York: Harper and Row.

Peterson, R. A., (1981), "Entrepreneurship and Organization." In W. H. Starbuck, and P. C. Nystrom (Eds.), *Handbook of Organizational Design*. New York: Oxford University Press, pp. 65–83.

Rogers, E. M., (1983), *The Diffusion of Innovations*, 3rd ed. New York: Free Press.

Schon, D. A., (1967), *Technology and Change*. New York: Delacorte Press.

Schumpeter, J. A., (1961), *Theory of Economic Development*. New York: Oxford University Press.

Schumpeter, J. A. (1964), *Business Cycles*. New York: McGraw-Hill.

Staw, B., (1977), "The Experimenting Organization." In B. Staw (Ed.), *Psychological Foundations of Organizational Behavior*. Santa Monica, CA: Goodyear.

Staw, B. and Ross, J. (1980), "Commitment in an Experimenting Society: A Study of the Attribution of Leadership from Administrative Scenarios." *Journal of Applied Psychology* 65:249–260.

Tansik, D. A. and Radnor, M. (1971), "An Organization Theory Perspective on the Development of New Organizational Functions." *Public Administration Review* 31:644–652.

von Hipple, E., (1976), "The Dominant Role of Users in the Scientific Instrumentation Process." *Research Policy* 5:212–239.

Williamson, O., (1975), *Markets and Hierarchies*. New York: Free Press.

Young, D., (1983), *If Not for Profit, for What?* Lexington, MA: Lexington Books.

Young, D., (1985), *Casebook of Management for Nonprofit Organizations: Entrepreneurship and Organizational Change in the Human Services*. New York: Haworth Press.

Chapter 10

INNOVATION AND PROPERTY RIGHTS IN INFORMATION:
AN EXPERIMENTAL APPROACH TO TESTING HYPOTHESES ABOUT PRIVATE R&D BEHAVIOR

R. Mark Isaac and Stanley S. Reynolds

I. INTRODUCTION

A. The Issues

How well do different regimes of private property rights in information provide appropriate incentives for research and development (R&D)? This central question has emerged after several decades of discussion by economists not only as to the process of innovation, but also to the criteria for evaluating the well-being of an economy. The purposes of this paper are first to review and analyze some different views of the innovative process and then to extend the inquiry using the relatively new technique of laboratory experimental economics.

The standard notion of economic efficiency has its origins in the nineteenth-century writing of Vilfredo Pareto. The Pareto efficiency criterion measures the effectiveness with which an economic system utilizes an existing set of resources

Advances in the Study of Entrepreneurship, Innovation, and Economic Growth, Volume 1, pages 129-156.
Copyright © 1986 by JAI Press Inc.
ISBN: 0-89232-703-0

to produce goods and services and distributes them to consumers. Many economists have stressed the benefits of a competitive market system in achieving Pareto efficiency. Note that this concept of economic efficiency is static; essentially it takes a "snapshot" of the economy at a point in time. Specifically, the resources which are assumed to be given for the purpose of the analysis include not only the natural resources of the economy, but also the state of knowledge about productive processes. In this snapshot world, innovation and investment are irrelevant concepts.

A more dynamic notion of economic efficiency originated with Joseph Schumpeter. Schumpeter (1950) stressed the role of technological innovation in contributing to improved living standards over time:

> "in capitalist reality as distinguished from its textbook picture, it is not that kind of competition (price competition) which counts but the competition from the new commodity, the new technology, the new source of supply, the new type of organization—competition which commands a decisive cost or quality advantage and which strikes not at the margins of the profits and the outputs of existing firms but at their foundations and their very lives.[1]

That is, in the Schumpeterian model, evaluation of an economic system does not occur as a snapshot, but rather more like a motion picture in which change via technological progress is observed across time.

Technological progress (through new products and processes) is based on the appearance and generation of new information. But information is a commodity and an economist would argue that the manner in which any scarce resource is allocated depends on the prevailing system of property rights in that commodity (in this case, the property rights to information). In the context of innovative behavior, property rights in information correspond to the appropriability of the gains from innovation. It is not only economists who have postulated a link between information appropriability and technological progress. The importance of information property rights was clearly on the minds of the framers of the U.S. Constitution, who established the patent powers of the Congress:

> Congress shall have the power . . . to promote the progress of science and useful arts, by securing for limited times to authors and inventors exclusive right to their respective writings and discoveries . . .[2]

Thus, the founding wisdom was that establishing property rights in information (e.g., patents for the innovator) could promote technological progress. However, such property rights are not costless (in the sense of Pareto efficiency) since they provide innovators with at least temporary monopoly power.

Given the importance of technological progress in contributing to economic welfare, economists have attempted to merge the Paretian and Schumpeterian viewpoints into comparative analyses of the efficiency across time of different systems of property rights in information. From these attempts, several key issues have emerged. One of these concerns the R&D incentives associated with different systems of private property rights in information. There are two principal arguments. One is that there will be underinvestment in R&D. The underinvestment argument focuses on the divergence between private and social gains from innovation. The most significant part of this divergence is consumer surplus, i.e., consumer benefit over and above the price(s) paid by consumers. When producers cannot perfectly bargain over price with each consumer of the product, some purchasers may pass less than the maximum amount which they would have been willing to exchange. This residual consumer benefit is a social gain from the innovation which is not appropriated by the innovator, even with complete patent protection. The divergence presumably will be greater under incomplete patent protection because even the gains reflected by the market price may be eroded by competition. Thus, the private incentives for investment in R&D are argued to be less than represented by the entire social benefits.

The other argument, made by Hirshleifer and Riley (1979), is that there will be overinvestment in information. They suggest that there is a "rush to invent" tendency because of the common property resource nature of undiscovered ideas when there are rewards (from the marketplace, from patent protection, etc.) for being the first to discover a new idea. This follows because some portion of each innovator's ideas would have been discovered later on anyway, by other innovators. However, in the presence of specific rewards for being the first, too much effort is put into innovative activity too soon. Hirshleifer and Riley suggest that this rush to invent could be corrected by assigning property rights in particular types of undiscovered ideas. However, they acknowledge the great practical difficulties of such a proposal.

Another important issue is the impact of market structure on the incentives for R&D. Elements of market structure include the number of buyers and sellers, the size distribution of buyers and sellers, barriers to entry, the extent of product differentiation, etc. Classical economists such as Ricardo, Malthus, and Mill tended to view technological advance as primarily exogenous from these features of the economic system. That is, technological advances occurred not as a result of decisions made by producers and consumers, but rather as a result of forces operating outside the economic system. Each advance was a "shock" to the system which, after a period of adjustment, led to a new equilibrium. Given this view of technological advance, perfect competition would appear to be best suited for promoting static and dynamic efficiency. Moreover, competitive forces would encourage rapid diffusion of new technologies once they appear.

In contrast, Schumpeter viewed technological progress as endogenous to the economic system. The role of technological progress and its character are determined by forces operating within the economic system. For example, the appearance of the Watt-Boulton steam engine was not, in this view, a simple business application of a randomly occurring invention or insight.[3] Rather, the development of the steam engine was the result of a series of economic decisions. These economic decisions were influenced by such underlying conditions as technological opportunities (in which chance may indeed have played a role), expected future demand levels, and the degree of appropriability of rewards. With such a model in mind, Schumpeter argued that large firms with at least some monopoly power are best suited for introducing innovations that benefit society:

> the perfectly competitive arrangement displays wastes of its own. The firm of the type that is compatible with perfect competition is in many cases inferior in internal, especially technological efficiency. . . What we have got to accept is that it (the large-scale establishment or unit of control) has come to be the most powerful engine of that progress, and in particular of the long run expansion of total output. . .[4]

Thus, monopoly profits are simply the rewards required to spur innovations. In addition, monopoly profits provide a source of funds for further investment in R&D. In Schumpeter's view, firms can achieve monopoly power only temporarily because a monopoly position lasts only until the next round of innovation.

We begin this paper with a review of the attempts of economists to formalize and analyze these different views of the innovative process. Following a discussion of the review, we will present the results of some laboratory economics experiments addressing the same questions. In doing so, we begin by elaborating on the use of laboratory experiments and then presenting a model of R&D behavior which has testable predictions about the influence of appropriability and market structure features on an economy. Following this, we present the actual data from the experiments, and close with our interpretation of the results of future research on innovation and technological progress.

B.   A Review of the Relevant Literature

This section focuses on how economic analysis has addressed the function of information appropriately and competitive forces in influencing technical progress. The relevant literature is broken down into three types: economic theory, simulation studies, and empirical studies.

Among the theoretical studies, Schumpeter was the first economist to present a comprehensive theory of endogenous technological progress. This theory describes a process of creative destruction, an economic evolution in which existing products and processes are continually supplanted by innovations. Recent theoretical work has attempted to make the model of the innovative process described by Schumpeter more rigorous.

Most early analytic models utilized a decision theoretic approach in which the decision making problem of a single potential innovator is formulated, regarding an exogenous specification of the innovator's environment as a given.[5] The questions addressed deal with the influence of various factors on the innovator's choice of the speed of development (or rate of R&D spending). Such factors include the degree of appropriability of the innovation (e.g., rewards for being first, rewards to imitation), properties of the development cost relationship (e.g., economies or diseconomies of scale, cost uncertainty, presence or absence of contractual requirements, etc.), and the perceived intensity of rivalry.

The principal hypotheses which emerge from this decision-theoretic approach are the following. The speed of development increases with the reward for being first. In other words, the rate of R&D spending will grow as the degree of appropriability of the innovation increases. Under this formulation, the fear of losses from rival innovation also speeds up development for the incumbent firm. The possibility of a rival's innovation also interacts in an interesting way with the form of development costs. The firm is more likely to undertake an R&D project when costs are noncontractual than when a contractual commitment is required. With no contract for development costs, the firm risks a smaller loss in the case if a rival innovates first. With no contractual commitment to a prespecified program of R&D spending, a firm has the option of stopping its R&D expenditures (and cutting its losses) if it loses a race to be first. Further, the perceived intensity of rivalry has an important effect on the potential innovator's speed of development. The greatest speed of development according to these models occurs under an intermediate level of competition, i.e., a market structure between perfect monopoly and perfect competition. As the environment moves toward perfect competition in which imitation is immediate, the incentives for R&D disappear because the effect appropriability of the gains from innovation disappear. On the other hand, if we started with virtually no competition, an increase in perceived rivalry spurs development because of the increased chance of rivals being first to innovate.

A weakness of the decision-theoretic approach is that only the decisions of one innovator out of a group of potential innovators are considered. This approach can generate misleading predictions. For example, suppose an increase in a parameter representing the probability of rival innovation causes a reduced rate of R&D investment by the firm. In this case, the decision-theoretic approach suggests that increased competition yields lower R&D investment. However, an increase in competition might cause an increase in aggregate R&D investment even if each individual firm lowers its own investment.[6]

An alternative view is the game-theoretic approach where the decisions of a group of potential innovators are considered simultaneously.[7] The prediction of such an analysis is the equilibrium of the game. Most commonly some version of the Nash Equilibrium concept is used. As in a decision-theoretic approach, each firm is assumed to adopt an R&D strategy which maximizes its expected (value of) returns given the environment. What is different about the Nash framework is that a critical part of that environment is assumed to be the simultaneous calculations of all the firms. Thus, the Nash equilibrium strategies have a mutual best-response property. That is, each firm's equilibrium R&D investment strategy is its best response to the equilibrium R&D investment strategies of all of its rivals. This equilibrium condition imposes a type of consistency on the behavior of a group of potential innovators.

Papers using a game-theoretic approach by Loury (1979), Dasgupta and Stiglitz (1980b), Lee and Wilde (1980), Mortensen (1982), Reinganum (1982), and Stewart (1983) have examined the case of a single product innovation produced by one of several identical firms. The timing of the innovation and the identity of the successful innovator are random variables that depend on the R&D spending of all of the firms. In Loury, Dasgupta and Stiglitz, and Lee and Wilde the innovator reaps the entire reward from the innovation (winner-take-all). With a fixed group of N firms, the following two predictions emerge from these winner-take-all models:

(P1) An increase in the number of firms raises aggregate industry investment in R&D in a Nash equilibrium;

(P2) If the private rewards from R&D equal the social rewards, then in a Nash equilibrium, firms overinvest in R&D relative to the social optimum.

In Loury and in Dasgupta and Stiglitz each firm incurs a one-time fixed cost for R&D. This is in essence a contractual commitment to a certain amount of R&D spending. In this case, an increase in the number of firms reduces investment by each individual firm but raises aggregate investment. In Lee and Wilde, each firm incurs constant investment flow costs until one firm innovates. There is no contractual commitment to a total amount of R&D spending. In this case, an increase in the number of firms raises both individual firm and aggregate investment rates.

Prediction (P2) above is an illustration of the overinvestment argument cited by Hirshleifer and Riley (1979). Loury shows that the overinvestment prediction also holds in a long run equilibrium with free entry of innovating firms if there is an initial interval of increasing returns to scale in R&D investment.

Mortensen, Reinganum and Stewart also consider the property rights issue, i.e., the effect of the appropriability of innovation on R&D spending. In each case, the following prediction emerges:

(P3) A reduction in appropriability for the innovator leads to reduced R&D spending by all participants.

In the context of game-theoretic models of R&D, a reduction in appropriability of rewards for the innovator means that more of the benefits from innovation spill over onto non-innovating firms. If the degree of appropriability for an innovator is so low that spillover effects are large, then either prediction (P1) and/or (P2) may be reversed. The result for (P1) is illustrated in Futia's (1980) model of repeated innovation in which a more competitive market structure (due to lower barriers to entry) tends to reduce the expected probability of innovation in the long run.[8] Regarding (P2), Mortensen and Stewart show that a property-rights system (i.e., a benefit sharing rule) exists where the Nash equilibrium outcome for a fixed group of N firms is socially optimal.

Game theoretic formulations of R&D competition are analytically tractable only for very stylized models. Simulation methods offer an alternative to purely analytical techniques, and they can be employed to explore the properties of much more realistic models of R&D competition. Simulation can also be used to evaluate the effects of various public policies toward innovative behavior. There are, however, two important limitations of the simulation approach. First, simulation results are obtained only for specific numerical choices of parameters. The behavior that emerges need not be robust over a wide range of parameter settings. Secondly, firm behavior in simulation studies is driven by ad hoc decision rules specified in advance. These decision rules are usually loosely based on interpretations of observed firm behavior. However, these prespecified decision rules may not describe the actions of self interested parties operating in a market environment.

Nelson and Winter have made several contributions to the R&D literature using simulation methods.[9] Their studies typically posit a dynamic oligopolistic market in which sellers make several decisions in each period. Each seller must decide on a price for its output, or simply select an output level. Each seller must also decide how much to invest in production capital, in innovation process R&D, and in imitative process R&D in each period. The focus of their analyses is on the dynamic competition among innovators and imitators. The outcome of the competitive process is shaped by technological and institutional conditions, some of which are influenced by government policy.

Nelson and Winter (1978, 1982a, 1982b) have conducted numerical simulation studies for various specifications of firms' behavior and of the economic environment. Values are set for parameters that determine the aggressiveness of capital investment, the proclivity for innovative as opposed to imitative R&D, ease of imitation, and the exogenous role of improvement in the underlying technology base. Nelson and Winter find that concentration within the industry increases over time in all of their simulation studies. This tendency towards increasing concentration is most pronounced in industries with rapidly expanding technological opportunities.

In the simulation studies conducted by Nelson and Winter, the behavior of firms is specified according to fixed decision rules. For example, a firm may be assigned a decision rule that sets innovative R&D spending at four percent of sales revenue and imitative R&D spending at two percent of sales revenue. These decision rules are not responsive to changes in the underlying economic environment. Because of this, it is difficult to draw any conclusions about the effects of appropriability or initial concentration on firms' R&D investment behavior.

Although there have been many empirical studies of R&D and innovation over the last 25 years, few have been closely linked to either game-theoretic or decision-theoretic analytical models of the innovative process.[10] Instead, the measures of "innovation" and the empirical hypotheses to be tested have been guided by the availability of data, not by any specific conceptual framework.[11] Relatively few empirical studies have examined the link between appropriability and innovation. The degree of appropriability of an innovation depends on the ability of firms to capture and protect the returns from new products and processes. This, in turn, depends upon several factors. One set of factors includes aspects of the legal environment (the patenting system, the breadth of patent rights, and the legal enforcement of patent protection are examples). Other factors such as secrecy, product or process complexity, steepness of the experience curve, and imitation lags can also influence effective appropriability.

Scherer (1984, Ch.13) provides indirect evidence of the impact of appropriability in his study of compulsory licensing. Firms subject to compulsory licensing decrees have their appropriability of a product or process directly reduced. Scherer finds no evidence that such decrees inhibit R&D spending in his study of large firms. However, Levin (1981) points out that appropriability depends upon several factors. Firms in some markets may resort to lawsuits leading to compulsory licensing decrees precisely because imitation is difficult in those markets. Levin employs simultaneous equations estimation methods to explore the relationships between private R&D, advertising, concentration, and profitability. The proxy variable used to measure appropriability has a positive but not statistically significant estimated effect on private R&D. Levin, Cohen, and Mowery (1985) utilize survey data at the line of business level to estimate the effects of appropriability, opportunity, and market structure on R&D and on a measure of innovative output. Single equation regressions were run with either an R&D-to-sales ratio or a measure of innovative output as the dependent variable. Appropriability is estimated to have the predicted positive relationship in both cases, although the estimated coefficient is statistically significant in the innovative output equation but not in the R&D equation.

The relationship between market structure and technological progress has been investigated in a large number of studies (see Kamien and Schwartz, 1982, Ch. 3 for a survey). Typically, these studies have estimated a single equation with R&D or some measure of technological progress as the dependent variable and a concentration measure as one of the independent variables. (This structure, of course, ignores the possibility that observed concentration in an industry might be simultaneously determined with R&D.) The studies typically find the estimated relationship between concentration and R&D to be weak or nonexistent, although some support exists for the hypothesis that an intermediate market structure between perfect competition and monopoly is most conducive to technological progress. Levin, Cohen, and Mowery (1985) show that the significance of coefficients for exogenous concentration variables is greatly reduced as exogenous variables representing appropriability and opportunity conditions are added.

II. RESULTS FROM LABORATORY MARKETS

In the laboratory tests described in this paper, we rely upon theoretical models which are Nash equilibrium, game-theoretic, stochastic invention models. Examples of this class of models include: Loury (1979), Dasgupta and Stiglitz (1980b), Futia (1980), Mortensen (1982), and Rogerson (1982). Of interest to us is that models in this class make direct predictions about the relationship between appropriability and R&D activity and between the number of firms in the market and R&D activity. The remainder of this paper reports on the results of our laboratory tests.

A. Methodological Issues

Laboratory experimental economics is a relatively new approach to economic analysis. Most of its development has taken place over the last twenty-five years. To our knowledge, the results presented here represent the first application of this methodology to hypotheses about research and development. We will not review here the fundamental methodological precepts of experimental economics. Instead, in this section we will discuss some issues which deal directly with our R&D experiments.[12]

To begin, it should be emphasized that the purpose of laboratory experimental economics is different than either computer simulation studies (as discussed in the previous section) or business simulation games. Our experiments utilize real people making real economic decisions for real money. Behavioral rules are not imposed ex ante, but are whatever flesh and blood human beings choose to do. Compared with business simulation games, our participants are not in an environment of "role playing." They are presented with relatively abstract market environments in which they have a chance to earn some money from their decisions. The profit, cost, and utility functions of economic theory are created by the process of induced valuation (Smith, 1976).

In the experiments reported here, participants were told that they were sellers of an unnamed commodity in a series of market periods, and that their market earnings depended upon whether they (and the other sellers) were "Type A" or "Type B" sellers. Each seller could become a "Type A" by earning at least one "success" in a random process. Each seller was free to purchase, at a cost of $.10 per draw, as many draws in a market period as he/she desired. While the experimenters knew that becoming a "Type A" seller in this process was the laboratory analog to being first to the market with a successful innovation, the words "innovation," "Nash Equilibrium," "R&D," were never used. Thus, it should be clear that it is not the purpose of these experiments to simulate or predict levels of R&D in any particular industry. Rather the experiments are designed to examine the usefulness of a family of predictions about appropriability and market structure from a particular class of economic theories. As noted above, our experiments draw upon a number of formalized mathematical models of the R&D process. When, as in this case, the experiments are guided by well developed theories, Smith (1982) says that the experiments are "nomothetic."

This leads immediately to a second important distinction. We say that we are guided by theories of R&D processes. Yet, economists use the term "theory" at several levels. At one level is the core theory (or "theorem") represented by the basic mathematical model. The "correctness" of this theory is proven at the logical/mathematical level by its internal consistency and mathematical reasoning. We take as a given that the Nash R&D models which form the basis for our research are "correct" at this level. The question which then might be asked of us is the following: "If the theories (theorems) are correct, what is there to test?" Or, put another way, what will the results of our experiments add to the theories discussed in the previous section? After all, if the results are consistent with the predictions of the theories, isn't that what one would have expected? Or, if the results are not consistent with the predictions, doesn't that mean that there is something wrong with the experiments (since we know that the theories are "correct")? Questions such as these fail to distinguish between the core theorem of the mathematical model and the operationalized economic theory which says that the model is supposed to have useful predictive power in an economic environment.

The mathematical models of R&D discussed here can, in this light, be seen as testable. There are a variety of reasons why, even though we give the theories a "fair shot," they might fail. Perhaps a Nash equilibrium is never obtained, or is obtained but is not behaviorally stable. Perhaps the assumption of noncooperative behavior breaks down. In any case, if the data turn out to be inconsistent with the theories, it is not "proven" that the theory will also fail in every other context, say in a field test of R&D in the semiconductor industry. Nevertheless, the burden of proof has been shifted by the nonconfirming data from the laboratory. Likewise, if the data are consistent with the theory, then our confidence in its predictive power is strengthened, and we can move to testing the robustness of the positive results [in what Smith (1982) has called searching for the boundaries of falsification].

The hypotheses of interest to us in the family of Nash stochastic invention models are the predictions about the influence of appropriability and market structure on R&D. In this paper, we will confine our attention to the results of twelve experiments we have conducted which look only at the appropriability issues. We turn now to a more complete description of the hypotheses, design, parameters, and results.

B. An Operational Model for Experimental Testing

The basic structure of the game-theoretic stochastic innovation models may be described as follows. There is a group of N potential innovators (or "firms"). Each firm must simultaneously and privately choose an R&D investment level without knowing the decisions made by its rivals. A random process then determines which of the firms, if any, is a successful (first) innovator. The probability of a firm becoming the successful innovator depends upon the underlying probability structure and upon the R&D decisions of all firms. The distribution of returns depends upon the property rights to the innovation and the resulting "payoffs" to being an innovator and to being an "imitator."

In operationalizing the stochastic innovation process, we chose to use a single-period variant of the discrete time formulations of Futia (1980) and Rogerson (1982). In their models, there is a stationary probability distribution over "success" in any time period. By adopting the Futia and Rogerson approach, we use a model different than the continuous time formulations of Loury (1979), Dasgupta and Stiglitz (1980b), and Stewart (1983) in which each firm's innovation program is assumed to be governed by an exponential probability distribution across time. While these models are analytically tractable, they are more difficult to operationalize in a laboratory setting. In economics experiments, participants are recruited for a fixed maximum length of time (say for two or three hours). A theory which allows (even if with very low probabilities) unbounded lengths of time to pass before an innovation occurs may not receive a fair test (or may have different theoretical interpretations) if an artificial boundary were added to insure that sufficient observations were gathered in the time constraints of the experiment.

Thus, our model is constructed as follows. Innovative success or failure in a given time period is determined by a lottery with probabilities determined conditionally by the R&D choices of the firms. Aggregate profits in a single time period due to an innovation can be represented by V. Let $V_w > 0$ be the payoff to a single winner. Let $V_\ell > 0$ represent the payoff to each of the losers (noninnovating firms) if there is a winner. Aggregate payoffs can then be written as:

$$V = V_w + (N-1)V_\ell$$

In a winner-take-all environment with a single winner, V_ℓ is zero and $V = V_w$. If the benefits from innovation are partially appropriable (i.e., there are spillover effects) then V_w is less than V, and V_ℓ is positive. Under partial appropriability, every firm receives a payoff of at least V_ℓ as long as some firm innovates.

In the model, each firm's decision is how many draws from the random process to purchase. Let x_i represent firm i's chosen number of innovation draws, and let c be the constant cost per draw. Then total R&D expenditure by firm i is cx_i. After each firm has chosen a level of R&D spending, a series of independent draws with replacement is made to determine which of the subjects, if any, is the winner. Let h represent the binomial probability of success on any one draw, so that if i elects to make x_i draws in a period, the probability of having at least one success in a period is

$$\theta (x_i) = 1 - (1 - h)^{x_i}$$

This probability θ is increasing and concave in R&D spending (where x_i is viewed as a continuous variable).[13] If firm i has at least one success and no other firm has any successes, then firm i is the sole winner of the innovation race and receives V_w. However, in discrete time we must consider the possibility of a tie.[14] There are two possible tie-breaking rules. One would conduct a second equal-probability lottery among the k successful firms to discover the single winner. The second approach awards each successful firm a payoff of $(V_w + (k - 1) V_\ell)/k$. These two tie-breaking rules are equivalent in expected value, but they are not necessarily equivalent in expected utility if some economic agents are risk averse. We chose the second method of dealing with ties, in which *all* those sellers who had successes shared equally in the total aggregate rewards from being a winner rather than a loser. This tie-breaking system is then analogous to a patent system in which "ties" (multiple innovators with equal claim to patent rights) are involved formally or informally in a patent-sharing arrangement.

Each market decision period in this model corresponds to one play of the stochastic innovation game. Expected profits for a subject in a given period may now be defined. Suppose that each of the N-1 rival subjects chooses x_j draws.[15] Then expected profit for firm i as a function of its own number of draws can be written as the following:

$$E[\pi_i(x_i, x_j)] = \theta(x_i) \sum_{m=1}^{N} \left\{ \left(\frac{V_w + (m-1)V_\ell}{m} \right) \binom{N-1}{m-1} \theta(x_j)^{m-1} \right.$$

$$\left. (1 - \theta(x_j))^{N-m} \right\} + (1 - \theta(x_i))V_\ell (1 - (1 - \theta(x_j))^{N-1}) - cx_i \qquad (1)$$

The expected profits function for firm i consists of three terms. The first term is expected profit, given that i has one or more successes. The second term is the expected profit if i has no successes. The third term is the certain constant cost of purchasing draws. If x_i is treated as a continuous variable, then the necessary conditions for expected profit maximization are:

$$0 = \left\{ -V_\ell(1 - (1 - \theta(x_j))^{N-1}) + \sum_{m=1}^{N} \left(\frac{V_w + (m-1)V_\ell}{m} \right) \binom{N-1}{m-1} \right.$$

$$\left. \theta(x_j)^{m-1} (1 - \theta(x_j))^{N-m} \right\} \frac{d\theta}{dx_i} - c \qquad (2)$$

Since θ is concave in x_i, this condition is also sufficient for a maximum. A symmetric noncooperative Nash equilibrium in R&D expenditures for a single period is defined by (2) with $x_i = x_j$.

Let the social value of the innovation be V_s. Suppose that an omniscient social planner could operate N R&D facilities with x being spent on R&D at each facility. The expected social welfare per period is given by:

$$E[S_N(x)] = V_s [1 - (1 - \Theta(x))^N] - Nxc \qquad (3)$$

This represents V_s times the probability of at least one success at any one of the facilities less the cost of operating N facilities. This equation also represents the expected value of joint profits if N innovating firms operated in a collusive manner, if $V = V_s$. Again treating x as a continuous variable, the necessary condition for maximizing expected social welfare (or, alternatively, expected joined profits if $V = V_s$) is given by:

$$0 = N \left\{ V_s((1 - \theta(x))^{N-1}) \frac{d\theta}{dx} - c \right\} \qquad (4)$$

Suppose that the rewards to innovation are fully appropriable so that $V_\ell = 0$.

Then, Eq. (2), the condition for noncooperative profit maximization may be written as (2′):

$$0 = V\left((1 - \theta(x_j))^{N-1}\right) \frac{d\theta}{dx_i} + \sum_{m=2}^{N} \left(\frac{V}{m}\right) \binom{N-1}{m-1} \theta(x_j)^{m-1}$$

$$\left((1 - \theta(x_j))^{N-m}\right) \frac{d\theta}{dx_i} - c \qquad\qquad (2')$$

Expressing the condition in this manner illustrates the incentives in this model for overinvestment in R&D in a symmetric Nash equilibrium when $V = V_s$. The second term in (2′) represents the marginal benefit to firm i as a result of innovation ties with its rivals. The possibility of being in a tie for innovative success represents a private return to the non-cooperating firms, since the gains from the innovation are shared among all the firms in the tie. However, this term is absent in Eq. (4), the condition for socially optimal (joint profit maximizing) R&D investment. That is, if two firms simultaneously perfect a better mousetrap, social welfare (joint profits) is not increased. Multiple successes simply represent duplication of effort. [Again, it is important to recall that this overinvestment argument necessarily holds only if rewards from the innovation are fully appropriable to the winner(s).]

This model of R&D behavior is associated with an environment which can be created in the experimental economics laboratory. Participants were recruited from undergraduate economic and business classes at the University of Arizona. After being paid $3.00 for arriving on time, they were given a copy of the instructions (which are reproduced here in the Appendix). Briefly, they were told that they were sellers of an unnamed commodity, and that their earnings were determined by whether they (and the other sellers) were Type A or Type B sellers. To become a Type A seller, each person had to buy a number of draws from a bingo cage and successfully draw the number 10. The total profits for each seller were determined by how many draws he purchased, whether he was a Type A or a Type B seller, and if he was a Type A seller, by how many other Type A sellers there were in that period.[16] All of the important parameters of this model are represented. N, the number of potentially innovating firms, could be altered by recruiting a different number of participants. The use of a bingo cage represents an easily understood binomial process with replacement. The binomial probability h can be changed by changing the number of balls in the cage. Finally, the returns from the innovation are set by the experimenters, and their distribution among Type A and Type B sellers represents different forms of innovation appropriability.

C. Experimental Design and Parameters

The experiments are organized in a two-by-two design with the treatment variables being market structure (number of firms) and appropriability of the rewards from innovation (distribution of payoffs to Type A and B sellers). For market structure, we will eventually look at groups of size 4 and 9, but all experiments report ed here have 4 participants. For appropriability, we examined both full app ropriability to innovators and also a partial diffusion payment scheme. A complete list of the parameters is given in Table 1.

With our operationalized version of a Nash stochastic invention model, and with our chosen parameters, the predictions of the theory correspond directly to predicting (P1) (aggregate industry investment increases with the number of firms), (P2) (overinvestment in R&D), and (P3) (reduction in appropriability reduces R&D for each firm). Here, we wish to discuss the results of 12 four-person experiments which allow us to concentrate on predictions about the effects of appropriability. The laboratory versions of predictions (P2) and (P3) are as follows:

(P2L) On average, firms will overinvest in draws relative to the social (joint profits) optimum under either appropriability condition.

(P3L) On average, firms will purchase more draws in the full appropriability condition than in the partial appropriability condition.

Table 1. Experimental Design and Parameterization

Two × Two Design

Appropriability

		Complete	Partial
Group Size	Small	Type I Experiments	Type II Experiments
	Large	Type III Experiments	Type IV Experiments

Parameters

Probability of success on one draw: $h = 0.1$
Cost per draw: $c = \$0.10$
Working capital: $W = \$5.00$
Aggregate profit: $V = V_s = \$5.90$
Reward to a single winner: $V_w = \$5.90$ (complete) or $\$3.50$ (partial)
Group size: $N = 4$ (small) or 9 (large)

The theoretical risk-neutral Nash equilibrium predictions and the joint-profit-maximizing values are presented in Table 2.[17] These predictions were obtained as follows. Given our choices of parameters, the theoretical equation defining the Nash equilibrium (Eq. 2) can be solved for a prediction using a simple computer routine. The numbers which emerge have precisely the Nash "best response" property. That is, the computer simulation tells us that if each of the sellers in the full appropriability setting purchases 9 draws, no seller will want to be the only one to switch to any other integer number of draws. Likewise, the computer routine calculated that if each seller chose precisely 4 draws, that would maximize the total combined profits to the 4 sellers. This divergence between the Nash predictions and the combined profit maximizing decisions is the substance of prediction (P2).

D. Experimental Results

A total of 12 four-firm, ten period experiments were conducted; six were run with full appropriability and six were run with partial appropriability. A summary of the results (representing average number of draws in each period) appears in Figure 1.

The impact of appropriability is clearly evident. The average number of draws is higher in every period under full appropriability (ranging from 6.88 to 8.08) than under partial appropriability (ranging from 4.67 to 5.79). Recall that draws represent R&D investment. The Nash equilibrium predictions and the socially efficient (joint profit maximizing) values are also depicted in Figure 1. Under both appropriability conditions, the average number of draws was indeed larger than the efficient level in all ten periods. In general, the numerical predictions of the risk neutral Nash model work reasonably well, although the outcomes from full appropriability tend to be in the 7 to 8 range rather than the predicted level of 9 draws.

The laboratory versions of the research predictions can be tested using standard hypothesis tests. Five t-tests are formulated, and the complete results are presented in Table 3. The following are brief descriptions of the results:

Table 2. Theoretical Predictions
(Single Period)

	Nash Equilibrium		Social Optimum	
Experiment Type	*Draws per Subject*	*Expected Profit per Subject*	*Draws per Subject*	*Expected Profit per Subject*
I	9	$0.542	4	$0.802
II	5	$0.796	4	$0.802

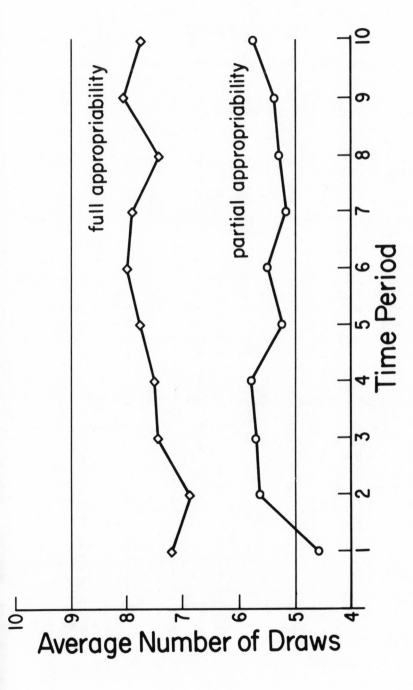

Figure 1. Summary of experimental results: Average number of draws per period.

Table 3. t-Statistics

Market Period

Hypothesis			1	2	3	4	5	6	7	8	9	10
A[a]	H_0:	$\mu_F \leq 4$	6.98**	5.42**	6.01**	8.25**	7.36**	5.93**	10.01**	7.58**	7.58**	5.03**
	H_1:	$\mu_F > 4$										
B[a]	H_0:	$\mu_P \leq 4$	1.48	5.82**	3.97**	2.78**	2.38**	6.71**	3.84**	5.13**	4.83**	3.46**
	H_1:	$\mu_P > 4$										
C[a]	H_0:	$\mu_F \leq \mu_P$	3.93**	2.08*	2.44*	2.22*	3.51**	3.52**	5.69**	4.12**	4.42**	2.21*
	H_1:	$\mu_F > \mu_P$										
D[b]	H_0:	$\mu_F = 9$	-3.93*	-3.99*	-2.67*	-3.54*	-2.35	-1.48	-2.75*	-3.50*	-1.71	-1.68
	H_1:	$\mu_F \neq 9$										
E[b]	H_0:	$\mu_P = 5$	-0.73	2.25	1.65	1.23	0.41	2.23	0.44	1.15	1.33	1.49
	H_1:	$\mu_P \neq 5$										

Notes:

[a]One-tailed test.

[b]Two-tailed test.

*H_0 can be rejected at the 95 percent confidence level.

**H_0 can be rejected at the 99 percent confidence level.

PREDICTION (P2L):   INVESTMENT GREATER THAN SOCIAL OPTI-
MUM

Hypothesis A: $\mu_F > 4$ (the mean of draws with full appropriability is greater than 4, the social optimum). The results are strongly consistent with this prediction. The (no-overinvestment) null hypothesis that $\mu_F \leq 4$ can be rejected at the 99% confidence level in every period.

Hypothesis B: $\mu_p > 4$ (the mean number of draws with partial appropriability is greater than 4). Overinvestment also appears with partial appropriability. The null hypothesis that $\mu_p \leq 4$ can be rejected with 99% confidence in periods 2–10.

PREDICTION (P3L):   APPROPRIABILITY MATTERS

Hypothesis C: $\mu_F > \mu_p$ (the mean number of draws is greater with full appropriability than with partial appropriability). The data provide strong support for this hypothesis. The null conjecture of a zero or negative difference ($\mu_F \leq \mu_P$) can be rejected at the 95% confidence level in every period and at the 99% confidence level in six periods.

PREDICTED LEVELS OF R&D INVESTMENT

Hypothesis D: $\mu_F = 9$ (the mean number of draws with full appropriability equals 9, the risk-neutral Nash equilibrium prediction). There is mixed support for this prediction from the risk-neutral version of the Nash model. In every period, μ_F is less than nine, although the hypotheses that $\mu_F = 9$ cannot be rejected in four of the last six periods.

Hypothesis E: $\mu_P = 5$ (the mean number of draws with partial appropriability equals 5, the risk-neutral Nash equilibrium prediction). While there was a tendency for μ_P to exceed 5, the hypothesis that $\mu_P = 5$ could not be rejected in any period at a 95% level of confidence.

III.   CONCLUSIONS

The experimental results support the hypothesis that the degree of appropriability of rewards has an impact on R&D spending. Average R&D investment (draws purchased by sellers) was consistently greater under full appropriability than under partial appropriability in the experiments. This is consistent with the Nash equilibrium predictions of game theoretic models of R&D. The strongly evident influence of appropriability in the experiments is an interesting result when one considers the high degree of uncertainty faced by subjects. Subjects in the experiments faced uncertainty with regard to the success or failure of their own R&D program and strategic uncertainty about rivals' decisions. The experimental results on appropriability are also useful in light of the dearth of empirical evidence on the impact of appropriability. As we noted earlier, in the non-laboratory world the degree of appropriability is a multi-faceted concept that is difficult to measure accurately.

The experimental results strongly support the hypothesis that firms overinvest in R&D relative to the social optimum in a winner-take-all environment (conditional on aggregate social benefit equaling aggregate private benefit). However, the extent of overinvestment in the full appropriability experiments was not quite as large as the Nash theory predicted.

The noncooperative, risk-neutral Nash equilibrium model performed quite well as a predictor of central tendencies in the experiments. There are two qualifications that emerged concerning the risk-neutral Nash predictions. The first concerns the variance of R&D investment draws. The risk-neutral Nash equilibrium prediction is identical for each seller, thus there is zero predicted variance in the distribution of draws across subjects. There is a positive variance in the distribution of draws under each appropriability condition from the experiments. Frequency distributions for subjects' draws are depicted graphically in Figure 2. The mode of the distribution for partial appropriability is 5 draws, the Nash prediction. The mode of the distribution for full appropriability is 8 draws, one draw less than the Nash prediction. (The χ^2 on the difference in the two appropriability conditions is 143.9, which is significant at 99 percent.)

A second qualification of the Nash predictions appears in the full appropriability setting. Subjects chose 7 to 8 draws on average rather than the Nash prediction of 9 draws in every period. One possible explanation for this divergence from risk-neutral Nash behavior is that subjects were risk-averse. We have run some numerical simulations of Nash equilibrium behavior of expected utility maximizing subjects using the exponential utility function,

$$u(y) = -\exp(-by).$$

The variable y represents the monetary reward and the positive parameter b is an index of risk aversion. With b equal to 0.5, the Nash prediction is 8 draws per subject. With b equal to 0.7, the Nash prediction falls to 7 draws per subject. So, under full appropriability, consideration of risk-averse behavior improves the Nash predictions. However, under partial appropriability, the risk-neutral Nash equilibrium yields better predictions than the risk-averse Nash equilibrium. With b equal to 0.5 and 0.7, the Nash predictions fall to 4 and 3 draws per subject, respectively. The average number of draws per subject in the experiments was slightly greater than the risk-neutral Nash prediction of 5 draws. So, we cannot simply appeal to risk aversion to reconcile these experimental results to the Nash

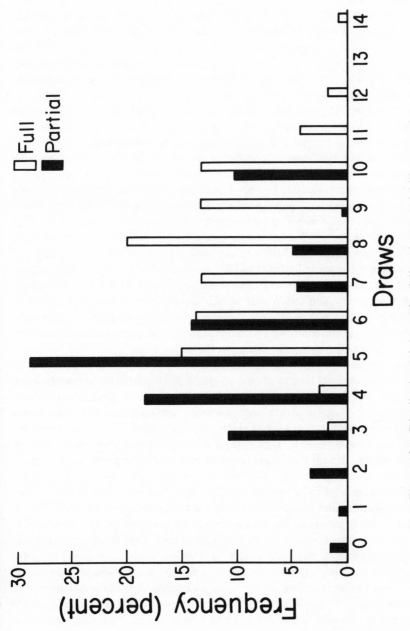

Figure 2. Distribution of draws for full and appropriability controls.

equilibrium theory. It may be the case that the risk sharing arrangement embodied in the partial appropriability setting induced subjects to alter their attitudes toward risk vis-à-vis their risk attitudes under full appropriability. This phenomenon merits further investigation.

The results reported above represent a first step in applying laboratory experimental methods to the economics of R&D. The predictions of the Nash equilibrium theory were found to perform quite well in these experiments. We plan to run another set of experiments using the same operational model with large groups of subjects (see Section II/C. above). This will allow us to examine the hypothesis about the effect of competition on R&D investment.

The most important direction for future research in this area is to integrate the experimental model of R&D into a framework in which the gains from innovation are determined directly by the profitability of the innovator operating in a full fledged market (i.e., making pricing decisions in a market with human buyers). In this type of integrated framework, firms would make decisions about pricing and production levels for their products. The private rewards to R&D in such a setting would be determined endogenously through the pricing and production decisions made by firms and by the purchasing decisions of the buyers. An experimental model of this type would be similar to the sort of dynamic model used by Nelson and Winter in their simulations. However, in laboratory experiments, the R&D investment, the selling and the buying decisions would be made by real people confronted with monetary incentives, rather than having decisions determined by fixed rules as in the simulations.

An integrated experimental framework would permit us to address several issues that we were not able to address adequately in our initial experiments. First, since the private rewards to R&D would be determined endogenously, a more meaningful evaluation of the overinvestment and underinvestment arguments would be possible. In our initial experiments, the private rewards are arbitrarily set to equal social rewards. That is, there is no representation of uncaptured consumer surplus. If real buyers are responding to and influencing sellers' pricing decisions, a divergence may develop between capturable private returns to the sellers and the total social rewards to innovation. Second, the impact of product market structure and institutions on R&D behavior could be evaluated. For example, is R&D behavior affected by whether the product market is organized as a "double oral auction" (which has active bids and offers from buyers and sellers and is similar to the trading rules used on stock exchanges), or by "seller posted offer pricing" (which has buyers shopping among sellers' listed prices and is used in most retail markets)? Third, an integrated model would allow us to investigate the effects of more realistic appropriability conditions in a controlled setting. For example, appropriability could be influenced by a patent grant on a new process that lasts a fixed number of market periods in the experiments.

Fourth, the level of competition could emerge endogenously based on R&D successes and failures of firms over time.

APPENDIX

The instructions for participants in the partial appropriability experiments are listed below. The full appropriability instructions are quite similar; the principal difference is the definition of market earnings in Part 3 of the instructions.

INSTRUCTIONS

1. Introduction

This is an experiment in the economics of decision-making under uncertainty. During this session we will create an environment in which you will be asked to make some choices regarding a simple investment procedure. The amount you earn will depend on the decisions that you and the other participants have made. The instructions are simple and if you follow them carefully and make good decisions, you might earn a considerable amount of money which will be paid to you in cash.

2. Probabilities

Your decisions will be influenced by a random process which will be explained fully below. As a first step in understanding this process, it is useful to introduce the notion of probability. Suppose that there are ten playing cards with one of the cards marked with an "X". If the cards are shuffled and then one card is selected at random, the probability of the "X" card being selected is one-tenth. If the card that was drawn is returned to the deck and the cards are reshuffled, then the probability of selecting the "X" card with a single random draw is again one-tenth. In this case the second draw is said to occur *with replacement*.

In the market experiment that you will be participating in, the market results (and your earnings) will be influenced by a series of random drawings with replacement. There are two possible outcomes for each draw: success or failure. The meaning of success and failure in the market experiment will be described below. The probability of success in any one draw is, as in the above example, one-tenth. In each decision period you will be able to purchase the number of draws you choose at a price of $.10 per draw. Remember, regardless of how many draws you choose, the probability of a success on any one draw is one-tenth.

3. Market Decision Periods

In the experiment, all of you are participating in a series of market decision periods. You can think of each of you as being a seller in a market with many buyers. Your market earnings will be determined by whether you and the other participants are Type A or Type B sellers. For each period, these market earnings are as follows:

		Total # of Type A Sellers				
		0	1	2	3	4
Per-Period Market Earnings of each Type A Seller	=	—	$3.50	2.15	1.70	1.48
Per-Period Market Earnings of each Type B Seller	=	$0	.80	.80	.80	—

Notice that if you are the only Type A seller, your earnings for that period are $3.50. If there are exactly three Type A sellers, each receives $1.70, etc. If you are a Type B seller and there are one or more Type A sellers, your earnings for that period are $.80. If you are a Type B seller and there are no Type A sellers, you earnings are zero for that period. What determines whether you are a Type A or a Type B seller? That is a good question and it will be answered in the next section.

4. Determining Type A and Type B Sellers

At the beginning of each period, each of you will be asked to choose the number of "investment draws" for that period. Each investment draw that you purchase costs $.10. Each investment draw is a random draw with a one-tenth probability of "success."

We will use a bingo cage to determine whether a draw is a success or a failure. There are 10 balls in the cage, numbered 1 through 10. If the ball marked "10" comes up then the draw is labeled a success. Otherwise, the draw is labeled a failure. Each draw from the bingo cage is made with replacement. After each of you have chosen how many investment draws to make in the decision period, we will conduct the appropriate number of drawings from the bingo cage for the period. Any seller with *at least one success* in his/her investment draws is a type A seller. Your total earnings in a decision period are your market earnings minus ($.10 × # of investment draws). Notice the following important points.

1.   If you choose *no* investment draws, you guarantee yourself total earnings of at least zero for that period.

2.   If you purchase one or more investment draws, your total earnings may be be positive or negative. For example, suppose that you have no successes on your draws in the market decisions period (Type B seller) and the other sellers

have no successes in the period. Then you lose an amount equal to $.10 times the number of draws you choose.

3. All it takes is one success to be a type A seller during a decision period. There is no earnings advantage to having more than one success in any one period.

4. The process begins all over again at the beginning of each period. Each of you selects the number of investment draws you wish to purchase for the period. The drawings from the bingo cage determine whether you will be a type A or a type B seller for the period. You *cannot* carry over "extra" successes from one period to the next.

5. You should keep track of your earnings on the seller's record sheet provided to you. The experimenter will be recording the results of the investment draws for each market decision period on the blackboard for you to see.

To make sure that everyone understands the process, we are going to demonstrate examples of series of randomly determined investment draws. After this, we will begin the first market decision period.

Because it is possible for you to have negative earnings, we will begin the experiment by giving each of you an initial endowment of $5.00.

Are there any questions?

INSTRUCTION SUPPLEMENT ON THE BINGO CAGE

Sitting on the table before you are 10 bingo balls with numbers 1–10. At this point, we would like you to choose from among yourselves one person to do the following:

1. examine the 10 balls
2. place the 10 balls in the bingo cage
3. examine the bingo cage
4. watch as we conduct four sample investment draws of 4, 9, 7, 1 purchases respectively

If during a turn a ball falls out the bottom of the cage, the turn is still good, but the ball which "counts" is the one appearing in the cup at the top. The errant ball will be replaced for the next turn. Any participant has the right to examine any ball as we read the number.

ACKNOWLEDGMENTS

We gratefully acknowledge financial support from the Karl Eller Center for the Study of the Private Market Economy, College of Business and Public Administration, University of Arizona.

NOTES

1. Schumpeter, (1950, p. 84).
2. U. S. Constitution, Article I, Section 8.
3. Scherer (1984, ch. 2) provides a detailed discussion of the development of the Watt-Boulton steam engine.
4. Schumpeter (1950, p. 106).
5. See Kamien and Schwartz (1982, ch. 4), for a detailed discussion of this approach and of the main hypotheses that emerge. It is typically assumed that a firm selects its R&D program to maximize the expected discounted present value of its profit stream.
6. Kamien and Schwartz (1982, pp. 107–108) point out that it may be very difficult for a firm to identify its potential innovative rivals since, for example, such rivals need not be in the same industry. In such cases, the decision theoretic approach makes sense since a firm does not know identity of rival "players."
7. Game theoretic models of new product development assume some technical uncertainty in the innovation process. Without the uncertainty, at most one firm from the group would undertake the innovation (see Dasgupta and Stiglitz 1980b).
8. Reinganum (1982), Rogerson (1982), Telser (1982), and Futia (1980) have analyzed game-theoretic models of repeated innovations. This permits consideration of incumbency effects on R&D and evolutionary changes in market structure over time.
9. See their 1978 and 1982 articles and 1982 book.
10. Among the topics studied are the relationship between research input and innovation output, the relationship between market structure and the rate of technological progress, the role of technological opportunity in innovation, and the role of demand-push forces in innovation. See Kamien and Schwartz (1982, ch. 3), for a survey of empirical studies. Also see the volume edited by Griliches (1984) for a good sample of recent studies.
11. An exception is Levin and Reiss (1984). The specification of their empirical model is based on the deterministic, game theoretic model of process innovation of Dasgupta and Stiglitz (1980a).
12. Those interested in exploring the central methodological issues of experimental economics might be interested in Smith's (1982) article on microeconomics as an experimental science, Plott's (1982) discussion of experimental economics and industrial organization, or Isaac's (1983) consideration of experimental applications to public policy issues.
13. This probabilistic formulation of the innovative process conforms to the initial model presented in Scherer (1984, ch. 4). Each draw can be interpreted as a particular approach to solving a given technical problem for a firm. Each potential approach has the same prior probability of success h. The success probability of any particular approach is assumed to be independent of the number and sequence of other approaches taken. There are two possible interpretations of R&D costs for a firm. Either the firm undertakes (and pays for) all approaches simultaneously or the firm tries a series of approaches sequentially, but is contractually committed to pay for a fixed number of approaches in advance. The Latter interpretation is consistent with the laboratory experiments.
14. A tie (simultaneous innovation by two or more firms) occurs with probability zero in the stochastic invention model with exponential distributions (e.g., see Loury, 1979). The event of a tie is *assumed* to occur with probability zero in the discrete time models of Futia (1980) and Rogerson (1982). However, it is difficult to rule out the possibility of two or more innovative successes in a discrete time model without imposing unreasonable assumptions on the random process which generates innovations.
15. The more general case in which different rivals make different choices is described below. Each participant i selects his/her number of draws from the set of nonnegative integers, $x_i \in I^+ = \{0,1,2, \ldots \}$. Let $R^i = \{1, \ldots, i-1, i+1, \ldots, N\}$ be the set of i's rival participants. Let R_k^i be a subset of R^i with k elements. Let $\mathcal{R}_k^i$ be the class of such distinct subjects; i.e., $\mathcal{R}_k^i = \{R_k^i : R_k^i \subset R^i\}$.

$$E\pi_i (x_1, \ldots, x_N) = \left\{ V_w \prod_{j\neq i} (1 - \theta(x_j)) + \sum_{k=1}^{N-1} \left(\frac{V_w + kV_\ell}{(k+1)} \right) \right.$$

$$\left. \sum_{R_k^i \varepsilon R_k^i} \left[\prod_{j\varepsilon R_k^i} \theta(x_j) \prod_{\substack{\ell\varepsilon R^i \\ \ell \not\in R_k^i}} (1 - \theta(x_\ell)) \right] \right\} \theta(x_i)$$

$$+ V_\ell(1 - \theta(x_i))(1 - \prod_{j\neq i} (1 - \theta(x_j))) - cx_i, \ i = 1, \ldots, N.$$

A Nash equilibrium is a vector of draws $(x_1^*, \ldots, x_N^*)$ such that $E\pi_i(x_1^*, \ldots, x_{i-1}^*, x_i^*, x_{i+1}^*, \ldots, x_N^*) \geq E\pi_i(x_1^*, \ldots, x_{i-1}^*, x_i, x_{i+1}^*, \ldots, x_N^*)$ for all $x_i \varepsilon I^+$ and for $i = 1, \ldots, N$.

16. In these experiments, each subject selected their current number of investment draws for a period without knowing how many draws their rivals would select for the period. However, the choices of all subjects and the identity of innovators for previous periods was available for all subjects to see. This information structure was used in order to give the Nash equilibrium theory its "best shot." An alternative information structure would allow subjects to know the identity of prior successful innovators, but not the amounts invested in R&D by rivals in previous periods. The static, mathematical models of R&D investment do not specify an information structure since players only make one decision. However, it is necessary to specify an information structure to be used for multi-period experiments using the operational model of R&D investment.

17. There is one Nash equilibrium for each appropriability condition. There are no asymmetric Nash equilibria for the operational model specified here.

REFERENCES

Dasgupta, P. and Stiglitz, J.E., (1980a), "Industrial Structure and the Nature of Innovative Activity." *Economic Journal* 90 (June): 266–293.

Dasgupta, P. and Stiglitz, J.E., (1980b), "Uncertainty, Industrial Structure and the Speed of R&D." *Bell Journal of Economics* 11, (Spring): 1–28.

Futia, C. A., (1980), "Schumpeterian Competition." *Quarterly Journal of Economics* 95, (June): 675–695.

Griliches, Z. (Ed.), (1984), *R&D Patents and Productivity* Chicago: University of Chicago Press.

Hirshleifer, J. and Riley, J., (1979), "The Analytics of Uncertainty and Information—An Expository Survey." *Journal of Economic Literature* 17: 1375–1421.

Isaac, R.M., (1983), "Laboratory Experimental Economics as a Tool in Public Policy Analysis." *Social Science Journal* 20, (July): 45–58.

Kamien, M.I. and Schwartz, N.L., (1982), *Market Structure and Innovation.* Cambridge: Cambridge University Press.

Lee, T. and Wilde, L., (1980), "Market Structure and Innovation: A Reformulation." *QuarterlyJournal of Economics* 94, (March): 429–436.

Levin, R.C., (1981), "Toward an Empirical Model of Schumpeterian Competition." Working PaperNo.43, Series A. Yale University, July.

Levin, R.C. and Reiss, P.C., (1984), "Test of a Schumpeterian Model of R&D Market Structure." In Z. Griliches (Ed.), *R&D, Patents and Productivity* Chicago: University of Chicago Press.

Levin, R.C., Cohen, W., and Mowery, D., (1985), "R&D Appropriability, Opportunity, and Maron Some Schumpeterian Hypotheses." *American Economic Re75, (May):* 20–24.

Loury, G., (1979), "Market Structure and Innovation." *Quarterly Journal of Economics* 93, (August): 395–410.

Mortensen, D., (1982), "Property Rights and Efficiency in Mating, Racing, and Related Games." *American Economic Review* 72, (December): 968–979.

Nelson, R. and Winter, S., (1978), "Forces Generating and Limiting Concentration Under Schumpeterian Competition." *Bell Journal of Economics* 9, (Autumn): 524–548.

Nelson, R. and Winter, S., (1982a), "The Schumpeterian Tradeoff Revisited." *American Economic Review* 72, (March): 114–132.

Nelson, R. and Winter, S., (1982b), *An Evolutionary Theory of Economic Change*. Cambridge, MA: Harvard University Press.

Pareto, V., (1879), *Cours d'Economie Politique,* Lausanne.

Plott, C.R., (1982), "Industrial Organization Theory and Experimental Economics." *Journal of Economic Literature* 20, (December): 1485–1527.

Reinganum, J.F., (1982), "A Dynamic Game of R&D: Patent Protection and Competitive Behavior." *Econometrica* 50, (May): 671–688.

Rogerson W., (1982), "The Social Costs of Regulation and Monopoly: A Game-Theoretic Analysis." *Bell Journal of Economics* 13, (Autumn): 391–401.

Scherer, F.M., (1984), *Innovation and Growth*. Cambridge, MA: The MIT Press.

Schumpeter, J.A., (1950), *Capitalism, Socialism and Democracy,* 3rd ed. New York: Harper & Brothers Publishers.

Smith, V.L., (1976), "Experimental Economics: Induced Value Theory." *American Economic Review* 66, (May): 274–279.

Smith, V.L., (1982), "Microeconomic Systems as an Experimental Science." *American Economic Review* 72, (December): 923–955.

Stewart, M., (1983), "Noncooperative Oligopoly and Preemptive Innovation without Winner-Take-All." *Quarterly Journal of Economics* 98, (November): 681–694.

Telser, L.G., (1982), "A Theory of Innovation and Its Effects." *Bell Journal of Economics* 13, (Spring): 69–92.

Chapter 11

ENTREPRENEURSHIP IN THE 1980s:
A STUDY OF SMALL BUSINESS IN INDIANA

Arne L. Kalleberg

I. INTRODUCTION

In the 1980s, there has been a renewed interest in the nature and correlates of entrepreneurship. Spurred by declines in productivity and the presumed links between entrepreneurship and technological change, economic development, and the creation of jobs, academics as well as business and government leaders have paid increasing attention to small businesses and to the people who start and run them. This has led to a growing body of writing and research related to entrepreneurs and entrepreneurship [for reviews of this literature, see, for example, the chapters in Kent, Sexton, and Vesper (Eds.), 1982]. Research on entrepreneurship is not new; as early as 1942, Arthur Cole wrote about the need for systematic research into the general question of the entrepreneur. Yet, as indicated in the introduction to this volume, there is still a need for additional research and understanding of this critical activity.

Several features of research on entrepreneurship have impeded a cumulation of well-tested findings about entrepreneurs and their businesses. Studies of entrepreneurship have been conducted in relative isolation from each other, and there are few attempts to integrate insights from diverse perspectives into an overall

Advances in the Study of Entrepreneurship, Innovation, and Economic Growth, Volume 1, pages 157-189.
Copyright © 1986 by JAI Press Inc.
ISBN: 0-89232-703-0

explanation of entrepreneurship. Rather, different writers have studied entrepreneurship with their own distinct sets of assumptions and disciplinary blinders. For example, psychologists often study the personal attributes of entrepreneurs without paying much attention to the social contexts within which they work; sociologists often focus on the environment for entrepreneurship without considering the nature of the entrepreneurial personality; and economists often view entrepreneurs as rational, isolated decision-makers without specifying the embedded nature of social behavior. Such "discipline-centered approaches to the subject of entrepreneurship almost always define away parts of the subject or oversimplify it to fit existing theoretical structures" (Shapero and Sokol, 1982:74).

Moreover, much of the writing on entrepreneurship is based on anecdotal information or is judgmental, and conclusions are often based on non-systematic samples drawn from populations that are not always clearly defined. For example, the inspirational biographies of successful entrepreneurs, which abound in the literature (see, e.g., Fucini & Fucini, 1985), do not lend themselves well to comparative research. In addition, comparisons among studies are hampered by the great variation in their methods of data collection. These problems have made it difficult to generalize about entrepreneurs and their activities (see Gasse, 1982).

As the science of entrepreneurship matures, it is necessary for researchers to become more sensitive to these limitations. Studies should incorporate insights from a variety of disciplines, including sociology, economics, psychology and history, in order to understand the multiplicity of forces acting upon entrepreneurs and their businesses. Moreover, researchers need to pay serious attention to issues of sampling, and collect data from diverse populations of entrepreneurs using well-defined conceptual schemes.

In this chapter, I present findings from a research program that illustrate some of these needed directions in the study of entrepreneurship. First, I identify several key research questions on the topic, and present a model which is useful in addressing them. I then report some results from a recent study of small business owner-operators in Indiana which shed light on these research questions. Finally, I outline a research agenda that is necessary to further advance our understanding of the nature of entrepreneurs and entrepreneurship.

II. DEFINING ENTREPRENEURSHIP

As illustrated by the differences in opinion expressed by writers in this volume over "what is entrepreneurship," there has not only been, but continues to be, a great deal of debate about the meaning of entrepreneurship. Webster's 3rd New International Dictionary (1961) defines an entrepreneur as "an organizer of an economic venture, especially one who organizes, owns, manages and assumes the risk of a business." This relatively broad and multidimensional definition includes different types of business activities: organizing, owning, managing and risk-taking. Taken together, these components constitute an ideal type of entrepreneurship, denoting what most people mean by the term. However, for research purposes, it is necessary to make some assumptions about which of these components is the "essence" of entrepreneurship. This question has generated considerable debate among academics as well as entrepreneurs themselves (see, for example, Brockhaus, 1982; Cochran, 1968; Harwood, 1982; Herbert and Link, 1982; Kent, 1984; Kilby, 1971; Livesay, 1982; Martin, 1982). The debates over the meaning of entrepreneurship can be summarized by several points of disagreement.

First, people differ in their assumptions about the appropriate unit of analysis for conceptualizing entrepreneurship. Some, following Schumpeter (1936, 1947), argue that it is a *function* or an event such as the creation of "new combinations" (see also Shapero and Sokol, 1982). Others maintain that characteristics of the *individual* businessperson are most critical for defining the entrepreneur (e.g., McClelland, 1961; Rustand, this volume).

Second, there is much disagreement about the role of *innovation* in defining entrepreneurship. This debate centers around Schumpeter's (1936, 1947) classic definition of the entrepreneur as the person who creates "new combinations" in the production and distribution of goods and services. According to Schumpeter, a person is an entrepreneur only when he or she is engaged in innovative behaviors, which constitute the "entrepreneurial function" (see also Kirzner, 1973). Others take a broader view of entrepreneurship. Schumpeter's colleague at Harvard, Arthur Cole, for example, considered entrepreneurship to include activities involved in the management of the enterprise, and McClelland (1961) viewed an entrepreneur as anyone who exercised control over production. This classic debate over the role of innovation in defining who is an entrepreneur is echoed elsewhere in this volume. Rosenberg, for example, adopts a view similar to Schumpeter's by arguing that entrepreneurship represents the introduction of new products. Others place less weight on the dramatic new invention as defining entrepreneurship. For example, Uselding sees product improvements as qualifying someone as an entrepreneur, and Freeman views entrepreneurship as the founding of new businesses.

Third, there has been disagreement over the role of *risk* in defining whether or not a person is an entrepreneur. Since Richard Cantillon's 18th-century view of the entrepreneur as a "bearer of uninsurable risk," a number of writers (e.g., Knight, 1921; Redlich, 1957), including some in this volume (e.g., Charles James), have equated risk with entrepreneurship. In contrast, Schumpeter and others argued that risking one's capital is not intrinsic to the entrepreneurial function; this is instead the role of the capitalist (see Gasse, 1982; Kanbur, 1980).

The role of risk in defining entrepreneurship is intimately related to disagreements over the *context* in which entrepreneurship occurs. Some argue that entrepreneurship can only exist in small businesses. As Kent (1984:4) puts it: "not all small firms are entrepreneurships, but most entrepreneurship begins in small firms.'' Moreover, recent heralders of the ''new spirit of enterprise'' in American society equate entrepreneurship with the small business sector of the economy (see, e.g., Gilder, 1984; Gevirtz, 1984). These writers argue that large companies are antithetical to the exercise of entrepreneurship (see the views of the small business entrepreneurs in this volume), both because of the lack of autonomy and control an individual is able to exercise, and the lack of financial risk involved in large companies. In contrast, other writers maintain that entrepreneurship can be found in large as well as small businesses (''intrapreneurship,'' or entrepreneurial activity in large organizations: see, for example, Kanter, 1983; Pinchot, 1985; Schollhammer, 1982).

These debates over the definition of entrepreneurship are likely to persist and to become more esoteric as the scientific study of entrepreneurship proceeds. In the meantime, the ambiguity surrounding what is entrepreneurship and who are entrepreneurs compels the researcher to be explicit about his or her assumptions regarding the nature of the ''heffalump'' (see Kilby, 1971) under investigation; I make several assumptions.

First, I assume that entrepreneurship refers *both* to an activity—the role behaviors associated with a particular status—and to the individual or small group of persons who engages in these activities. It is impossible to conceive of entrepreneurial activities without considering the individuals who perform them. Moreover, the characteristics of the individual and the company become increasingly intertwined, making it difficult to separate one from the other: ''a new business revolves around the entrepreneur so that his or her strengths and weaknesses become those of the firm'' (Cooper, 1982:200).

Second, I assume that entrepreneurship is a *continuum;* some activities or individuals are more ''entrepreneurial'' than others. The entrepreneur is not simply a self-employed businessperson (Kent, 1984); what determines the degree to which an activity or a person is entrepreneurial is the degree of *innovativeness.* Thus, Henry Ford or Ray Kroc, by virtue of their creative and profitable use of assembly-line techniques and product standardization, are generally regarded as more innovative (and hence more entrepreneurial) than the thousands of other inventors who had relatively little impact on modern society. A sufficient condition for defining entrepreneurship, then, is innovation.

Third, I assume that there are two necessary conditions that qualify one to be potentially regarded as an entrepreneur. One necessary condition is that the person's activity must involve *risk,* specifically the economic risks associated with the *ownership* of a business. This suggests that the small business setting is most conducive to the study of entrepreneurial activity, since it is most likely to involve such risk-taking. The second necessary condition for defining entrepreneurship involves the exercise of *control* over the business: potential entrepreneurs are those who are in effective control of a business unit. This is another reason why the small business, in which such control is easier to obtain, is a particularly appropriate context for studying entrepreneurship.

In summary, I assume that entrepreneurship is a multidimensional concept. A potential entrepreneur is someone who exercises both ownership and control over the firm. All owner-operators may be regarded as entrepreneurs to some degree, in the sense that they all have created or taken over a business (see the Freeman paper in this volume). However, some activities and persons are more entrepreneurial than others; they have been more involved in the creation of innovations and "new combinations." I will refer to the small business owners as "owner-operators," saving the term "entrepreneur" for those who have actually engaged in innovative activities (see also Carland et al. 1984).

III. STUDYING ENTREPRENEURSHIP

A. Overview

As is the case with defining entrepreneurship, there is great diversity in the kinds of questions that have been deemed important to study. Some researchers have focused their attention on the social context or the environment for entrepreneurship. Others are more concerned with understanding the nature of the individual entrepreneur (see Vesper, 1982). The present research project addresses some of the key questions raised by each of these approaches.

First, we investigate the determinants of innovation, and ask what makes some business owners more "entrepreneurial" than others? This issue raises two more specific questions: what features of social contexts make it easier or more difficult to engage in innovative behaviors; and what personality characteristics are associated with innovation? A second set of questions addressed by this research refers to the determinants of business performance. This also has two components: what affects a company's performance such as its market share, profits and earnings; and, what are the determinants of an individual's success, or the economic and psychic rewards received by small business owners? Finally, we examine the attributes of owner-operators of small businesses: who are they; what are their backgrounds and work histories; why did they decide to become self-employed; and, what are the differences between men and women small business owners?

These questions are important for both theoretical and practical reasons. Theoretically, they shed light on the nature of an increasingly important organizational form in modern societies—the small business. They also inform us about the characteristics of a unique and important "class" in industrial societies—entrepreneurs. Practically, answers to these questions would suggest ways in which entrepreneurial education can be improved. Such academic inquiries can also help those in the private sector to increase their yield of innovations (Sexton, 1982).

Unfortunately, research on these questions related to entrepreneurship is still in its formative stages, and is characterized by the absence of both a definitive set of precepts and a universally accepted methodology to address them (Perryman, 1982). In view of this diversity, it is especially important for the researcher to be explicit about his or her theoretical and methodological assumptions about the determinants of entrepreneurship.

First, I assume that entrepreneurship needs to be investigated in relation to its *social context*. Entrepreneurs and entrepreneurial activities are embedded in a complex system of social relations. These features of the social context need to be specified clearly and used to explain entrepreneurial outcomes (e.g., Aldrich and Zimmer, 1986). For example. it is necessary to consider the impacts on entrepreneurship of differences in product markets, government policies, social networks of contacts, structures of opportunities, consumer tastes for particular kinds of products and services, organizational constraints, and so on.

Second, I assume that the social context of entrepreneurship is formed by structures operating at many different levels of analysis. Entrepreneurs and entrepreneurial roles are embedded in organizational structures, which in turn are nested within more macroscopic industrial structures (for a discussion of the multi-level nature of work-related structures, see Kalleberg and Berg, 1987). In the present research, the primary social context of entrepreneurship is the *industry*. This is appropriate, since industries group together businesses that produce similar products or services, and are thereby subject to similar product market conditions, supply and demand regimes, business problems, and other environmental features.

Third, I assume that entrepreneurial outcomes (innovations and related events such as business and personal successes and failures) need to be explained by *both* characteristics of individuals and features of their social contexts. This follows from the view of entrepreneurship as both an activity and a person. For example, innovations result from the *interplay* between the skills and efforts of individuals and the nature of their environments.

B.   A Model of Entrepreneurship

These assumptions form the basis of the model of entrepreneurship represented by Figure 1.

The model outlines the basic sets of factors involved in our study of entrepreneurship. The social context of entrepreneurship is primarily defined by the industry, which denotes differences in products and services as well as in the nature of competition, types of business problems and changes that affect the

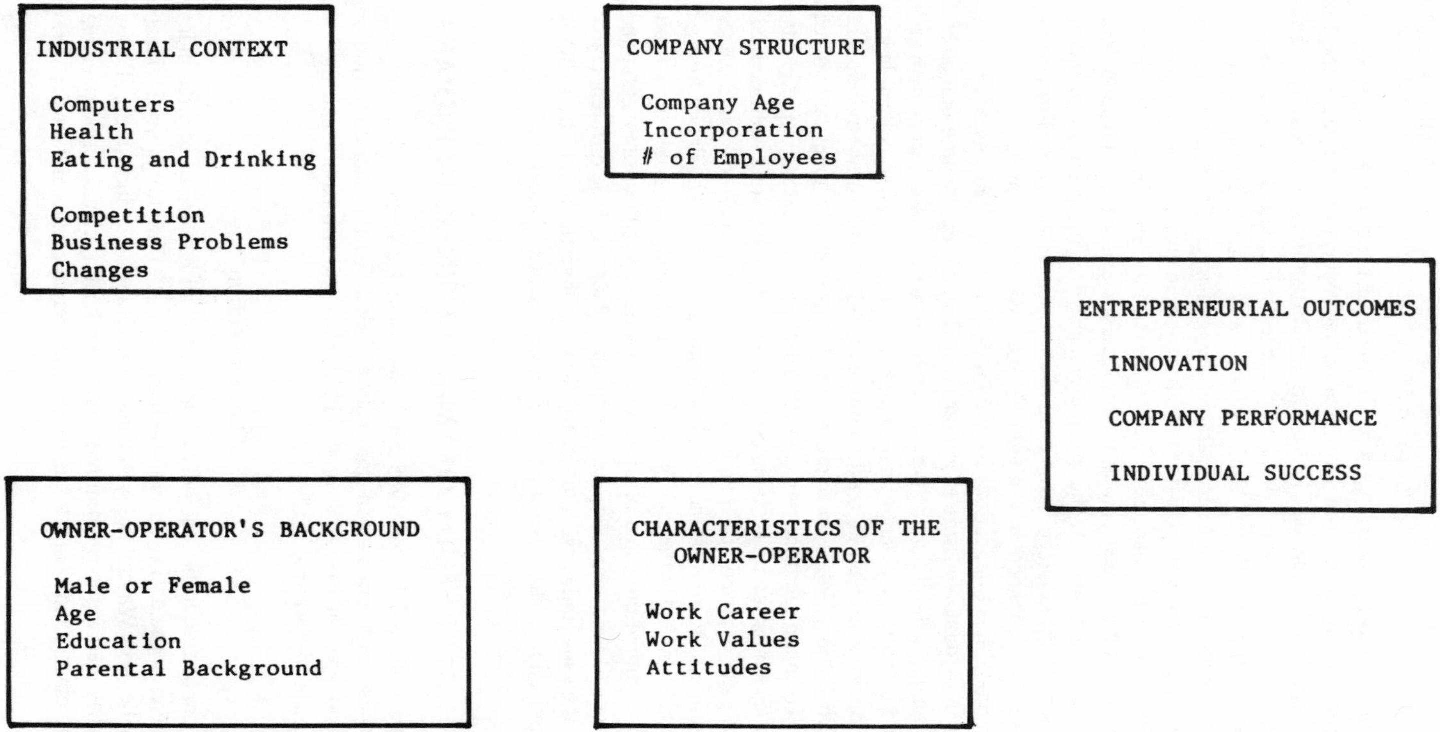

INDUSTRIAL CONTEXT

Computers
Health
Eating and Drinking

Competition
Business Problems
Changes

COMPANY STRUCTURE

Company Age
Incorporation
# of Employees

ENTREPRENEURIAL OUTCOMES

INNOVATION

COMPANY PERFORMANCE

INDIVIDUAL SUCCESS

OWNER-OPERATOR'S BACKGROUND

Male or Female
Age
Education
Parental Background

CHARACTERISTICS OF THE OWNER-OPERATOR

Work Career
Work Values
Attitudes

Figure 1. A model of entrepreneurship

operation of the business. A second context of entrepreneurship refers to the background of the owner-operator (gender, age, education, parental background, and so on). These contextual factors, in turn, affect the structure of the company (for example, its size, incorporation and age) and characteristics of the owner-operator such as his or her work history, work values, and attitudes.

The attributes of the owner-operator, the industry and the company, then, are assumed to be jointly responsible for differences in outcomes such as innovation, business performance and individual success. Moreover, these outcomes are assumed to be interrelated among themselves: for example, innovations may enhance the performance of the company; successful companies and individuals may consequently engage in more innovative behaviors; the performance of the company may enhance an individual's success; and so on.

This model has implications for the kinds of data needed to study how attributes of individuals and structural contexts affect entrepreneurial outcomes. The unit of analysis should be the person as well as the company, since both are integral to the definition of entrepreneurship. Hence, we need to collect data on the owner-operator as well as on the company and its industrial environment (see also Brockhaus, 1982). In addition, the sample should meet certain requirements. The main sampling unit should be the owner-operator of a particular company; these units should be sampled systematically from some well-defined population, as opposed to being convenience samples of say, successful entrepreneurs. Moreover, the sample of companies should be drawn from a number of different industries, so as to permit the comparative study of how product markets, competition, and other industrial structures affect innovation and performance. At the same time, the sample should also include different companies within the same industry, in order to allow the investigation of how differences in organizational structures influence entrepreneurial outcomes.

IV.   1985 STUDY OF SMALL BUSINESS IN INDIANA

The data collected by the 1985 Study of Small Business in Indiana generally meets these requirements. In this section, I describe the data collection procedures and give an overview of the industries, the companies and the owner-operators in the sample.

A.   Data Collection

The population to be studied was defined as all businesses in three industries that were located in several Indiana cities: Bloomington; Indianapolis; Evansville; Fort Wayne; Lafayette; and Terre Haute. The industries, all of which were fairly well represented in Indiana, were: health-related services; eating and drinking places; and computer hardware and software sales and service. Drawing mainly upon the yellow pages from these cities, we constructed lists of the businesses in each of the three industries. We then selected a systematic sample of companies in each industry. In the eating and drinking industry, which was represented by the largest number of businesses, we selected a random sample of firms. In the other two industries, we chose most of the companies that were available.

We next sent letters describing and endorsing the study to each of the sampled companies. This letter was followed several weeks later by a telephone call to the company, at which time we attempted to learn the name of its owner-operator. If the owner was not the operator, we excluded the company from the sample. If there were multiple owner-operators, we selected for interview the one that was available. We then tried to arrange a telephone interview with the owner-operator. Interviews with 411 owner-operators were conducted by a professional group of graduate students and staff trained by the Center for Survey Research at Indiana University during the Spring of 1985. The average overall time for the telephone interviews was 47 minutes, with average times of 38 minutes in eating and drinking; 45 minutes in computers; and 60 minutes in the health industry.

In general, the response rates were fairly high: 136 interviews were completed in the computer industry for a response rate of 68%; 127 in health-related businesses (63.5%); and 148 in eating and drinking establishments (55%). (These response rates were computed as the number of completed interviews divided by the number of persons interviewed plus those who refused, who were out of town for the duration of the study, or who were persistently unavailable after repeated tries. The response rates exclude those with nonworking telephone numbers, businesses which had no eligible owners, or those ineligible for other reasons.)

Given the systematic way in which it was selected, this sample appears to be fairly representative of small businesses in these three industries in Indiana, and, perhaps, elsewhere in the United States. Moreover, the research design insures that we will be able to examine differences among industries in entrepreneurial outcomes as well as investigate organizational and individual differences within the same industry. However, this is clearly a restricted sample of small businesses, in that it is confined to three service industries. In addition, these companies are relatively successful, since they are still in business. These features of the research design imply that we will not presently be able to address certain types of questions. For example, we can not study the determinants of business failures; or compare these owner-operators to the general population; or be able to understand why some people become self-employed and others do not. In addition, the cross-sectional nature of these data implies that we can not examine how changes in business environments or in individuals' motivations or beliefs influence entrepreneurial outcomes. Nevertheless, the sample appears to be a reasonable one for a preliminary investigation of the kinds of questions that we are exploring here.

B.   The Industries, the Companies and the Owner-Operators:
An Overview

The Industries

The basic source of differences in products and services is, of course, the industry. Within an industry, each of the companies provided a variety of goods and services. In the health industry, most companies provide either nutrition counseling, physical treatments or Western exercise. Other companies provide health food, medical care, Eastern exercise and cosmetic services.

All of the businesses in the eating and drinking industry serve food, though almost all of them also provide other products and services. Over three-quarters serve alcoholic beverages, about 40% offer catering services, a third provide banquet facilities and about a quarter provide entertainment.

In the computer industry, about three-quarters of the companies sell software and 60% sell or rent hardware. In addition, almost 80% provide systems consultation, 63% furnish educational services, and nearly half provide word and/or data processing services.

The Companies

Table 1 presents some descriptive information on the companies and owner-operators in the sample. The average ages of the companies range from a median of 5.5 years in computers to 7.4 years in health. These companies are therefore relatively successful, since only about 1 of 3 new firms survive the first four years of their existence (Dun & Bradstreet, 1967). Moreover, the majority of the businesses in the computer and eating and drinking industries are incorporated, and have been so for a median of about 5 years.

As expected, these companies are relatively small, ranging from a median of 1 (health) to 5.5 (computers) full-time employees. Businesses in the eating and drinking industry have the largest average number of part-time employees (a median of 3.5). While small, the sizes of these companies are representative of the vast majority of businesses in the United States, 79% of which have fewer than 5 employees (1972 Enterprise Statistics, 1977).

The Owner-Operators

The proportion of owner-operators who are sole owners of their businesses varies from a low of 47% in the computer industry to almost 70% in the health industry. Moreover, many of these people own and are actively involved in other businesses as well: this varied from over 40% of those in the computer industry to less than 30% of those in the health industry.

Men outnumber women in each industry, with the lowest proportion of women in the sample found in the computer industry and the highest in the health

Table 1.   The Companies and the Owner-Operators

	Computers	*Health*	*Eating and Drinking*
The Companies			
COMPANY AGE (in years)	8.9 (5.5)[b]	12.1 (7.4)	12.8 (6.5)
% INCORPORATED	87	42	73
YEARS INCORPORATED	7.2 (4.6)[b]	9.3 (5.5)	7.6 (4.9)
# FULL TIME EMPLOYEES	13.5 (5.5)[b]	3.5 (1.1)	10.3 (4.8)
# PART TIME EMPLOYEES	2.9 (1.2)[b]	6.4 (1.1)	8.3 (3.5)
The Owner-Operators			
% SOLE OWNER OF COMPANY	47	69	55
# MALES	122	84	106
# FEMALES	14	43	42
AGE (in years)	41.5 (9.6)[a]	42.4 (12.1)	46.6 (11.3)
EDUCATION (0 = none, 20 = doctorate)	16.0 (2.3)[a]	16.6 (3.2)	13.7 (2.6)
YEARS IN INDUSTRY	13.5 (9.3)[a]	12.3 (9.6)	14.5 (12.8)
% OWNING OTHER BUSINESSES	42	29	32
ANNUAL EARNINGS	39872 (37083)[b]	26674 (17143)	22438 (16750)

Notes: [a]Mean (standard deviation)
        [b]Mean (median)

industry. Since one of our concerns in the present research was to compare men and women small business owners, we purposely selected certain industries (i.e., health and eating and drinking places) which we knew had a relatively high proportion of women. This was necessary in order to obtain an adequate number of women, since they control only about 5% of all the businesses in the United States (Reagan, 1982).

The mean age of the owner-operators is slightly over 41 years in computers and health and almost 47 years in the eating and drinking industry. Assuming that the majority of these owner-operators became self-employed a number of years before our survey, this is in line with Brockhaus' (1982) estimate that most people make the decision to become entrepreneurs between the ages of 25 and 40. In addition, these small business owner-operators are relatively highly educated, with those in computers and health averaging more than a college degree (= 16). The average length of experience in the industry is roughly equal among the different kinds of businesses, ranging from about 12 years (health) to 14.5 years (eating and drinking). Finally, those in the computer industry earned the highest average salaries from their businesses during the past year (their median earnings were more than $37,000), while those in the eating and drinking industry earned the least.

In order to explain the entrepreneurial outcomes that are the main dependent variables in this research (innovation, company performance, individual success), we need to take a closer look at the characteristics of these industries and owner-operators.

C. The Industries: Problems, Competition, Changes

Business Problems

Companies in the three industries share some common business problems. From Table 2, we see that relatively large proportions of owner-operators in each industry report that they have "great" problems with managing their time. This undoubtedly reflects the pressures produced by being responsible for the large variety of activities related to owning and operating a small business. The severity of other problems varies by industry. For example, those in the computer industry appear to be most concerned with "financial matters," while those in the health and eating and drinking industries are more likely to view "government regulations" as a problem for their business. In contrast, relatively few of the owner-operators regarded "dealing with clients and customers" and "maintaining a high quality of service" as great problems, perhaps because these activities reflect things that they can actually do something about.

Several additional business problems were specific to particular industries. For example, over half of those in the eating and drinking industry said that the weather was either a "great problem" or "somewhat of a problem" for their business, while others were concerned with issues such as inadequate physical space and mandatory "carding" of minors. On the other hand, many of those in the computer industry were concerned with keeping up with rapid technological change and with "computer fear" in the population.

Competition

Competition is a key feature of industries which has important implications for entrepreneurial outcomes. As expected, industries differ in the extent of competition and in the degree to which competition affects their businesses (see Table 2). For example, owners of eating and drinking places most often reported that there is a "great deal" of competition in their product markets. However, owner-operators in the computer industry are most likely to report that competition is a "great" problem for their businesses. Competition in the computer industry stems from several main sources, including: large companies such as IBM and AT&T; small hardware and software companies; and independent consultants.

Table 2.   The Industries (Competition, Problems) and the Companies
(Innovations, Performance)

	Computer	Health	Eating and Drinking
Competition			
% There is a "great deal" of competition in the market	56	47	72
% Competition is a "great" problem	21	16	17
Business affected by increased competition from large companies	49	34	44
% Business affected by increased competition from small companies	49	36	29
Problems (% reporting "great" problems with):			
Inadequate demand	4	6	5
Financial matters	27	12	14
Dealing with clients and customers	2	2	1
Employee relations	4	2	6
Government regulation	7	14	22
Maintaining high quality of service	4	0	3
Time management	36	22	15
Innovations			
% New products	74	54	73
% New services	68	55	35
% New advertising	48	56	42
% New management	37	31	35
% New physical changes	51	47	46
% Other innovations	18	19	11
% Expanded product/services	83	69	57
% Failed new product/service	37	21	25
% Edge is unique product/service	13	13	14
Company Performance			
% Expanded market share	79	67	66
% Lost market share	14	25	32
% Increased profits/sales	92	79	70
% Decreased profits/sales	18	26	41
Company Gross Earnings	53770 (64130)[a]	48000 (63393)	52292 (64052)

Note: [a]Mean (median)

Changes in the Industries

Companies in each industry have experienced a variety of *changes* in the past two years which have affected the nature of their business. In the computer industry, 83% of the owner-operators noted the importance of an expanded computer market, which has increased demand for their goods and services. Moreover, over 70% cited as key factors affecting their business: the rise in personal computing; improvements in hardware and software; and higher consumer expectations. In the health industry, the important changes included: the increased public awareness of health; the development of new technology in the medical area; and the closer cooperation between physicians and insurance companies. Those in the eating and drinking industry most frequently cited as factors affecting their business: the increase in people eating out; greater health consciousness by consumers; increased demand for interesting surroundings; and specialized cuisines.

D.   The Owner-Operators: Backgrounds, Careers and Values

Since our sample includes only owner-operators of small businesses, we are unable to draw conclusions about differences or similarities between these self-employed individuals and those not in business for themselves. With this caveat in mind, we note that the backgrounds of many of these owner-operators fit the descriptions provided by past studies. For example, a majority (56% of the men and 60% of the women) were Indiana natives. This is consistent with the findings of Collins and Moore's (1970) study of entrepreneurs in Michigan, which noted that almost ⅔ were born in that state. Their interpretation seems to fit our results as well: these persons didn't want to leave family and friends and chose small business ownership as a means of remaining at home. Moreover, about a third of these owner-operators were the oldest children in their families (cf. Sarachek, 1978).

There is also evidence that the decision of these owner-operators to become self-employed was influenced by parental role models, especially by their fathers: over 40% of the men and 36% of the women had fathers who were self-employed, while less than 10% had mothers that were in business for themselves (see also Shapero and Sokol, 1982: 83–4). Those in the health industry were most likely, and those in the computer industry least likely, to have fathers that were self-employed.

These owner-operators also reported that they are relatively religious: about 60% say that they belong to or regularly attend a church or synagogue. This is consistent with Gilder's (1984:255) observation that entrepreneurs emerge from a culture shaped by religious values, since "secular culture has yet to produce a satisfactory rationale for a life of work, risk, and commitment oriented toward the needs of others—a life of thrift and trust leading to investments with uncertain rewards."

Starting the Business

How did these owner-operators get started in their current businesses? Did he or she start the business, alone or with a partner?; or, did he or she buy an existing business, either alone or with someone else? In this sample, men (41%) were more likely than women (35%) to have started their business themselves, while women more often bought it with a partner (16% vs. 12%). Similar percentages of men and women started the business with a partner (25%) or bought it by themselves (15%). The ways these owner-operators got started in their businesses varied by industry: those in the eating and drinking industry were least likely to have started the business themselves (19%, as opposed to about half of those in computers and health), reflecting in part the greater capital investment required to start a restaurant or bar. Rather, these owner-operators were the most likely to have bought the business from someone else, either by themselves (23%) or with a partner (29%). In contrast, those in computers were most likely to have started the business with a partner (32% vs. 24% in health and 20% in eating and drinking).

Where did these owner-operators get the financing necessary to start their businesses? In each industry, the most common source of start-up financing was one's personal resources, which were used by 88% of those in computers, 79% in eating and drinking, and 66% of those in health. The next common source of financing was bank loans. And, a relatively large number relied on loans from friends and family (19% in computers, 43% in health, 27% in eating and drinking). In contrast, only about 6% of those in computers and eating and drinking and 3% of those in health received loans from the Small Business Administration to start their businesses. Moreover, only 4% of those in eating and drinking received loans from venture capital organizations, as did only 1% of those in computers and health.

Work Careers

These owner-operators worked previously for an average of three different employers. However, a sizable proportion were self-employed prior to owning their current businesses: over 40% of the men and a quarter of the women were previously self-employed; 23% of the men and 21% of the women were self-employed in their work activity immediately preceding their current one. This varied by industry: for example, those in the health industry were the least likely to have been self-employed previously (32%) and on their immediately prior work activity (16%).

Why did these owner-operators become self-employed? Our findings, taken together, suggest that independence and control are the major reasons why they become and continue to be self-employed (see also Boyd and Gumpert, 1983; Hornaday and Aboud, 1971). For example, men most often cited the independence and flexibility associated with self-employment as their major reasons for going into business for themselves. The second most common response given for why they became self-employed was because of opportunities to make money (men) and family reasons (women). Only 10% of the men and 2% of the women cited "entrepreneurship" as the main reason they became self-employed. These motivations for becoming self-employed were paralleled by the work values of these owner-operators (see Table 3), which indicate that they place greater importance on "being your own boss" and "developing new ways of doing things" than on rewards such as money or job security. Moreover, when asked about the advantages of self-employment, owner-operators typically responded by citing reasons such as: "independence and control;" "having your name on the door;" "flexibility;" "freedom of choice;" "you can be yourself;" "you can create your own vision;" being able to do "what works for you;" "you don't have to answer to anyone else;" and so on.

Why did these owner-operators decide to become self-employed in their particular industry? Our main conclusion is that, having decided to become self-employed, they chose a business in which they had prior experience (39% of men and 34% of women—see also Brockhaus, 1982:52). One's background and experience were especially important in the computer industry (57%). The reason cited most often for starting a business in the health industry was "personal interest" (40%). In the eating and drinking industry, the most common reasons were one's prior background and support from family and/or friends (26% each).

What best prepared owner-operators for their present work? Men (46%) more often than women (36%) cited experience gained in the present industry. This differed among industries: over half of those in the computer industry mentioned their experience in the industry, while only 30% of those in the health-related businesses found their previous experiences in that industry to be most useful. Relatively few of the owner-operators cited their educational experiences as being most useful in preparing them for their present work (30% in health, 14% in computers, 10% in eating and drinking). While educational experiences may well be potentially useful sources of preparation for self-employment, then, these results point to the importance of "learning by doing" (see also Copulsky and McNulty, 1974).

An important factor affecting one's decision to become self-employed is whether he or she receives encouragement from significant others (see Shapero and Sokol, 1982). Who encouraged these owner-operators to become self-employed? Almost all of the men cited business partners (99%) and potential clients (96%) as encouraging them to go into business for themselves. Moreover, 80% of the men also said that they were encouraged by spouses, parents, siblings and friends. The only source of discouragement cited by men was their previous employers. The greatest sources of encouragement for women to become self-employed came from their spouses (62%), clients (58%) and friends (54%). In contrast to men, relatively few women reported that they were encouraged to become self-employed by their parents (39%) or by their siblings (35%).

Table 3. Attitudes of the Owner-Operators
[Means (Standard Deviations)]

	Men	*Women*
Work Values (1 = not very important; 3 = somewhat important; 5 = very important)		
MONEY (high income)	3.47 (1.26)	3.12 (1.30)
BEBOSS (being your own boss)	4.35 (1.13)	4.23 (1.20)
JOB SECURITY	3.34 (1.73)	4.03 (1.48)
NEWWAYS (developing new ways of doing things)	4.02 (1.14)	4.19 (1.14)
Satisfaction (1 = not very satisfied; 3 = somewhat satisfied; 5 = very satisfied)		
LIFE	3.76 (1.30)	3.63 (1.30)
HOME	4.18 (1.20)	3.94 (1.44)
WORK	4.07 (1.14)	4.09 (1.12)
BE SELF-EMPLOYED AGAIN (1 = no; 3 = second thoughts; 5 = yes)	4.60 (.93)	4.56 (.97)
RECOMMEND BUSINESS TO FRIEND (1 = advise vs. it; 3 = some doubts; 5 = recommend it)	3.84 (1.46)	3.76 (1.58)
BUSINESS MEASURES UP TO EXPECTATIONS (1 = no; 3 = somewhat; 5 = yes)	3.71 (1.13)	3.71 (1.08)
Work as Central Life Interest		
% of TIME devoted to business	65 (16)	58 (20)
OTHER ACTIVITIES more important than business (1 = agree; 3 = undecided; 5 = disagree)	3.99 (1.65)	3.69 (1.77)
MOST IMPORTANT things involve family, not business (1 = agree; 3 = undecided; 5 = disagree)	2.47 (1.76)	2.21 (1.64)
PREFER OTHERS JUDGE me by business, not other accomplishments (1 = disagree; 3 = undecided; 5 = agree)	2.47 (1.69)	2.29 (1.63)
Confidence		
I have BETTER IDEA about RUNNING my BUSINESS than most of my competitors (1 = disagree; 3 = undecided; 5 = agree)	4.03 (1.40)	3.65 (1.44)
I am relatively SUCCESSFUL in my present business (1 = disagree; 3 = undecided; 5 = agree)	4.14 (1.41)	4.43 (1.14)
Risk Taking ("I am a person who likes to take chances"—1 = disagree; 3 = undecided; 5 = agree)	4.00 (1.58)	3.89 (1.67)

Women, then, are less likely than men to receive encouragement from significant others to become self-employed. Nevertheless, over half of the women, as opposed to less than 40% of the men, felt that women have a better opportunity to succeed by going into their own business than by working for others. However, only 21% of the women owner-operators, and only 8% of the men, believed that women are more likely than men to be successful in small business. This suggests that women who become self-employed are disadvantaged compared to men (see also Table 6).

Attitudes

When interpreting our findings regarding the attitudes of these owner-operators, we must again keep in mind that we can not draw any conclusions about how they differ from the general population, since we lack a group of people who are not self-employed against whom to compare them. Nevertheless, some of the attitudes of these owner-operators are consistent with descriptions provided by previous studies. For example, the results support the view of the small business owner-operator as one who is a "workaholic," who is "driven," and who "never wastes a minute" (see also Boyd & Gumpert, 1983). That is, these small businesspeople are very work oriented, with men regarding work as more of a central life interest than women: the men estimated that they spend 65% of their time during a typical week on their business, compared to 58% for women (see Table 3). Men were also more likely than women to feel that they did not have other activities more important than their business, to disagree that the most important things that happened to them involved their family and not their business, and to prefer that others judge them by their business, not by their other accomplishments.

Moreover, the owner-operators in this sample may be described as "moderate" risk takers (see also Brockhaus, 1980; Hornaday, 1982; McClelland, 1961). For example, the average response to the question "I am a person who likes to take chances" (where 1 = disagree, 3 = undecided, 5 = agree) is a "4" for men and only slightly lower for women (see Table 3). In addition, the answers to a question about the odds of success it would take for them to invest their life savings in their business indicated that they would do so with an average 60% probability of success. Hence, they appear not to be willing to take wild chances but to take calculated risks—risks that have good chances of success.

Finally, these owner-operators tended to express confidence in their ability to run their businesses (see Table 3). While men were more likely than women to agree that they had a better idea of running their business than their competitors, women were more likely than men to feel that they were relatively successful in their present business (see also Hornaday, 1982).

These characteristics of industries and owner-operators are key explanations of entrepreneurial outcomes, to which I now turn.

V. INNOVATION

Innovation is both the essence of entrepreneurship and an activity that is generally identified with small businesses. Since Schumpeter, small companies have been regarded as the sources of innovative behavior, and the recent interest in small businesses is largely due to the belief that they are primarily responsible for entrepreneurship and innovation (see, e.g., Arrow, 1983). For example, a study sponsored by the National Science Foundation found that firms with less than 100 employees accounted for four times more major innovations per dollar spent on research and development than medium-size or large firms.

Innovation, like entrepreneurship, is a multidimensional concept. Drucker (1985) regards innovation as the "specific tool of entrepreneurs, the means by which they exploit change as an opportunity for a different business or a different service". An oft-cited definition of innovation is provided by Prager and Omenn (1980:379):

> The overall innovation process encompasses a spectrum of activities from basic research to commercial application and marketing. For the innovation process to be productive, the generation of new knowledge and the translation of that knowledge into commercial products and services must be linked.

The broadness of these definitions suggests that innovation refers to different kinds of things. Thus, Schumpeter (1936) identified five types of entrepreneurial innovations: (1) the introduction of new goods; (2) the introduction of new methods of production; (3) the opening of new markets; (4) the opening of new sources of supply; and (5) industrial reorganization. Some of these innovative behaviors (for example, opening new sources of supply and industrial reorganization) are not as applicable to small businesses as they are to large organizations. Nevertheless, the owner-operators in our sample reported that they were involved in a variety of innovative behaviors.

In the analysis to follow, I classify the innovative activities of the companies in our sample into several groups: the introduction of new products; the introduction of new services; the use of new advertising techniques; innovations related to the restructuring of the management of the business; improvements in the physical aspects of the business; expansions of product and/or service lines; and "other" innovations. Since we do not presently have detailed information on these innovative behaviors, we are unable to differentiate the "long leap" innovations (see Krasner, 1982) from the more mundane.

The percentages of owner-operators in each of the industries who reported that they were involved in the various types of innovative activities are listed in Table 2. In general, the proportion of owner-operators who said that they introduced new products and/or services is rather high. It is unclear how many of these were "dramatic" new inventions, though it is unlikely that most were of this character.

Overall, those in the computer industry appear to be the most "entrepreneurial:" they most often reported that they developed new products and (especially) services during the past two years, and were most likely to have expanded their product and service lines. Moreover, those in the computer industry most often reported that they tried new products or services that failed. This is an important indicator of entrepreneurial activity, since the process of innovation is generally accompanied by considerable trial and error. Examples of innovations in the computer industry included: developing new software programs; altering hardware so as to make it compatible with other machines; introducing timesharing on a privately-owned mainframe computer, and developing networking. Perhaps reflecting the competitive nature of the computer industry, a number of owner-operators refused to discuss their innovative ideas and did not reveal some of their recent innovations.

Those in the health and eating and drinking industries differ in their kinds of innovative behaviors: owner-operators in the health industry were more likely to have provided new services; while those in the eating and drinking industry were more likely to have introduced new products. This reflects differences in the nature of the activities in these two industries. The commodity sold by companies in the health industry is basically a service—exercise, tanning, reflexology, medical care, and chiropractory. Innovations in the health industry included the provision of these services as well as their timing. For example, an emergency physician's service in Bloomington provided health care on weekends and holidays, which is not the usual practice among health care providers. In contrast, the commodity sold in the eating and drinking industry is basically a product. Most of the innovations in this industry involved changes in the menu, such as new types of food and presentations of food. Other innovations cited by owner-operators in this industry included physical renovations, adding entertainment such as comedy shows or movies, and improving customer relations by increasing the quantity and security of parking facilities.

Relatively few (about 13–14%) of the owner-operators in any of the industries felt that they had a unique product or service that gave them an "edge" over their competitors. Rather, other factors besides innovation were stressed as ways of obtaining such a competitive edge: in the computer industry, most of the respondents felt that their "customer orientation" gave them an edge (38%—see Peters and Waterman, 1982). In health, characteristics of the owner (29%) and customer orientation (28%) were mentioned most often. In eating and drinking, a "quality product" was most frequently cited (36%).

What accounts for differences in the incidence of innovative behaviors among owner-operators and industries? As noted previously, our analysis of the determinants of innovation assumes that: (1) there are features associated with the social context (i.e., characteristics of industries and companies) that provide both the opportunity and need for innovations; and (2) some owner-operators are more likely than others to engage in innovative behaviors because of their personality traits and other personal attributes. Accordingly, our variables include character-istics of the person (gender, age, experience, risk-taking and so on), of the firm (size, incorporation), and the industry (nature of competition).[1] And, since the rate of innovation may be affected by company and individual performance, we include measures of company success (profits/sales—see note 2) and an individual's business-related rewards (earnings).

Table 4 presents the results of our regression analyses of the determinants of innovation. Three measures of innovation are used: whether ($=1$) or not ($=0$) the firm developed new products within the past two years; whether or not it developed new services; and a composite measure of the number of "other" in-novations in which the company has been involved (new advertising, new man-agement, new physical changes, and "other" innovations). Not surprisingly, our equations are unable to explain most of the differences in innovation among owner-operators (see the coefficients of explained variation, which range from 8.4% to 14.6%). Nevertheless, the different kinds of innovations are related in predictable ways to the other variables in the model.

There continue to be differences among industries in rates of innovation even when the other variables are taken into account. Each of the industries can be regarded as the most "entrepreneurial" for a particular kind of innovative behav-ior: owner-operators in the eating and drinking industry are most likely to have introduced new products; those in the computer industry are most likely to have introduced new services; and those in the health industry are the most "entrepre-neurial" with regard to "other" innovative behaviors (such as new advertising, management structures, and so on). On the other hand, owner-operators in the computer industry are least likely to have engaged in "other" innovations, those in the eating and drinking industry least likely to have provided new services, and those in the health industry least likely to have introduced new products.

Our conclusions as to how characteristics of the owner-operator and of the company's context affect innovation depend on the kind of innovative behavior that is considered. For example, the introduction of new products is related pri-marily to industry membership and attributes of the individual owner-operator: those who perceive themselves as being persons who like to take chances and who place high importance on new ways of doing things are more likely to have introduced new products; while those who place great importance on "being the boss" appear less likely to report having engaged in this kind of innovative activ-ity. Finally, owner-operators who reported that their companies increased their profits and/or sales within the last two years are more likely to say that they have introduced new products.

Our results suggest that there is a decline in innovative activity with increasing age. For example, the introduction of new services is negatively related to both the ages of the company and its owner-operator: older companies and persons are less likely to have engaged in this type of innovation. On the other hand, people with more experience in the industry are more likely to have introduced new ser-

Table 4. Determinants of Innovation
(Standardized Coefficients, N = 411)

Independent Variables	New Products	New Services	Other Innovations
The Industries			
Computer (= 1)	.014	.169**	−.107†
Health (= 1)	−.157**	.069	.135*
Eating and Drinking (= 1)	.144*	−.235**	−.030
Competition	.079	.017	.127**
The Companies			
Incorporated (= 1)	.063	.007	.084
Company Age	−.074	−.197**	−.006
# Full Time Employees	.068	.072	.255**
Venture (= 1)	−.074	.027	−.114*
The Owner-Operators			
Sole Owner (= 1)	.049	−.024	.047
Gender (1 = F)	−.029	.022	.024
Age	−.041	−.127*	−.152**
Education	−.032	.020	.072
Years in Industry	.033	.182**	.039
Confidence	.035	.123**	.131**
Work as CLI	−.014	.036	.109*
Risk Taking	.100*	.014	.085†
Beboss	−.135**	−.070	−.081†
Newways	.144**	.141**	.122**
Profits	.123**	.059	.043
(1n) Earnings	.019	.004	.019
R^2(adj)	.084	.145	.146

Notes: **$p \leq .01$;
        *$p \leq .05$;
        †$p \leq .10$

vices, suggesting that more "know how" in the business gained through experience results in new ways of serving the public. Finally, new services are more likely to have been provided by owner-operators who are more confident about their business success and those who value new ways of doing things.

Companies in highly competitive industries are more likely to have developed innovations other than new products and services: new advertising techniques, physical restructuring, new management, and so on. This result, together with our results for the question about what gives these companies an "edge" over their competitors, suggests that these owner-operators primarily respond to competitive pressures in their industries not by introducing new products or services, but by improving the ways that they sell their existing products and services.

Larger companies are more likely than smaller ones to have engaged in "other" innovations, probably because of the greater need for management reorganization and advertising in larger firms. In addition, those who received start-up financing from venture capital organizations are less likely to have been involved in innovations other than new products or services. We included this variable primarily because of the concern of other writers in this volume with the role of venture capital in starting small businesses. Our results suggest that such sources of capitalization do not necessarily result in innovative behaviors.

Characteristics of the owner-operators are also salient for predicting whether he or she was involved in "other" kinds of innovations. Those who feel confident in their abilities, who like to take chances, who regard work as more of a central life interest, and those who place a high importance on new ways of doing things are more likely to engage in these other types of innovations. On the other hand, older owner-operators and those more concerned with "being the boss" are less likely to do so.

In sum, our analysis of the determinants of innovative behaviors suggests several conclusions. First, most of the differences in innovation are unexplained by the variables in our model. Second, owner-operators of eating and drinking places are most entrepreneurial with regard to introducing new products, those in computers are most entrepreneurial in introducing new services, and those in the health industry most often innovate in ways other than by introducing new products or services. Third, there is a link between one's personality attributes and innovative behaviors. In particular, confidence in one's ability as a businessperson, one's propensity for risk-taking, and valuing new ways of doing things appear to enhance innovative behaviors. Finally, the social context also affects the incidence of innovative activity, with larger companies and those in competitive markets being more likely to engage in innovative behaviors other than the introduction of new products and services.

VI. COMPANY PERFORMANCE

Each week, thousands of small businesses in the United States fail. Judged by this criterion, all of the companies in our sample are relatively successful, with most being in the early and late growth stages identified by Vesper (1979). Our investigation into the differential success of companies, then, looks at variations within a relatively favored group. I use three indicators of a company's performance: (1) whether the firm increased its share of the market during the past two years; (2) whether the company increased its profits and/or sales during this period; and (3) the log of the company's gross earnings during the past year.[2]

Table 2 presents the overall results for the three industries on each of these dimensions of a company's performance. It appears that companies in the computer industry are the most successful: they have the highest average gross earnings; are most likely to have expanded their share of the market (and least likely to have lost market share); and are most likely to have increased their profits or sales.

Why are some of these businesses more successful than others? Our analysis of the determinants of company performance again relies on two sets of factors: characteristics of the company and industrial contexts; and attributes of the owner-operator (see note 1). I also include as independent variables: (1) a measure of innovation (computed as the sum of six types of innovative behaviors— new products, services, advertising, management, physical changes and "other" innovations); and (2) measures of an individual's business success (earnings or job satisfaction). The results of this analysis are presented in Table 5.

Table 5. Determinants of Company Performance
(Standardized Coefficients, N = 411)

Independent Variables	Market Share	Profits/ Sales	(ln) Gross
The Industries			
Computer (= 1)	.127*	.212**	−.059
Health (= 1)	−.032	.021	.005
Eating and Drinking (= 1)	−.093	−.229**	.053
Competition	−.214**	−.213**	.120**
The Companies			
Incorporated (= 1)	.081	−.001	.111*
Company Age	−.018	.006	.029
# Full Time Employees	−.032	−.012	.103†
Venture (= 1)	.076	.026	−.140**
The Owner-Operators			
Sole Owner (= 1)	−.115*	−.108*	.022
Gender (1 = F)	−.056	−.036	−.034
Age	−.076	−.114*	−.041
Education	.011	−.049	.124*
Years in Industry	−.116*	−.077	.120*
Confidence	.144**	.088†	.042
Work as CLI	−.012	.059	.090†
Risk Taking	.110**	.029	.010
Beboss	−.013	.014	−.058
Newways	.006	.053	−.141**
Innovate	.129**	.092†	−.023
(ln) Earnings	.095†	.094†	—
Job Satisfaction	—	—	.125**
R²(adj)	.187	.156	.074

Notes: **p ≤ .01;
  *p ≤ .05;
  †p ≤ .10

As with innovation, our equations are unable to explain the bulk of the variation in company performance. However, there are a number of important and significant predictors of a company's success. While the amount of money grossed by companies during the past year does not differ among industries, there continue to be industry differences in the other two measures of performance even when the other variables are taken into account. Thus, the companies in the computer industry are most successful in terms of increased market share and profits/sales; while companies in the eating and drinking industry are most likely to have experienced a decrease in profits/sales.

Companies in highly competitive product markets are less likely to have increased their share of those markets or to have increased their profits/sales. This illustrates the meaning of market competition: if markets are competitive, single firms should be unable to dominate them or to be unusually successful for very long. However, we also find that companies in more competitive markets obtain higher annual earnings. This helps to account for why some markets are highly competitive in the first place: the relatively high economic rewards available in such markets encourage people to enter them (see also Table 6).

Differences among owner-operators help explain differences in the performance of their companies. For example, owner-operators who are more confident about their business success (see Hornaday and Bunker, 1970) and who like to take chances, are more likely to report that they have increased their share of the market. In addition, those with more industry experience are less likely to have done this, and older persons are less likely to have increased their profits/sales. Finally, being the sole owner of the company is negatively related to its success, as reflected in both growth in market share and in profits/sales.

There also appears to be a ''payoff'' to innovation in terms of increased market share and profits/sales. Those who report high levels of innovative activity (as measured by the scale of all six types of innovations) also tend to say that they have increased their share of the market in the last two years and to report that they have increased their profits/sales. To the extent that innovations entail risks, then, these results support Knight's (1921) classic definition of profits as rewards that owners of businesses receive for bearing risks. Finally, our indicator of individual success, one's annual earnings, is positively related to these two measures of company performance.

The structure of the company is also related to its level of earnings. For example, incorporated companies earn more than those that are not incorporated, and those that were started with venture-capital financing earn less than those which did not use this source of capitalization. In addition, the size of the company is positively related to its gross earnings (see also Cooper, 1982).

Inequality in company earnings is also generated by differences in the characteristics of the owner-operators. In particular, those with more education and experience in the industry report that their company earned more, a finding consistent with previous research [e.g., Hoad and Rosko's (1964) study of new

Table 6.   Determinants of Individual Performance
(Standardized Coefficients, N = 411)

Independent Variables	(ln) Earnings	Job Satisfaction
The Industries		
Computer (= 1)	.083	−.068
Health (= 1)	.046	.117†
Eating and Drinking (= 1)	−.128*	−.051
Competition	.109*	−.146**
The Companies		
Incorporated (= 1)	.170**	.011
Company Age	.091†	−.019
# Full Time Employees	.155**	−.009
Venture (= 1)	−.097*	.011
The Owner-Operators		
Sole Owner (= 1)	.104*	.030
Gender (1 = F)	−.154**	.023
Age	−.019	.111*
Education	.115*	−.003
Years in Industry	.157**	.038
Confidence	.155**	.216**
Work as CLI	.073	−.071
Risk Taking	−.056	−.004
Beboss	.017	.153**
Newways	−.040	.052
(ln) Earnings	—	.144**
Innovate	.020	−.013
Profits	.086†	.172**
R^2(adj)	.230	.187

Notes: **$p \le .01$;
  *$p \le .05$;
  †$p \le .10$

manufacturing firms in Michigan]. In addition, owner-operators who view work as more of a central life interest report higher company earnings, perhaps because they put in more effort to help their company to succeed. Further, while people who place high importance on new ways of doing things may engage in more innovative activities (see Table 4), their companies earn less. Similarly, there is no relationship between our scale of innovation and company earnings. Finally, there continues to be a positive association between individual and company performance: owner-operators who are more satisfied with their work also report that their companies earned more money.

VII. INDIVIDUAL SUCCESS

The final entrepreneurial outcomes examined in this research are the rewards that owner-operators receive from their work. We investigate the determinants of two kinds of individual success: the annual earnings that the owner-operator obtained from the business during the past year; and his or her degree of job satisfaction. Our measure of economic rewards is a straightforward one: the log of the earnings that the owner-operator obtained from the business during the past year.

The concept of job satisfaction is more complex. We use it as an overall indicator of one's quality of work experience, reflecting whether or not the person feels that his or her work values are fulfilled through the work situation. It thus refers to the adequacy of extrinsic rewards such as earnings as well as of psychic rewards derived from work. Our scale of job satisfaction is computed as the sum of the four items listed in Table 3 (divided by four): how satisfied the person is with his or her work; whether the person would be self-employed if he or she could "do it over again;" whether the person would recommend his or her business to a friend; and whether the business measures up to his or her initial expectations (see also Kalleberg, 1977).

My analysis of the determinants of earnings and job satisfaction is guided by the same assumptions underlying my investigation of the other types of entrepreneurial outcomes. That is, I assume that an owner-operator's personal success is also determined by his or her personal attributes as well as by characteristics of the company's social context. In addition, I include as predictors the six-item innovation scale used in the last section as well as the "profits/sales" indicator of a company's performance. Table 6 presents the results of the analysis of the determinants of earnings and job satisfaction.

Those in the eating and drinking industry earn, on average, less than owner-operators in the other two industries. The absence of a significant positive effect for those in the computer industry in this equation suggests that their earnings advantage observed in Table 1 is accounted for by the other variables in the model. One of these explanatory variables appears to be competition: those in highly competitive markets earn more; and the level of competition appears to be highest in the computer industry.

Incorporated and larger companies provide higher earnings for their owner-operators. Moreover, we find again that those who received start-up financing from venture capital organizations obtained lower earnings. Further, sole owners of businesses receive higher earnings than those who must share their company's profits with others. In addition, women owner-operators earn less than their male counterparts, a finding which parallels that found in studies of gender differences in the labor force more generally. Also consistent with the literature on economic inequality are the positive relations between earnings and one's education and experience in the industry. Furthermore, owner-operators of companies which have increased their profits or sales receive higher earnings, again highlighting the positive relationship between company and individual success. Finally, we find once again that engaging in innovative behaviors does not appear to increase earnings; in this case, those of the owner-operator.

The results for job satisfaction indicate that owner-operators in the health industry are the most satisfied with their work, despite their not having unusually high earnings. Moreover, owner-operators in highly competitive industries are less satisfied with their work, again pointing to the mixture of advantages and disadvantages associated with running businesses in competitive environments. That is, owning and operating a business in highly competitive markets result in higher earnings, but the stresses, strains and other factors related to competition result in lower job satisfaction.

Several other results mirror those found by previous studies. For example, older owner-operators are more satisfied with their work than younger ones, and earnings are positively related to one's level of satisfaction. Moreover, people who are more confident in their business success are also more satisfied with their work. In addition, owner-operators of successful companies (measured by whether it increased its profits or sales) are more satisfied, again demonstrating the positive relationship between company and individual success.

Since job satisfaction is determined by the interplay between what one wants from work and what he or she actually receives (see, e.g., Kalleberg, 1977), one's work values, or what the person considers important in the work activity, affect one's level of job satisfaction. We have previously noted that the main work value expressed by these owner-operators is having independence and control over one's work, or "being the boss." This is one work value that is attained by all of these owner-operators, since they are all the "bosses" of their respective businesses. Our results support this argument, as we find that those who place the most importance on being the boss are most satisfied with their work.

VIII.   TOWARD A RESEARCH AGENDA ON ENTREPRENEURSHIP

The research reported in this chapter has addressed some key questions related to the study of the nature and consequences of entrepreneurship. I have focused on three entrepreneurial outcomes associated with the ownership and operation of small businesses: innovation; company performance; and individual success. In general, the analyses suggest that each outcome is affected by characteristics of both the social context (the nature of the industry and the structure of the company) and the owner-operators (demographic characteristics and more subjective personality attributes).

These findings must be evaluated in light of the limitations imposed by our sample, data collection procedures and measurement of key concepts. I have undoubtedly raised as many questions as I have answered. Rather than providing definitive answers to these questions, the research-reported here is intended to illustrate some of the elements of a research agenda that is needed to advance our understanding of the causes and consequences of entrepreneurial activity. In the interests of furthering the scientific study of entrepreneurship, it is instructive to point out some of the limitations of the present research and to suggest how they could be overcome in future efforts.

First and foremost, our sample is limited because it is cross-sectional, providing only a "snapshot" of companies and owner-operators at a single point in time. Hence, while this research enables us to draw conclusions about why some small businesses engage in more innovative behaviors than others, it says little about the dynamic processes that produce changes in innovation and success. It may well be, for example, that business cycle fluctuations influence rates of innovation. And, of course, we are unable to say anything about the factors that contribute to the survival or the failure of small businesses, a critical question for both academics and practitioners. This limitation of the present study characterizes research on entrepreneurship more generally. As Hornaday (1982) points out, a definitive investigation of the dynamic interplay between psychological and sociological factors in determining entrepreneurial events such as innovation has yet to be carried out.

The cross-sectional nature of our data has imposed another important limitation on the analysis: it has not been possible to test some of our key causal assumptions. I have assumed, for example, that changes in profits/sales cause innovations; that confidence in one's business success causes high company performance, earnings and job satisfaction, and so on. However, the causality among these variables may well be the reverse: for example, one's confidence in his or her business success could well result from good company and individual performance. While it is always necessary to make some causal assumptions for purposes of analysis, cross-sectional data are particularly inadequate for testing the implications of different causal assumptions. Since entrepreneurship is inherently a dynamic process, we should study it using longitudinal data. As Brockhaus (1982:56) notes, "what is needed most is a comprehensive longitudinal study of a comparative nature. Ideally, information should be obtained from a population of potential entrepreneurs before the entrepreneurial decision is made." Panel studies of small businesses are needed to disentangle the complex set of factors related to entrepreneurial activity.

Another limitation of the present study is that we sacrificed in-depth knowledge of a few specific businesses and owner-operators in order to obtain comparative information on a large number of them. Since the vast majority of studies of entrepreneurship are of the intensive, "case study" variety, a comparative approach is needed. However, a merger of quantitative and qualitative approaches is likely to provide greater insights into the nature of entrepreneurs and entrepreneurship than is possible using a single strategy.

In order to overcome some of the limitations of the present study, we intend to re-interview these 411 owner-operators annually for the next two years. Subsequent interviews will elicit information on future innovative behavior and performance and will enable us to investigate how attributes of these owner-operators and their companies, measured in 1985, affect future innovations and performance. This will strengthen the reasonableness of our causal assumptions: for example, we can safely assume that characteristics measured in 1985 are causally prior to outcomes observed in later years. Moreover, we will extend this research by focusing in greater depth on those owner-operators we have identified as being especially "entrepreneurial" and/or successful. Such intensive interviews with carefully selected owner-operators are likely to provide additional insights into the nature of entrepreneurship.

The research described here, then, is part of an ongoing investigation of entrepreneurship in the 1980s. A longitudinal panel study of these owner-operators and their companies is likely to greatly improve the utility of the present data set for addressing these questions. However, this study is but one component of the kind of research program needed in order to develop a cumulative science of entrepreneurship. We need to design studies of other industries, covering other areas of the United States and the world. We also need to study entrepreneurial activity in large as well as small business contexts. These studies need to be based on insights from diverse intellectual perspectives and need to take into account both the social context of entrepreneurship as well as characteristics of the entrepreneurs themselves. Only by such concerted efforts can we hope to develop a more complete understanding of the causes, correlates and consequences of entrepreneurship.

NOTES

1. The industry variables were coded so that the coefficients represent deviations of that industry from the overall sample mean on the entrepreneurial outcome studied. "Competition" is a scale computed as the sum of the four competition questions (divided by four) listed in Table 2. "Incorporated" and "venture" are dichotomous variables coded "1" if the business is incorporated and received start-up financing from venture capital organizations, respectively, and "0" if not. Company age and age of the owner-operator are measured in years. "# full-time employees" is the actual number of such employees. "Sole owner" is coded "1" if the owner-operator is the only owner of the company and "0" otherwise. "Gender" is coded: male = 0; female = 1. "Education" is scored on a scale from "0" = no education, to "20" = doctorate. "Years in industry" reflects the number of years the owner-operator has worked in his or her present industry. "Confidence," "risk-taking," "beboss" and "newways" are defined in Table 3. Finally, "work as CLI" is a scale computed as the sum of the four items listed in Table 3 (divided by four). (In computing this scale, the percent of time spent on business activities was multiplied by .1).

2. The "market share" measure was coded "1" if the owner-operator reported that the company increased its share of the market in the past two years, " − 1" if it lost market share, and "0" if it both expanded and lost market share during this period or if it neither increased nor decreased its share of the market. Similarly, the "profits/sales" measure was coded "1" if the company increased

its profits or sales during the past two years, " − 1" if profits or sales decreased, and "0" if it both increased and decreased profits or sales at different times during this period or if profits and/or sales neither increased or decreased. Since some owner-operators reported that their profits and/or sales both increased and decreased during the past two years, the sums of "%increased profits/sales" and "%decreased profits/sales" in Table 2 exceed 100%.

REFERENCES

Aldrich, H. and Zimmer, C. (1986), "Entrepreneurship through Social Networks." In Raymond Smilor and Donald Sexton (Eds.), *Entrepreneurship*. New York: Ballinger, pp. 3–23.

Arrow, K. J. (1983), "Innovation in Large and Small Firms." In Joshua Ronen (Ed.), *Entrepreneurship*. Lexington, MA: D.C. Heath, pp. 15–28.

Boyd, D. P. and Gumpert, D. E. (1983), "Coping with Entrepreneurial Stress." *Harvard Business Review* 61:44–63.

Brockhaus, R. H., Sr. (1980), "Risk Taking Propensity of Entrepreneurs." *Academy of Management Journal* 23:509–520.

Brockhaus, R. H., Sr. (1982), "The Psychology of the Entrepreneur." In Calvin A. Kent, Donald L. Sexton, and Karl H. Vesper (Eds.), *Encyclopedia of Entrepreneurship*. Englewood Cliffs, NJ: Prentice-Hall, pp. 39–57.

Carland, J. W., Hoy, F., Boulton, W. R., and Carland, J. C. (1984), "Differentiating Entrepreneurs from Small Business Owners: A Conceptualization." *Academy of Management Review* 9:354–359.

Cochran, T. C. (1968), "Entrepreneurship." In David L. Sills (Ed.), *International Encyclopedia of the Social Sciences*. New York: Macmillan and Free Press, pp. 87–90.

Cole, A. H. (1942), "Entrepreneurship As An Area of Research." *The Task of Economic History*, supplement to *Journal of Economic History* 2:118–126.

Collins, O. F. and Moore, D. G. (1970), *The Organization Makers: A Behavioral Study of Entrepreneurs*. New York: Meredith.

Cooper, A. C. (1982), "The Entrepreneurship-Small Business Interface." In Calvin A. Kent, Donald L. Sexton, and Karl H. Vesper (Eds.), *Encyclopedia of Entrepreneurship*. Englewood Cliffs, NJ: Prentice-Hall, pp. 193–205.

Copulsky, W. and McNulty, H. W. (1974), *Entrepreneurship and the Corporation*. New York: Anacom.

Drucker, P. F. (1985), *Innovation and Entrepreneurship: Practice and Principles*. New York: Harper and Row.

Dun and Bradstreet (1967), *Patterns for Success in Managing a Business*. New York: Dun and Bradstreet.

Fucini, J. J. and Fucini, S. (1985), *Entrepreneurs: The Men and Women Behind Famous Brand Names and How They Made It*. Boston: G. K. Hall and Company.

Gasse, Y. (1982), "Elaborations on the Psychology of the Entrepreneur." In Calvin A. Kent, Donald L. Sexton, and Karl H. Vesper (Eds.), *Encyclopedia of Entrepreneurship*. Englewood Cliffs, NJ: Prentice-Hall, pp. 57–66.

Gevirtz, D. (1984), *The New Entrepreneurs: Innovation in American Business*. New York: Penguin Books.

Gilder, G. (1984), *The Spirit of Enterprise*. New York: Simon and Schuster.

Harwood, E. (1982), "The Sociology of Entrepreneurship." In Calvin A. Kent, Donald L. Sexton, and Karl H. Vesper (Eds.), *Encyclopedia of Entrepreneurship*. Englewood Cliffs, NJ: Prentice-Hall, pp. 91–98.

Hebert, R. F. and Link, A. N. (1982), *The Entrepreneur: Mainstream Views and Radical Critiques*. New York: Praeger.

Hoad, W., and Rosko, P. (1964), *Management Factors Contributing to the Success or Failure of New Small Manufacturers*. Ann Arbor: University of Michigan.

Hornaday, J. A. (1982), "Research about Living Entrepreneurs." In Calvin A. Kent, Donald L. Sexton, and Karl H. Vesper (eds.), *Encyclopedia of Entrepreneurship*. Englewood Cliffs, NJ: Prentice-Hall, pp. 20–34.

Hornaday, J. A. and Aboud, J. (1971), "Characteristics of Successful Entrepreneurs." *Personnel Psychology* 24:141–153.

Hornaday, J. A. and Bunker, C. S. (1970), "The Nature of the Entrepreneur." *Personnel Psychology* 23:47–54.

Kalleberg, A. L. (1977), "Work Values and Job Rewards: A Theory of Job Satisfaction." *American Sociological Review* 42:124–143.

Kalleberg, A. L. and Berg, I. (1987), *Work and Industry: Structures, Markets and Processes*. New York: Plenum Press.

Kanbur, S. M. (1980), "A Note on Risk-Taking, Entrepreneurship and Schumpeter." *History of Political Economy* 12:489–498.

Kanter, R. M. (1983), *The Changemasters: Innovation for Productivity in the American Corporation*. New York: Simon and Schuster.

Kent, C. A. (1984), "The Rediscovery of the Entrepreneur." In Calvin A. Kent (Ed.), *The Environment for Entrepreneurship*. Lexington, MA: D.C. Heath, pp. 1–19.

Kent, C. A., Sexton, D. L., and Vesper, K. H. (Eds.), (1982), *Encyclopedia of Entrepreneurship*. Englewood Cliffs, NJ: Prentice-Hall.

Kilby, P. (1971), "Hunting the Heffalump." In Peter Kilby (Ed.), *Entrepreneurship and Economic Development*. New York: Free Press, pp. 1–43.

Kirzner, I. M. (1973), *Competition and Entrepreneurship*. Chicago: University of Chicago Press.

Knight, F. (1921), *Risk, Uncertainty and Profit*. New York: Harper and Row.

Krasner, O. J. (1982), "The Role of Entrepreneurs in Innovation." In Calvin A. Kent, Donald L. Sexton, and Karl H. Vesper (Eds.), *Encyclopedia of Entrepreneurship*. Englewood Cliffs, NJ: Prentice-Hall, pp. 277–281.

Livesay, H. C. (1982), "Entrepreneurial History." In Calvin A. Kent, Donald L. Sexton, and Karl H. Vesper (Eds.), *Encyclopedia of Entrepreneurship*. Englewood Cliffs, NJ: Prentice-Hall, pp. 7–15.

Martin, A. (1982), "Additional Aspects of Entrepreneurial History." In Calvin A. Kent, Donald L. Sexton, and Karl H. Vesper (Eds.), *Encyclopedia of Entrepreneurship*. Englewood Cliffs, NJ: Prentice-Hall, pp. 15–18.

McClelland, D. C. (1961), *The Achieving Society*. New York: Free Press.

Perryman, M. R. (1982), "Commentary on Research Methodology in Entrepreneurship." In Calvin A. Kent, Donald L. Sexton, and Karl H. Vesper (Eds.), *Encyclopedia of Entrepreneurship*. Englewood Cliffs, NJ: Prentice-Hall, pp. 377–379.

Peters, T. J. and Waterman, Jr., R. H. (1982), *In Search of Excellence: Lessons from America's Best-Run Companies*. New York: Harper and Row.

Pinchot, III, G. (1985), *Intrapreneuring: Why You Don't Have to Leave the Corporation to Become an Entrepreneur*. New York: Harper and Row.

Prager, D. J. and Omenn, G. S. (1980), "Research, Innovation and University-Industry Linkages." *Science* 207:379–384.

Reagan, R. (1982), *The State of Small Business: A Report of the President*. Washington, DC: U.S. Government Printing Office.

Redlich, F, (1957), "Toward a Better Theory of Risk." *Explorations in Entrepreneurial History* 10:33–39.

Sarachek, B. (1978), "American Entrepreneurs and the Horatio Alger Myth." *Journal of Economic History* 38:439–456.

Schollhammer, H. (1982), "Internal Corporate Entrepreneurship." In Calvin A. Kent, Donald L. Sexton, and Karl H. Vesper (Eds.), *Encyclopedia of Entrepreneurship*. Englewood Cliffs, NJ: Prentice-Hall, pp. 209–223.

Schumpeter, J. (1936), *The Theory of Economic Development*. Cambridge, MA: Harvard University Press (reprinted by Oxford, 1961).

Schumpeter, J. (1947), *Capitalism, Socialism and Democracy*. London: George Allen and Unwin (reprinted by Harper and Row, 1950; Simon and Schuster, 1958).

Sexton, D. L. (1982), "Research Needs and Issues in Entrepreneurship." In Calvin A. Kent, Donald L. Sexton, and Karl H. Vesper (Eds.), *Encyclopedia of Entrepreneurship*. Englewood Cliffs, NJ: Prentice-Hall, pp. 383–389.

Shapero, A. and Sokol, L. (1982), "The Social Dimensions of Entrepreneurship." In Calvin A. Kent, Donald L. Sexton, and Karl H. Vesper (Eds.), *Encyclopedia of Entrepreneurship*. Englewood Cliffs, NJ: Prentice-Hall, pp. 72–90.

United States Bureau of the Census (1977), *Enterprise Statistics 1972*. Washington, DC: U.S. Government Printing Office.

Vesper, K. H. (1979), "Commentary." In D. Schendel and C. Hofer (Eds.), *Strategic Management: A New View of Business Policy and Planning*. Boston: Little, Brown.

Vesper, K. H. (1982), "Introduction and Summary of Entrepreneurship Research." In Calvin A. Kent, Donald L. Sexton, and Karl H. Vesper (Eds.), *Encyclopedia of Entrepreneurship*. Englewood Cliffs, NJ: Prentice-Hall, pp. xxxi–xxxviii.

Chapter 12

RESEARCH BIBLIOGRAPHY ON ENTREPRENEURSHIP, INNOVATION AND VENTURE CAPITAL

THE ECONOMICS OF TECHNICAL CHANGE REFERENCES

Adkins, L. (1982), "Creating a Climate for Productivity." *Duns Business Monthly* 119:69.

Arrow, K. J. (1962), "The Economic Implications of Learning by Doing." *The Review of Economic Studies* 29:155–75.

Atkinson, A. and J. Stiglitz (1969), "A New View of Technical Change." *Economic Journal* 79:573–8.

Baldwin, W. L. and G. L. Childs (1969), "The Fast Second and Rivalry in Research and Development." *Southern Economic Journal* 36:18–24.

Barzel, Y. (1968), "Optimal Timing of Innovation." *Review of Economics and Statistics* 50:348–55.

Bass, F. M. (1980), "The Relationship between Diffusion Rates, Experience Curves, and Demand Elasticities for Consumer Durable Technological Innovations." *Journal of Business* 53:52–67.

Batelle-Columbus Laboratories (1973), *Interaction of Science and Technology and the Innovative Process.* Washington, DC: National Science Foundation.

Baumol, W. J. (1967), "The Macro Economics of Unbalanced Growth." *American Economic Review* 57:415–26.

Berle, A. A. and G. C. Means (1932), *The Modern Corporation and Private Property.* New York: Macmillian Co.

Binks, M. and J. Coyne (1983), *The Birth of Enterprise.* London: Institute of Economic Affairs.

Birch, D. L. (1981), "Who Creates Jobs?" *The Public Interest* 65:3–14.

Advances in the Study of Entrepreneurship, Innovation, and Economic Growth, Volume 1, pages 191-213.
Copyright © 1986 by JAI Press Inc.
ISBN: 0-89232-703-0

Boskin, M. et al. (1980), *The Impact of Inflation on U.S. Productivity and International Competitiveness*. Washington, DC: National Planning Association.

Box, G. E. P. and N. R. Draper (1969), *Evolutionary Operation: A Method for Increasing Industrial Productivity*. New York: Wiley.

Brown, L. A. (1975), "The Market and Infrastructure Content of Adoption: A Spatial Perspective on the Diffusion of Innovation." *Economic Geography* 51:185–216.

Brown, M. and J. Popkin (1962), "A Measure of Technological Change and Returns to Scale." *The Review of Economics and Statistics* 44:402–11.

Burger, R. M. (1977), *An Analysis of the National Science Foundation's Innovation Centers Experiment: An Effort to Promote Technological Innovation and Entrepreneurship in Academic Settings*. Washington, DC: U.S. Government Printing Office.

Burns, R. O. (1975), *Innovation*. Lexington, MA: Lexington Books.

Chandler, A., Jr. (1977), *The Visible Hand:The Managerial Revolution in American Business*. Cambridge, MA: Harvard University Press.

Charpie, R. et al. (1967), *Technological Innovation: Its Environment and Management*. Washington DC: U.S. Government Printing Office.

Coase, R. H. (1937), "The Theory of the Firm." *Economica N. S.* 4:368–405.

Cochran, T. C. (1972), *Business in American Life: A History*. New York: McGraw-Hill.

Cole, A. F. (1959), *Business Enterprise in Its Social Setting*. Cambridge, MA: Harvard University.

Colton, R. M. and G. G. Udall (1976), "The National Science Foundation's Innovation Centers —An Experiment in Training Potential Entrepreneurs and Innovators." *Journal of Small Business Management* 14:11–20.

Commerce Technical Advisory Board (1976), *The Role of New Technical Enterprises in the U. S. Economy*. Washington, DC: U. S. Department of Commerce.

David, P. A. (1974), *Technical Change, Innovation and Economic Growth*. London: Cambridge University Press.

Davis, L. E. and D. C. North (1971), *Institutional Change and American Economic Growth*. Cambridge: Cambridge University Press.

Dasgupta, P. and J. Stiglitz (1980), " Industrial Structure and the Nature of Innovative Activity." *Economic Journal* 90:266–93.

Dasgupta, P. and J. Stiglitz (1980), "Uncertainty: Industrial Structure and the Speed of R&D." *Bell Journal of Economics* 11:1–28.

Domar, E. D. (1961), "On the Measurement of Technological Change." *Economic Journal* 71:709–29.

Duvall, R. D. and J. R. Freeman (1983), "The Techno-Bureaucratic Elite and the Entrepreneurial State in Dependent Industrialization." *American Political Science Review* 77:3.

Ewers, H. J. and R. W. Wettman (1980), "Innovation – Oriented Regional Policy." *Regional Studies* 14:161–79.

Ferguson, E. S. (1979), "The American-ness of American Technology." *Technology and Culture* 20:3–24.

Freeman, C. (1974), *The Economics of Industrial Innovation*. Baltimore, MD: Penguin Books.

Frey, R. S. (1984), "Need for Achievement, Entrepreneurship, and Economic Growth: A Critique of the McClelland Thesis." *The Social Science Journal* 21:125–134.

Gellman Research Associates, Inc. (1976), *Indicators of International Trends in Technological Innovation*. Washington, DC: National Science Foundation.

Goldstein, J. (1981), "Entrepreneuring in Appropriate Technology." In K. H. Vesper (Ed.), *Frontiers of Entrepreneurship Research*. Wellesley, MA: Babson College.

Greenfield, S. M. and A. Strickon (1981), "A New Paradigm for the Study of Entrepreneurship and Social Change." *Economic Development and Cultural Change* 29:467-99.

Grossman, G. M. (1984), "International Trade, Foreign Investment, and the Formation of the Entrepreneurial Class." *American Economic Review* 74:605–14.

Hagen, E. E. (1971), "How Economic Growth Begins: A Theory of Social Change." In P. Kilby (Ed.), *Entrepreneurship and Economic Development.* New York: Free Press.

Hammeed, K. A. (1974), *Enterprise: Industrial Entrepreneurship in Development.* London: Sage Publications.

Harris, J. R. (1973), "Entrepreneurship and Economic Development ." In G. Cain and P. Uselding (Eds.), *Business Enterprise and Economic Change.* Kent, OH: Kent State University.

Hartman, R. S. and D. R. Wheeler (1979), "Schumpeterian Waves of Innovation and Infrastructure Development in Great Britain and the United States: The Kondratieff Cycle Revisited." In P. Uselding (Ed.), *Research in Economic History,* Vol. 4. Greenwich, CT: JAI Press.

Hayek, F. (1945), "The Use of Knowledge in Society." *American Economic Review* 35:519–530.

Hill, C. T. and J. M. Uherback (1979), *Technological Innovation for a Dynamic Economy.* New York: Pergamon.

Hirschman, A. E. (1958), *The Strategy of Economic Development.* New Haven: Yale University Press.

Hoselitz, B. F. (1960), *Sociological Aspects of Economic Growth.* Glencoe, NY: Free Press.

Hughes, J. (1968), "Industrialization: Economic Aspects." In D. L. Sills (Ed.), *International Encyclopedia of the Social Sciences.* New York: MacMillan.

Ihori, T. (1979), "Entrepreneurs' Capital Accumulation Behavior and Long-Run Equilibrium." *Journal of Macroeconomics* 1:295–307.

Jenks, L. H. (1949), *Change and the Entrepreneur.* Cambridge, MA: Harvard University Press.

Jewkes, J., D. Sawyers, and R. Stillerman (1971), *Sources of Invention.* New York: Norton.

Johnson, P. S. and D. G. Cathcart (1979), "New Manufacturing Firms and Regional Development: Some Evidence from the Northern Region." *Regional Studies* 13:269–280.

Kamien, M. I. and N. L. Schwartz (1972), "Timing of Innovation Under Rivalry." *Econometrica* 40:43–60.

Kanbur, S. M. (1982), "Entrepreneurial Risk Taking, Inequality, and Public Policy: An Application of Inequality, Decomposition Analysis to the General Equilibrium Effects of Progressive Taxation." *Journal of Political Economy* 90:1–21.

Kennedy, C. and A. P. Thirtwall (1972), "Technical Progress: A Survey." *Economic Journal* 82:11–72.

Kirchhoff, B. A. and W. E. Knight (1981), "Government's Role in Research and Development." In K. H. Vesper (Ed.), *Frontiers of Entrepreneurship Research.* Wellesley, MA: Babson College.

Kirzner, I. M. (1982), "The Theory of Entrepreneurship in Economic Growth." In C. A. Kent, et al. (Eds.), *Encyclopedia of Entrepreneurship.* Englewood Cliffs, NJ: Prentice-Hall.

Kirzner, I. M. (1983), "Entrepreneurship and the Future of Capitalism." In J. Backman (Ed.), *Entrepreneurship and the Outlook for America.* New York: Free Press.

Krasner, O. J. (1982), "The Role of Entrepreneurs in Innovation." In C. A. Kent, et al. (Eds.), *Encyclopedia of Entrepreneurship.* Englewood Cliffs, NJ: Prentice-Hall.

Kuhn, T. S. (1970), *The Structure of Scientific Revolutions.* Chicago: University of Chicago Press.

Kunkel, J. H. (1965), "Values and Behavior in Economic Development." *Economic Development and Cultural Change* 13:257–77.

Kunkel, J. H. (1974), "Patent Life and R&D Rivalry." *American Economic Review* 64:183–7.

Kunkel, J. H. (1975), "Market Structure and Innovation: A Survey." *Journal of Economic Literature* 13:1–37.

Kunkel, J. H. (1978), "Potential Rivalry, Monopoly Profits, and the Pace of Inventive Activity." *Review of Economic Studies* 45:547–57.

Kuznets, S. (1954), *Economic Change.* London: William Heineman.

Kuznets, S. (1961), *Capital in the American Economy*. Princeton, NJ: Princeton University Press.

Landes, D. (1949), "French Entrepreneurship and Industrial Growth in the Nineteenth Century." *Journal of Economic History* 9:45–61.

Leff, N. H. (1979), "Entrepreneurship and Economic Development: The Problem Revisited." *Journal of Economic Literature* 17:46–64.

Leibenstein, H. (1968), "Entrepreneurship and Development." *American Economic Review* 58:72–83.

Leibenstein, H. (1978), *General X-Efficiency Theory and Economic Development*. New York: Oxford University Press.

Litvak, I. A. and C. J. Maule (1976), "Comparative Technical Entrepreneurship: Some Perspectives." *Journal of International Business Studies* 7:31–38.

Livesay, H. C. (1979), *American Made: Men Who Shaped the American Economy*. Boston: Little Brown.

Macdonald, R. (1971), "Schumpeter and Max Weber: Central Visions and Social Theories." In P. Kilby (Ed.), *Entrepreneurship and Economic Development*. New York: Free Press.

Machlup, F. (1962), *The Production and Distribution of Knowledge in the United States*.

Maidique, M. A. (1980), "Entrepreneurs, Champions, and Technological Innovation." *Sloan Management Review* 21:59–76.

Mansfield, E. (1968), *Industrial Research and Technological Innovation: An Econometric Analysis*. New York: W. W. Norton.

Mansfield, E. et al. (1968), *The Economics of Technological Change*. New York: W. W. Norton.

Mansfield, E. (1969), "Industrial Research and Development: Characteristics, Tradeoffs, and Diffusion of Results." *American Economic Review* 59(2):65–71.

Mansfield, E. et al. (1971), *Research and Innovation in the Modern Corporation*. New York: W. W. Norton.

Mansfield, E. (1975), "International Technology Transfer: Problems, Costs, Policies." *American Economic Review* 65(2):372–376.

Mansfield, E. and S. Wagner (1975), "Organizational and Strategic Factors Associated with Probabilities of Success in Industrial R and D." *Journal of Business* 48(2):179–198.

Mansfield, E. et al. (1977), *The Production and Application of New Industrial Technology*. New York: W. W. Norton.

Mansfield, E. et al. (1977), "Social and Private Rates of Return from Industrial Innovations." *Quarterly Journal of Economics* 91(2):221–240.

Mansfield, E. (1980), "Basic Research and Productivity Increase in Manufacturing." *American Economic Review* 70(5):863–873.

Mansfield, E. (1980), "Innovation in the United States: Its State of Health." *Innovation and the American Economy*. Philadelphia: Franklin Institute. (Also published in *Interdisciplinary Science Reviews*, Vol. 5, No. 3, 1980.)

Mansfield E. (1981), "Composition of R and D Expenditures: Relationship to Size of Firm, Concentration, and Innovative Output." *Review of Economics and Statistics* 63(4):610–614.

Mansfield, E., M. Schwartz, and S. Wagner (1981), "Imitation Costs and Patents: An Empirical Study." *Economic Journal* 91:907–918.

Mansfield, E. (1983), "Technological Change and Market Structure: An Empirical Study." *American Economic Review* 73(2):205–209.

Mansfield, E. (1984), "R and D Innovation: Some Empirical Findings." In Z. Griliches (Ed.), *R and D, Patents, and Productivity*. National Bureau of Economic Research.

Marquis, D. G. (1981), "The Anatomy of Successful Innovations." In R. R. Rothberg (Ed.), *Corporate Strategy and Product Innovation*. New York: Free Press.

McClelland, D. C. (1961), *The Achieving Society*. Princeton, NJ: D. Van Nostrand Co.

McClelland, D. C. (1971), "The Achievement Motive in Economic Growth." In P. Kilby (Ed.), *Entrepreneurship and Economic Development*. New York: Free Press.

McCullagh, C. (1984), "Entrepreneurship and Development: An Alternative Perspective." *Economic and Social Review* 15:109–24.

Miller, D. and P. H. Friesen (1982), "Innovation in Conservative and Entrepreneurial Firms: Two Models of Strategic Momentum." *Strategic Management Journal* 3:1–25.

Morse, R. S. (1978), *The Changing National Environment for Innovation.* Cambridge, MA: Sloan School of Management, M.I.T.

Mueller, D. C. (1972), "A Life Cycle Theory of the Firm." *Journal of Industrial Economics* 20:199–219.

National Science Foundation (1976), *Indicators of International Trends in Technological Innovation.* Washington, DC: U. S. Government Printing Office.

Nelson, R. R. (1959), *The Economics of Invention: A Survey of the Literature.* Santa Monica, CA: The RAND Corporation.

Nelson, R. R. (1972), "Issues and Suggestions for the Study of Industrial Organization in a Regime of Rapid Technological Change." In V. R. Fuchs (Ed.), *Policy Issues and Research Opportunities in Industrial Organization.* New York: Columbia University Press.

Nelson, R. (1974), "Neoclassical vs. Evolutionary Theories of Growth." *Economic Journal* 84:886–905.

Nelson, R., S. Winter, and H. Schuette (1977), "Technical Change in an Evolutionary Model." *Quarterly Journal of Economics* 90:90–118.

Nelson, R. R. and D. Yates (1978), *Innovation and Implementation In Public Organizations.* Lexington, MA: Lexington Books.

Nelson, R. R. and S. G. Winter (1982), *An Evolutionary Theory of Economic Change.* Cambridge, MA: Belknap Press.

Norris, W. C. (1981), "Developing Corporate Policies for Innovation: A Program of Action." *Long Range Planning.* 14:34–42.

North, D. C. (1978), "Structure and Performance: The Task of Economic History." *Journal of Economic Literature* 16:963–978.

Nystrom, H. (1979), *Creativity and Innovation.* New York: Wiley-Interscience.

Obermayer, J. H. (1981), "Government R&D Funding and Startups." In K. H. Vesper (Ed.), *Frontiers of Entrepreneurship Research.* Wellesley, MA: Babson College.

O'Donnell, L. A. (1973), "Rationalism, Capitalism and the Entrepreneur: The Views of Veblen and Schumpeter." *History of Political Economy* 5:199–214.

Pelz, D. C. (1967), "Creative Tensions in the R&D Climate." *Science* 157:160–5.

Peterson, P. G. (1965), "Some Approaches to Innovation in Industry." In G. A. Steiner (Ed.), *The Creative Organization.* Chicago: The University of Chicago Press.

Porter, G. (1973), *The Rise of Big Business, 1860–1910.* Arlington Heights, IL: AHM Publishing Corporation.

Prager, D. J. and D. S. Omean (1980), "Research Innovation and University – Industry Linkages." *Science* 207(January):379–384.

Quinn, J. B. (1979), "Technological Innovation, Entrepreneurship, and Strategy." *Sloan Management Review* 20:19–30.

Robertson, T. S. (1971), *Innovative Behaviour and Communication.* New York: Holt, Rinehart and Winston.

Rodgers, E. M., and F. F. Shoemaker (1971), *Communication of Innovations..* New York: Free Press.

Rodgers, E. M. (1962) *Diffusion of Innovations.* New York: Free Press.

Romeo, A. (1977), "The Rate of Imitation of a Capital-Embodied Process Innovation." *Economica* 44:63–70.

Ronen, J. (1983), "Toward Operation Models of Entrepreneurship"; and "Organizational Innovation: The Transaction-Cost Approach." In J. Ronen (Ed.), *Entrepreneurship.* Lexington, MA: Lexington Books.

Ronstadt, R. and R. J. Kramer (1983), "Internationalizing Industrial Innovation." *Journal of Business Strategy* 3:3–15.

Rosenberg, N. (1972), *Technology and American Economic Growth.* New York: Harper and Row.

Rosenberg, N. (1977), "American Technology: Imported or Indigenous?" *American Economic Review* 67:21–26.

Rossini, F. and B. Bozeman (1977), "National Strategies for Technological Innovation." *Administration and Society* 9:81–110.

Schatz, S. P. (1971), "N Achievement and Economic Growth: A Critical Appraisal." In P. Kilby (Ed.), *Entrepreneurship and Economic Development.* New York: Free Press.

Schon, D. A. (1967), *Technology and Change.* New York: Delacorte Press.

Schumpeter, J. A. (1939), *Business Cycles.* New York: McGraw-Hill.

Schumpeter, J. A. (1942), *Capitalism, Socialism and Democracy.* New York: Harper and Row.

Schumpeter, J. A. (1947), "The Creative Response in Economic History." *Journal of Economic History* 7:149–159.

Schumpeter, J. A. (1949), *The Theory of Economic Development.* Cambridge, MA: Harvard University Press.

Schumpeter, J. A. (1954), *History of Economic Analysis.* New York: Oxford University Press.

Simon, H.A. (1978), "Rationality as Process and Product of Thought." *American Economic Review* 68:1–16.

Solow, R. M. (1957), "Technical Change and the Aggregate Production Function." *The Review of Economics and Statistics* 39:312–20.

Solow, R. M. (1962), "Technical Progress, Capital Formation and Economic Growth." *American Economic Review* 52:76–86.

Spicer, E. H. (Ed.), (1952), *Human Problems in Technological Change.* New York: Russell Sage Foundation.

Stigler, G. J. (1951), "The Division of Labor is Limited by the Extent of the Market." *Journal of Political Economy* 56:185–193.

Stumpe, W. R. (1982), "Entrepreneurship in R&D–A State of Mind." *Research Management* 25:13–16.

Udell, G. (1982), "Elaboration on Entrepreneurs and Innovation." In C. A. Kent et al. (Eds.), *Encyclopedia of Entrepreneurship.* Englewood Cliffs, NJ: Prentice-Hall.

United States Congress. Joint Economic Committee (1985), *Climate for Entrepreneurship and Innovation in the United States: Hearings before the Joint Economic Committee, Congress of the United States, Ninety-eighth Congress.* Washington, DC: U.S. Government Printing Office.

Uselding, P. and B. Juba (1973), "Based Technical Progress in American Manufacturing." *Explorations in Economic History* 11:55–72.

Uselding, P. and B. Juba (1981), "Measuring Techniques and Manufacturing Practice." In O. Mayr (Ed.), *The American System of Manufacturing.* Washington, DC: The Smithsonian Institution.

Williams, E. E. (1983), "Entrepreneurship, Innovation and Economic Growth." *Technovation* (Netherlands) 2:3–15

Young, F. W. (1971), "A Macrosociological Interpretation of Entrepreneurship." In P. Kilby (Ed.), *Entrepreneurship and Economic Development.* New York: Free Press.

FINANCE AND VENTURE CAPITAL REFERENCES

Anreder, S. S. (1980), "Up the Entrepreneur: The World of Finance is Beating a Path to His Door." *Barron's* 60:4–5, 24.

Arrowsmith, J. W. (Ed.), (1966), *Financing for Small Business.* Ann Arbor, MI: Institute of Continuing Legal Education.

Baker, H. K. (1981), "The Cost and Availability of Credit Venture Capital." In *Economic Research* on *Small Business: The Environment for Entrepreneurship and Small Business, Summary Analysis of the Regional Research Reports*. Washington, DC: U. S. Government Printing Office.

Boskin, M. J. (1984), "The Fiscal Environment for Entrepreneurship." In C. A. Kent (Ed.), *The Environment for Entrepreneurship*. Lexington, MA: D. C. Heath.

Brophy, D. J. (1981), "Flows of Venture Capital 1977–1980." In K. H. Vesper (Ed.), *Frontiers of Entrepreneurship Research*. Wellesley, MA: Babson College.

Brophy, D. J. (1982), "Venture Capital Research." In C. A. Kent et al. (Eds.), *Encyclopedia of Entrepreneurship*. Englewood Cliffs, NJ: Prentice-Hall.

Brophy, D. J., E. Amonsen, and P. Bontrager (1982), "Analysis of Structuring and Pricing of Venture Capital Investment Proposals." In K. H. Vesper (Ed.), *Frontiers of Entrepreneurship Research*. Wellesley, MA: Babson College.

Bruno, A. V. and T. T. Tyebjee (1984), "The Entrepreneur's Search for Capital." In J. A. Hornaday, F. A. Tardley, Jr., J. A. Timmons, and K. H. Vesper (Eds.), *Frontiers of Entrepreneurship Research*. Wellesley, MA: Babson College.

Buskirk, R. H. (1982), "The Dangers of Overcapitalization in the Startup Stage." In K. H. Vesper (Ed.), *Frontiers of Entrepreneurship Research*. Wellesley, MA: Babson College.

Bygrave, W. D., J. A. Timmons, and N. D. Fast (1984), "Seed and Startup Venture Capital Investing in Technological Companies." In J. A. Hornaday, F. A. Tardley, Jr., J. A. Timmons, and K. H. Vesper (Eds.), *Frontiers of Entrepreneurship Research*. Wellesley, MA: Babson College.

Fast, N. D. (1982), "Venture Capital Investment and Technology Development." In K. H. Vesper (Ed.), *Frontiers of Entrepreneurship Research*. Wellesley, MA: Babson College.

Gasse, Y. (1984), "Attitudes Toward External Financing: A Comparison of Canadian Entrepreneurs and Owner-Managers." In J. A. Hornaday, F. A. Tardley, Jr., J. A. Timmons, and K. H. Vesper (Eds.), *Frontiers of Entrepreneurship Research*. Wellesley, MA: Babson College.

Gillingham, D.W. and K. E. Loucks (1982), "Forming New Entrepreneurial Ventures Through the Use of Venture Group Sessions." *Journal of Small Business Management* 20:5–12.

Goldstein, J. (1984), "Undercapitalization As a Winning Entrepreneurial Strategy." In J. A. Hornaday,, F. A. Tardley, Jr., J. A. Timmons, and K. H. Vesper (Eds.), *Frontiers of Entrepreneurship Research*. Wellesley, MA: Babson College.

Green, J. R. and J. B. Shoven (1983), "The Effects of Financing Opportunities and Bankruptcy on Entrepreneurial Risk Bearing." In J. Ronen (Ed.), *Entrepreneurship*. Lexington, MA: D. C. Heath.

Gumpert, D. E. (1979), "Venture Capital Becoming More Widely Available." *Harvard Business Review* 57:178–92.

Hills, G. E. (1984), "Market Analysis and Marketing in New Ventures: Venture Capitalists' Perceptions." In J. A. Hornaday, F. A. Tardley, Jr., J. A. Timmons, and K. H. Vesper (Eds.), *Frontiers of Entrepreneurship Research*. Wellesley, MA: Babson College.

Hoffman, C. A. (1972), "The Venture Capital Decision Process." Ph.D. dissertation, University of Texas.

Jensen, M. C. and W. H. Meckling (1976), "The Theory of the Firm: Managerial Behaviour, Agency Costs and Ownership Structure." *Journal of Financial Economics* 3:305–60.

Kelly, A. J., et al. (1971), *Venture Capital, A Guidebook for New Enterprises*. Chestnut Hill, MA: The Management Institute, Boston College.

Kravitz, L. (1984), "The Venture Capital 100." *Venture* 6:60–8.

Larson, J. A. (1982), "Venturing Into Venture Capital." *Business Horizons* 25:18–23.

Liles, P. R. (1977), *Sustaining the Venture Capital Firm*. Cambridge, MA: Management Analysis Center, Inc.

McMullan, W. E. (1982), "In Interest of Equity: Distributing Equity to Many New Venture Employees." In K. H. Vesper (Ed.), *Frontiers of Entrepreneurship Research*. Wellesley, MA: Babson College.

McMullan, W. E., R. Long, and J. Tapp (1984), "Entrepreneurial Share Transaction Strategies." In

J. A. Hornaday, F. A. Tardley, Jr., J. A. Timmons, and K. H. Vesper (Eds.), *Frontiers of Entrepreneurship Research*. Wellesley, MA: Babson College.

Mitton, D. G. (1982), "The Anatomy of High Leverage Buyout." In K. H. Vesper (Ed.), *Frontiers of Entrepreneurship Research*. Wellesley, MA: Babson College.

Much, M. (1978), "Who's Financing the U. S. Entrepreneur?" *Industry Week* 199:119–120.

Murray, T. J. (1982), "Venture Capital: The Game Gets Riskier." *Duns Business Monthly*, 119.

Patrick, T. (1980), "Employees as a Source of Funds." *Journal of Small Business* 18:55–57.

Rind, K. W. (1982), "Venture Capital in High Tech Acquisitions." *Mergers and Acquisitions* 17:40.

Ruby, L. (1984), "The Role of the Venture Capitalist in the Entrepreneurial Process." In Raymond W. Smilor and Robert Lawrence Kuhn (Eds.), *Corporate Creativity*. New York: Praeger Publishers.

Schell, D. W. (1984), " The Development of the Venture Capital Industry in North Carolina: A New Approach." In J. A. Hornaday, F. A. Tardley, Jr., J. A. Timmons, and K. H. Vesper (Eds.), *Frontiers of Entrepreneurship Research*. Wellesley, MA: Babson College.

Shames, W. H. (1974), *Venture Management: The Business of the Inventor, Entrepreneur, Venture Capitalist and Established Company*. New York: Free Press.

Shatto, G. M. (1981), "The Cost and Availability of Credit and Venture Capital: A Southwest Survey." *Texas Business Review* 55:14–18.

Stigler, G. J. (1967), "Imperfections in the Capital Market." *Journal of Political Economy* 75:287–92.

Timmons, J. A. (1981), "Survey of the Most Active Venture Capital Firms." In K. H. Vesper (Ed.), *Frontiers of Entrepreneurship Research*. Wellesley, MA: Babson College.

Timmons, J. A. and D. E. Gumpert (1982), "Discard Many Old Rules about Getting Venture Capital." *Harvard Business Review* 60:152–56.

Tyebjee, T. T. and A. V. Bruno (1981), "Venture Capital Decision Making." In K. H. Vesper (Eds.), *Frontiers of Entrepreneurship Research*. Wellesley, MA: Babson College.

U. S. General Accounting Office (1982), *Government-Industry Cooperat ion Can Enhance the Venture Capital Process*. Washington, DC: General Accounting Office.

Von Hippel, E. (1981), *Increasing Innovators' Returns from Innovation*. Cambridge, MA: M.I.T.

Walker, E. W. and J. W. Petty, II (1978), *Financial Management of the Small Firms*. Englewood Cliffs, NJ: Prentice-Hall.

Welsh, J. A. and J. F. White (1976), "Keeping Score in Business — An Accounting Primer for Entrepreneurs." *Journal of Small Business Management* 14:29–40.

Wetzel, W. E., Jr. (1982), "Project ICE: An Experiment in Capital For mation." In K. H. Vesper (Ed.), *Frontiers of Entrepreneurship Research*. Wellesley, MA: Babson College.

Wetzel, W. E., Jr. (1984), "Venture Capital Network, Inc.: An Experiment in Capital Formation." In J. A. Hornaday, F. A. Tardley, Jr., J. A. Timmons, and K. H. Vesper (Eds.), *Frontiers of Entrepreneurship Research*. Wellesley, MA: Babson College.

White, M. J. (1980), "Public Policy Toward Bankruptcy: Me-First and Other Priority Rules." *Bell Journal of Economics* 11:550–564.

ENTREPRENEURSHIP AND INTRAPRENEURSHIP REFERENCES

Aitken, H. G. J., (1965), *Explorations in Enterprise*. Cambridge, MA: Harvard University Press.

Alexander, A. P. (1967), "The Supply of Industrial Entrepreneurship." *Exploration in Entrepreneurial History* 2:134–49.

Ansoff, H. I. and J. M. Stewart (1981), "Strategies for a Technology-Based Business." In R. R. Rothberg (Ed.), *Corporate Strategy and Product Innovation*. New York: Free Press.

Arrow, K. J. (1963), "Control in Large Organizations." *Management Science* 10:397–408.

Arrow, K. J. (1983), "Innovation in Large and Small Firms." In J. Ronen (Ed.), *Entrepreneurship*. Lexington, MA: D.C. Heath.

Avruck, K. (1982), "New Markets and Good Deeds: On Altruism and Exemplary Entrepreneurship." *Anthropological Quarterly* 55:211–223.

Backman, J. (1983), "Entrepreneurship: An Overview." In J. Backman (Ed.), *Entrepreneurship and the Outlook for America*. New York: The Free Press.

Bailey, J. E. (1984), "Intrapreneurship — Source of High Growth Startups or Passing Fad?" In J. A. Hornaday, F. A. Tardley, Jr., J. A. Timmons, and K. H. Vesper (Eds.), *Frontiers of Entrepreneurship Research*. Wellesley, MA: Babson College.

Baumann, D. M. (1981), "Second Generation Innovation Center Entrepreneurs." In K. H. Vesper (Ed.), *Frontiers of Entrepreneurship Research*. Wellesley, MA: Babson College.

Baumback, C. M. (1981), *Baumback Guide to Entrepreneurship*. Englewood Cliffs, NJ: Prentice-Hall.

Baumol, W. J. (1962), "On the Theory of Expansion of the Firm." *American Economic Review* 52:1078–87.

Baumol, W. J. (1968), "Entrepreneurship in Economic Theory." *American Economic Review* 58:64–71.

Baumol, W. J. (1983), "Toward Operational Models of Entrepreneurship." In J. Ronen (Ed.), *Entrepreneurship*. Lexington, MA: D. C. Heath.

Baumol, W. J. and M. Stewart (1971), "On the Behavioral Theory of the Firm." In R. Morris and A. Wood (Eds.), *The Corporate Economy: Growth, Competition and Innovation Potential*. Cambridge, MA: Harvard University Press.

Bearse, P. J. (1982), "A Study of Entrepreneurship by Region and SMSA Size." In K. H. Vesper (Ed.), *Frontiers of Entrepreneurship Research*. Wellesley, MA: Babson College.

Beattie, L. E. (1984), "The Entrepreneurial Woman." *Business & Economic Review* 31:3–6.

Becker, S. W. and T. L. Whistler (1967), "The Innovative Organization: A Selective View of Current Theory and Research." *The Journal of Business* 40:462–469.

Bekey, M. (1984), "Serving Entrepreneurs." *Venture* 6:144.

Benson, G., and J. Chasin (1976), *The Structure of New Product Organization*. New York: Amacom.

Bettencourt, E. (1980), "Competencies Validated for Entrepreneurial Training of Secondary Vocational Students." Ph.D. dissertation, Rutgers University.

Bickerstaffe, G. (1982), "The Disillusioned Entrepreneur." *International Management* (UK) 37:18–19.

Bird, B. J. (1983), "Intentional Maps of Entrepreneurs." Ph.D. dissertation, University of Southern California.

Blowett, K. R. (1979), "Marketing for the Technical Entrepreneur." In D. S. Scott and R. M. Blair (Eds.), *The Technical Entrepreneur*. Ontario, Canada: Press Porcepic Limited.

Bower, M. (1965), "Nurturing Innovation in an Organization." In G. A. Steiner (Ed.), *The Creative Organization*. Chicago: The University of Chicago Press.

Boyd, D. P. and D. E. Gumpert (1983), "Coping with Entrepreneurial Stress." *Harvard Business Review* 61:44–64.

Boyd, D. P. and D. E. Gumpert (1984), "The Loneliness of the Start-Up Entrepreneur." In J. A. Hornaday, F. A. Tardley, Jr., J. A. Timmons, and K. H. Vesper (Eds.), *Frontiers of Entrepreneurship Research*. Wellesley, MA: Babson College.

Brereton, P. R. (1974), "The Qualifications for Entrepreneurship." *Journal of Small Business Management* 12:1–3.

Brinner, R. (1978), *Technology, Labor and Economic Potential*. Lexington, MA: Data Resource, Inc.

Broat, I. G. (1978), *Entrepreneur*. New York: Antheum Publishing.

Brockhaus, R. H. (1980), "Risk Taking Propensity of Entrepreneurs." *Academy of Management Journal* 23:509–520.

Brockhaus, R. H. (1981), "The Authoritarian Entrepreneur." In K. H. Vesper (Ed.), *Frontiers Of Entrepreneurship Research*. Wellesley, MA: Babson College.

Brockhaus, R. H. (1982), "The Psychology of the Entrepreneur." In C.A. Kent et al. (Eds.), *Encyclopedia of Entrepreneurship*. Englewood Cliffs, NJ: Prentice-Hall.

Brockhaus, R. H. and W. R. Nord (1979), "An Exploration of Factors Affecting the Entrepreneurial Decision: Personal Characteristics vs. Environmental Conditions." In R. C. Hoseman (Ed.), *Academy of Management Proceedings*. Athens, GA: University of Georgia.

Brown, D. J. and J. H. Atkinson (1981), "Cash and Share Renting: An Empirical Test of the Link Between Entrepreneurial Ability and Contractual Choice." *Bell Journal of Economics* 12:296–299.

Brown, P. B. (1984), "Entrepreneurship 101." *Forbes* 134:174–178.

Brown, W. S. (1982), "Commentary on Entrepreneurship Education." In C. A. Kent et al. (Eds.), *Encyclopedia of Entrepreneurship*. Englewood Cliffs, NJ: Prentice-Hall.

Brown, W. S. (1982), "The Utah Innovation Center: An Experiment in Entrepreneurship." In K. H. Vesper (Ed.), *Frontiers of Entrepreneurship Research*. Wellesley, MA: Babson College.

Bruno, A. V. and T. T. Tyebjee (1982), "The Environment for Entrepreneurship." In C. A. Kent et al. (Eds.), *Encyclopedia of Entrepreneurship*. Englewood Cliffs, NJ: Prentice-Hall.

Bruun, M. O. (1980), "Technology Transfer and Entrepreneurship." In D. Sahal (Ed.), *Research Development and Technological Innovation*. Lexington, MA: Lexington Books.

Buchanan, J. M. and A. D. Pierro (1980), "Cognition, Choice and Entrepreneurship." *Southern Economic Journal* 46:693:701.

Buchanan, J. M. and R. L. Faith (1981), "Entrepreneurship and the Internalization of Externalities." *Journal of Law and Economics* 24:95–111.

Buckeye, J. G. (1984), "How Entrepreneurs' Perceptions of the Personal Risks and Rewards of Starting a Business Relate to the Firm's Performance." Ph.D. dissertation, University of Minnesota.

Buckley, R. J. (1985), "The New Bourgeoisie — A Threat to Entrepreneurship." *Vital Speeches* 51:178–180.

Burgelman, R. A. (1983), "Corporate Entrepreneurship and Strategic Management: Insights from a Process Study." *Management Science* 29:1349–1364.

Burgelman, R. A. (1984), "Designs for Corporate Entrepreneurship in Established Firms." *California Management Review* 26:154–166.

Burns, S. (1981), "Rebirth of the Entrepreneurial Spirit." *New England Business* 3:42–44.

Bush, R. C. (1983), "Planning and the Entrepreneurial Spirit." *Manage* 35:28–30.

Bylinsky, G. (1976), *The Innovation Millionaires: How They Succeed*. New York: Charles Scribner's Sons.

Calvo, G. A. and S. Wellisz, (1980), "Technology, Entrepreneurs, and Firm Size." *Quarterly Journal of Economics* 95:663–77.

Carbone, T. C. (1983), "The Entrepreneurs' Economy." *Management World* 12:34–35.

Carland, J. W. et al. (1984), "Differentiating Entrepreneurs from Small Business Owners: A Conceptualization." *Academy of Management Review* 9:354–359.

Carson, C. R. (1982), "How G. E. Grows Entrepreneurs." *Management Review* 71:29–32.

Carstensen, F. and M. Morris (1978), "Credit, Infrastructure, and Entrepreneurial Opportunity in Developing Regions." *Journal of Economic History* 38:262–265.

Caves, R. (1980), "Corporate Strategy and Structure." *Journal of Economic Literature* 18:64–92.

Cawelti, J. G. (1965), *Apostles of the Self-Made Man*. Chicago: University of Chicago Press.

Chamley, C. (1983), "Entrepreneurial Abilities and Liabilities in a Model of Self-Selection." *Bell Journal of Economics* 14:70–80.

Chandler, A. D. (1962), *Strategy and Structure*. Cambridge, MA: MIT Press.

Chandler, A. D. (1977), *The Visible Hand: The Managerial Revolution in American Business.* Cambridge, MA: Harvard University Press.

Charboneau, F. J. (1981), "The Woman Entrepreneur." *American Demographics* :21–23.

Chilton, K. W. (1984), "Regulation and the Entrepreneurial Environment." In C. A. Kent (Ed.), *The Environment for Entrepreneurship.* Lexington,MA: D. C. Heath.

Christensen, L. R. (1971), "Entrepreneurial Income: How Does It Measure Up?" *American Economic Review* 61:575–85.

Clark, B. W. et al. (1984), "Do Courses in Entrepreneurship Aid in New Venture Creation?" *Journal of Small Business Management* 22:26–31.

Cochran, T. and W. Miller (1951), *The Age of Enterprise.* New York: Macmillan.

Cole, A. H. (1959), *Business Enterprise is Its Social Setting.* Cambridge, MA: Harvard University Press.

Cole, A. H. (1968), "The Entrepreneur: Introductory Remarks." *American Economic Review* 63:60–63.

Coleman, J. et al. (1957), "The Difference of an Innovation Among Physicians." *Sociometry* 20:253–270.

Comegys, C. (1976), "Cognitive Dissonance and Entrepreneurial Behavior." *Journal of Small Business Management* 14:1–6.

Comerford, R. A. (1981), "Trying to Implement a New Venture Course." In K. H. Vesper (Ed.), *Frontiers of Entrepreneurship Research.* Wellesley, MA: Babson College.

Cooper, A. C. (1975), "Technical Entrepreneurship: What Do We Know?" In C. Baumback and J. Mancuso (Eds.), *Entrepreneurship and Venture Management.* Englewood Cliffs, NJ: Prentice-Hall.

Cooper, A. C. and W. C. Dunkelberg (1981), "A New Look at Business Entry." In K. H. Vesper (Ed.), *Frontiers of Entrepreneurship Research.* Wellesley, MA: Babson College.

Cooper, A. C. (1984), "Contrasts in the Role of Incubator Organizations in the Founding of Growth-Oriented Firms." In J. A. Hornaday, F. A Tardley, Jr., J. A. Timmons, and K. H. Vesper (Eds.), *Frontiers of Entrepreneurship Research.* Wellesley, MA: Babson College.

Cyert, R. M. and J. G. March (1963), *A Behavioral Theory of the Firm.* Englewood Cliffs, NJ: Prentice-Hall.

Dandridge, T. C. (1982), "Encouraging Urban Entrepreneurship." In K. H. Vesper (Ed.), *Frontiers of Entrepreneurship Research.* Wellesley, MA: Babson College.

Dart, J. and L. L. Pendleton (1984), "The Role of Advertising Agencies in Entrepreneurial Education." *Journal of Small Business Management* 22:38–44.

Davies, S. (1980), "Diffusion, Innovation and Market Structure." In D. Sahal (Ed.), *Research Development and Technological Innovation.* Lexington, MA: Lexington Books.

Davison, J. L. (1984), "Entrepreneur MBAs Are a Bit Different from Their Peers." *New England Business* 6:30–32.

DeCarlo, J. F. and P. R. Lyons (1980), "Toward a Contingency Theory of Entrepreneurship." *Journal of Small Business Management* 18:37–42.

Demsetz, H. (1983), "The Neglect of the Entrepreneur." In J. Ronen (Ed.), *Entrepreneurship.* Lexington, MA: D. C. Heath.

DeVries, M. K. (1977), "The Entrepreneurial Personality — A Person at the Crossroads." *Journal of Management Studies* (UK) 14:34–57.

Dickson, H. (1983), "How Did Keynes Conceive of Entrepreneurs' Motivation? Notes on Patinkin's Hypothesis." *History of Political Economy* 15:229–47.

Distelhorst, G. F. (1985), "When Associations Become Entrepreneurs." *Association Management* 37:109–111.

Doutriaux, J. and B. F. Peterman (1982), "Technology Transfer and Academic Entrepreneurship." In K. H. Vesper (Ed.), *Frontiers of Entrepreneurship Research.* Wellesley, MA: Babson College.

Doutriaux, J. (1984), "Evolution of the Characteristics of (High-Tech) Entrepreneurial Firms." In J.

A. Hornaday, F. A. Tardley, Jr., J. A. Timmons, and K. H. Vesper (Eds.), *Frontiers of Entrepreneurship Research*. Wellesley, MA: Babson College.

Dresang, D. L. (1973), "Entrepreneurialism and Development Administration." *Administrative Science Quarterly* 18:76–85.

Drucker, P. F. (1984), "Our Entrepreneurial Economy." *Harvard Business Review* 62:59–64.

Drucker, P. F. (1985), "Entrepreneurial Strategies." *California Management Review* 27:9–25.

Drucker, P. F. (1985), "A Prescription for Entrepreneurial Management." *Industry Week* 22:33–40.

Drucker, P. F. (1985), "The Entrepreneurial Society." *Industry Week* 22:52–55.

Duffy, P. B., and H. H. Stevenson (1984), "Entrepreneurship and Self-Employment: Understanding the Distinctions." In J. A. Hornaday, F. A Tardley, Jr., J. A. Timmons, and K. H. Vesper (Eds.), *Frontiers of Entrepreneurship Research*. Wellesley, MA: Babson College.

Dunkelberg, W. C. and A. C. Cooper (1982). "Entrepreneurial Typologies." In K. H. Vesper (Ed.), *Frontiers of Entrepreneurship Research*. Wellesley, MA: Babson College.

Durand, D. E. (1974), "Training and Development of Entrepreneurs — A Comparison of Motivation and Skill Approaches." *Journal of Small Business Management* 12:23–26.

Durand, D. and D. Shea (1974), "Entrepreneurial Activity as a Function of Achievement Motivation and Reinforcement Control." *Journal of Psychology* 88:57–63.

Dutton, J. M. and R. D. Freedman (1980), *Calculating and Experimenting in a Theory of a Firm*. New York: New York University.

Ebrill, L. P. and D. G. Hartman (1983), "The Corporate Income Tax, Entrepreneurship, and the Noncorporate Sector." *Public Finance Quarterly* 11:419–436.

Eisenhardt, K. M. and N. Forbes (1984), "Technical Entrepreneurship: An International Perspective." *Columbia Journal of World Business* 19:31–38.

Elliott, S. J. (1985), "Goldhirsh: The Entrepreneur's Entrepreneur." *Advertising Age* 56:4, 74.

Farrell, K. (1984), "A Federal Program for Entrepreneurs." *Venture* 6:188.

Fast, N. D. and S. E. Pratt (1981), "Individual Entrepreneurship and Large Corporations." In K. H. Vesper (Ed.), *Frontiers of Entrepreneurship Research*. Wellesley, MA: Babson College.

Feinberg, A. (1984), "Inside the Entrepreneur." *Venture* 6:80–86.

Fellner, W. (1983), "Entrepreneurship in Economic Theory: The Scientific Method and Vicarious Introspection." In J. Backman (Ed.), *Entrepreneurship and the Outlook for America*. New York: The Free Press.

Foreman, T. (1984), "A Strategy for the Entrepreneur." *Accountancy* (UK) 95:98–99.

Freeman, J. R. and R. D. Duvall (1984), "International Economic Relations and the Entrepreneurial State." *Economic Development & Cultural Change* 32:373–400.

Freudenberger, H. (1970), "An Exploration in Entrepreneurial Motivation and Action." *Explorations in Economic History* 7:433–49.

Frohlich, N. and J. A. Oppenheimer (1974), "The Carrot and the Stick: Optimal Program Mixes for Entrepreneurial Political Leaders." *Public Choice* 19:43–61.

Ganz, C. (1981), "Linkages Between Knowledge, Creation, Diffusion and Utilization." In Robert Rich (Ed.), *The Knowledge Cycle*. Beverly Hills, CA: Sage Publications.

Gasse, Y. and G. d'Amboise (1981), "Managerial Problems of Entrepreneurs." In K. H. Vesper (Ed.), *Frontiers of Entrepreneurship Research*. Wellesley, MA: Babson College.

Gasse, Y. (1982), "Elaborations on the Psychology of the Entrepreneur." In C. A. Kent et al. (Eds.), *Encyclopedia of Entrepreneurship*. Englewood Cliffs, NJ: Prentice-Hall.

Gasse, Y. (1982), "Entrepreneurs and University Graduates: Expectations and Evaluations." In K. H. Vesper (Ed.), *Frontiers of Entrepreneurship Research*. Wellesley, MA: Babson College.

Gatewood, E., F. Hoy, and C. Spindler (1984), "Functionalist vs. Conflict Theories: Entrepreneurship Disrupts the Power Structure in a Small Community." In J. A. Hornaday, F. A. Tardley, Jr., J. A. Timmons, and K. H. Vesper (Eds.), *Frontiers of Entrepreneurship Research*. Wellesley, MA: Babson College.

Geiger, A. H. (1984), "Innovation and Entrepreneurialism in the Educational Setting: Evaluating the Ohio University Innovation Center's Potential Resources and Services to Clients and Prospective Clients and their Risk Preferences." Ph.D. dissertation, Ohio University.

Gerschenkron, A. (1953), "Social Attitudes, Entrepreneurship and Economic Development." *Explorations in Entrepreneurial History* 5:1–19.

Gevirtz, D. L. and J. Kotkin (1984), "Suppporting the Entrepreneurial Process: The Soundest American Industrial Economic Policy." *New Management* 1:39–43.

Gibson, W. D. (1985), "Budding Entrepreneurs Show the Way." *Chemical Week* 136:36–39.

Gilad, B. (1982), "An Interdisciplinary Approach to Entrepreneurship: Locus of Control and Alertness." Ph.D. dissertation, New York University.

Gilad, B. (1982), "On Encouraging Entrepreneurship: An Interdisciplinary Analysis." *Journal of Behavioral Economics* 11:132–63.

Gill, M. D. (1984), "A Status Report on Selected Segments of the Venture Capital Industry." In *Technology Venturing: American Innovation and Risk Taking.* Austin, TX: The Institute for Constructive Capitalism.

Glade, W. (1967), "Approaches to a Theory of Entrepreneurial Formation." *Explorations in Entrepreneurial History* 4:245–59.

Goldhirsh, B. A. (1985), "America's Entrepreneurial Environment — The New Industries." *Vital Speeches* 51:402–406.

Goodman, S. R. (1976), "Using Return on Investment for New Product Development." In *Corporate Strategy and Production Innovation.* New York: Free Press.

Greenhut, M. (1966), "The Decision Process of Entrepreneurial Returns." *Manchester School* 34:247–67.

Gregg, G. (1984), "Investing in Entrepreneurs." *Venture* 6:46–50.

Gregg, G. (1984), "Banking's Minority Entrepreneurs." *Venture* 6:64–71.

Gregory, F. W. and I. D. Neu (1952), "The American Industrial Elite in the 1870's: Their Social Origins." In William Miller (Ed.), *Men In Business: Essays in the History of Entrepreneurship.* Cambridge, MA: Harvard University Press.

Greiner, L.E. (1972), "Evolution and Revolution as Organizations Grow." *Harvard Business Review* 50:37–46.

Gumpert, D. E. (1982), "Entrepreneurship: A New Literature Begins." *Harvard Business Review* 60:50–60.

Guttman, J. M. (1982), "Can Political Entrepreneurs Solve the Free-Rider Problem?" *Journal of Economic Behavior and Organization* 3:357–66.

Hankin, R. N., and W. J. B. (1985), "Entrepreneur: A Growing Plan: A Written Outline for Success." *Management World* 14:42–43.

Hannah, L. (1984), "Entrepreneurs and the Social Sciences." *Economica* 51:219–34.

Harris, M. (1969), "Shifts in Entrepreneurial Functions in Agriculture." *American Journal of Agricultural Economics* 51: 517–29.

Harwood, E. (1982), "The Sociology of Entrepreneurship." In C. A. Kent et al. (Eds.), *Encyclopedia of Entrepreneurship.* Englewood Cliffs, NJ: Prentice-Hall.

Hay, D. R. and M. R. Wolff (1982), "Birth and Growth of Entrepreneurial Groups." In K. H. Vesper (Ed.), *Frontiers of Entrepreneurship Research.* Wellesley, MA: Babson College.

Heller, R. (1981), "Lessons of the Entrepreneur." *Management Today* (UK) (April): 54–59, 139.

Henderson, J. V. (1985), "The Tiebout Model: Bring Back the Entrepreneurs." *Journal of Political Economy* 93:248–264.

Herbert, V. H. and A. Bisio (1981), "Venture Analysis: The Assessment of Uncertainty and Risk." In *Corporate Strategy and Product Innovation.* New York: Free Press.

Hill, R. M. and J. D. Hlavacek (1972), "The Venture Team: A New Concept in Marketing Organization." *Journal of Marketing* 36:44–50.

Hisrich, R. D. and M. P. Peters (1984), "Internal Venturing in Large Corporations: The New Business Venture Unit." In J. A. Hornaday, F. A. Tardley, Jr., J. A. Timmons, and K. H. Vesper (Eds.), *Frontiers of Entrepreneurship Research*. Wellesley, MA: Babson College.

Hlavacek, J. D. (1974), "Toward More Successful Venture Management." *Journal of Marketing* 38:56–60.

Hoadley, W. E. (1982), "The Spirit of Entrepreneurial Capitalism is Very Much Alive, Despite Recession." *Dun's Business Month* 120:43.

Holland, P. (1984), *The Entrepreneur's Guide*. New York: G. P. Putnam's Sons.

Hornaday, J. and K. H. Vesper (1981), "Alumni Views of an Entrepreneurship Course After Five to Seven Years." In D. L. Sexton and P. M. Van Auken (Eds.), *Entrepreneurship Education*. Wayco, TX: Baylor University.

Hornaday, J. A. (1982), "Research about Living Entrepreneurs." In C. A. Kent, D. L. Sexton, and K. H. Vesper (Eds.), *Encyclopedia of Entrepreneurship*. Englewood Cliffs, NJ: Prentice-Hall.

Hornaday, J. A. and K. H. Vesper (1982), "Entrepreneurial Education and Job Satisfaction." In K. H. Vesper (Ed.), *Frontiers of Entrepreneurship Research*. Wellesley, MA: Babson College.

Horton, T. R. (1984), "Entrepreneurialism Lives!" *Credit & Financial Management* 86:29–30.

Hosmer, L. T. et al. (1977), *The Entrepreneurial Function*. Englewood Cliffs, NJ: Prentice-Hall.

Hosmer, L. T., A. C. Cooper, and K. H. Vesper (1977), *The Entrepreneurial Function*. Englewood Cliffs, NJ: Prentice-Hall.

Huang, Y. (1973), "Risk, Entrepreneurship and Tenancy." *Journal of Political Economy* 81:1241–1244.

Hughes, J. R. T. (1965), *The Vital Few: American Economic Growth and Its Protagonists*. Boston: Houghton Mifflin.

Hull, D. L. et al. (1980), "Renewing the Hunt for the Heffalump: Identifying Potential Entrepreneurs by Personality Characteristics." *Journal of Small Business Management* 18:11–18.

Hutt, R. W. and T. S. Mescon (1982), "Classifying Ventures in the Service Sector." In K. H. Vesper (Ed.), *Frontiers of Entrepreneurship Research*. Wellesley, MA: Babson College.

Hutt, R. W. and W. E. Miller (1981), "New Ventures in the Food Industry." In K. H. Vesper (Ed.), *Frontiers of Entrepreneurship Research*. Wellesley, MA: Babson College.

Hutt, R. W. (1984), "Preferred Activities of an Entrepreneurs' Organization Start-up and Early Stage Firms vs. Established Firms." In J. A. Hornaday, F. A. Tardley, Jr., J. A. Timmons, and K. H. Vesper (Eds.), *Frontiers of Entrepreneurship Research*. Wellesley, MA: Babson College.

Hutton, T. J. (1985), "Recruiting the Entrepreneurial Executive." *Personnel Administrator* 30:35–41.

Janowiak, R. M. (1976), "New Venture Management." *IEEE Transactions on Engineering Management* EM-23:47–50.

Jeromin, L. S. (1984), "Management Attitude and Responsibility Toward Skills Training in Entrepreneurial Companies." Ph.D. dissertation, Claremont Graduate School.

Kahn, J. P. (1985), "Portrait of a Compulsive Entrepreneur." *Inc.* 7:78–88.

Kahn, S. A. (1973), "The Entrepreneur Revisited." *Appraisal Journal* 41:113–118.

Kahneman, D. and A. Tversky (1979), "Prospect Theory: An Analysis of Decision Under Risk." *Econometrica* 41.

Kanbur, S. M. (1979), "Of Risk Taking and the Personal Distribution of Income." *Journal of Political Economy* 87:769–97.

Kanbur, S. M. (1980), "A Note on Risk Taking, Entrepreneurship and Schumpter." *History of Political Economy* 12:489–98.

Kanter, R. M. (1983), *The Change Masters: Innovation for Productivity in the American Corporation*. New York: Simon and Schuster.

Kasdan, L. (1971), "Family Structure, Migration, and the Entrepreneur." In P. Kilby (Ed.), *Entrepreneurship and Economic Development*. New York: Free Press.

Katz, J. A. (1984), "Entry Strategies of the Self-Employed: Individual Level Characteristics and Organizational Outcomes." In J. A. Hornaday, F. A. Tardley, Jr., J. A. Timmons, and K. H. Vesper (Eds.), *Frontiers of Entrepreneurship Research*. Wellesley, MA: Babson College.

Kazanjian, R. K. (1984), "Operationalizing Stage of Growth: An Empirical Assessment of Dominant Problems." In J. A. Hornaday, F. A. Tardley, Jr., J. A. Timmons, and K. H. Vesper (Eds.), *Frontiers of Entrepreneurship Research*. Wellesley, MA: Babson College.

Keirns, H. (1984), "Flexibility and Stability in a Growing Company." In Raymond W. Smilor and Robert Lawrence Kuhn (Eds.), *Corporate Creativity*. New York: Praeger Publishers.

Kent, C. A. (1982), "Entrepreneurship in Economic Development." In C. A. Kent et al. (Eds.), *Encyclopedia of Entrepreneurship*. Englewood Cliffs, NJ: Prentice-Hall.

Kent, C. A. (1984), "The New Entrepreneurs." In C. A. Kent (Ed.), *The Environment for Entrepreneurship*. Lexington, MA: D. C. Heath.

Kent, C. A. (1984), "The Rediscovery of the Entrepreneur." In C. A. Kent (Ed.), *The Environment for Entrepreneurship*. Lexington, MA: D. C. Heath.

Kent, C. A. (1984), "Taxation and the Entrepreneurial Environment." In C. A. Kent (Ed.), *The Environment for Entrepreneurship*. Lexington, MA: D. C. Heath.

Kent, C. A. et al. (1982), "Managers and Entrepreneurs: Do Lifetime Experiences Matter?" In K. H. Vesper (Ed.), *Frontiers of Entrepreneurship Research*. Wellesley, MA: Babson College.

Kierulff, H. E. (1979), "Finding – and Keeping: Corporate Entrepreneurs." *Business Horizons* 22:6–15.

Kierulff, H. E. (1981), "Turnabouts of Entrepreneurial Firms." In K. H. Vesper (Ed.), *Frontiers of Entrepreneurial Research*. Wellesley, MA: Babson College.

Kierulff, H. E. (1982), "Additional Thoughts on Modeling New Venture Creation." In C. A. Kent et al. (Eds.), *Encyclopedia of Entrepreneurship*. Englewood Cliffs, NJ: Prentice-Hall.

Kihlstrom, R. E. and J. Laffront (1979), "A General Equilibrium Entrepreneurial Theory of Firm Formulation Based on Risk Aversion." *Journal of Political Economy* 89:719–748.

Kilby, P. (1983), "An Entrepreneurial Problem." *American Economic Review* 73:107–11.

Kimsey, J. (1984), "Business as Usual: Unusual for Entrepreneurs." *Advertising Age* 55:34–35.

Kirzner, I. M. (1973), *Competition & Entrepreneurship*. Chicago: University of Chicago Press.

Kirzner, I. M. (1979), *Perception, Opportunity, and Profit: Studies in the Theory of Entrepreneurship*. Chicago: University of Chicago Press.

Kirzner, I. M. (1979), "Comment: X-Inefficiency, Error, and the Scope for Entrepreneurship." In Mario Rizzo (Ed.), *Time, Uncertainty and Disequilibrium*. Lexington, MA: Heath.

Kirzner, I. M. (1983), "The Entrepreneurs and the Entrepreneurial Function: A Commentary." In J. Ronen (Ed.), *Entrepreneurship*. Lexington, MA: D. C. Heath.

Kirzner, I. M. (1984), "The Entrepreneurial Process." In C. A. Kent (Ed.), *The Environment for Entrepreneurship*. Lexington, MA: D. C. Heath.

Knight, F. H. (1921), *Risk, Uncertainty and Profit*. New York: Harper & Row.

Komives, J. L. (1972), "A Preliminary Study of the Personal Values of High Technology Entrepreneurs." In A. Cooper and J. Komives (Eds.), *Technical Entrepreneurship: A Symposium*. Milwaukee, WI: The Center for Venture Management.

Koolman, G. (1971), "Say's Conception of the Role of the Entrepreneur." *Economica* 38:269–86.

Kourilsky, M. (1980), "Predictors of Entrepreneurship in a Simulated Economy." *The Journal of Creative Behavior* 14:175–198.

Krasner, O. J. and C. L. Wood (1981), "Free Trade Zones and Entrepreneurship." In K. H. Vesper (Ed.), *Frontiers of Entrepreneurship Research*. Wellesley, MA: Babson College.

Kurz, M. (1983), "Entrepreneurial Activity in a Complex Economy." In J. Ronen (Ed.), *Entrepreneurship*. Lexington, MA: D. C. Heath.

Lavenstein, M. C. and W. Skinner (1980), "Formulating a Strategy of Superior Resources." *Journal of Business Strategy* 1:4–10.

Lee, F. E. (1976), "Entrepreneurial Marketing Management." *Industrial Marketing Management* 5:169–173.

Leibenstein, H. (1979), "The General X-Efficiency Paradigm and the Role of the Entrepreneur." In Mario Rizzo (Ed.), *Time, Uncertainty and Disequilibrium*. Lexington, MA: Heath.

Lessem, R. (1979), "Training Entrepreneurs." *Industrial and Commercial Training* (UK) 11:464–466.

Lessem, R. (1983), "The Art of Entrepreneurship." *Journal of General Management* (UK) 8:39–49.

Levy, B. D. (1983), "The Industrial Economics of Entrepreneurship and Dependent Development." Ph.D. dissertation, Harvard University.

Link, A. N. (1980), "Firm Size and Efficient Entrepreneurial Activity: A Reformulation of the Schumpeter Hypothesis." *Journal of Political Economy* 88:771–782.

Litvak, I. A. and C. J. Maule (1976), "Comparative Technical Entrepreneurship — Some Perspectives." *Journal of International Business Studies* 7:31–38.

Livesay, H. C. (1977), "Entrepreneurial Persistence through the Bureaucratic Age." *Business History Review* 51:416–43.

Livesay, H. C. (1979), *American Made: Men Who Shaped the American Economy*. Boston: Little, Brown.

Livesay, H. C. (1982), "Entrepreneurial History." In C. A. Kent, D. L. Sexton, and K. H. Vesper (Eds.), Englewood Cliffs, NJ: Prentice-Hall.

Loasby, B. J. (1984), "Entrepreneurs and Organization." *Journal of Economic Studies* (UK) 11:75–88.

Long, W. (1983), The Meaning of Entrepreneurship." *American Journal of Small Business* 8:47–56.

Long, W. and W. E. McMullan (1984), "Mapping the New Venture Opportunity Identification Process." In J. A. Hornaday, F. A Tardley, Jr., J. A. Timmons, and K. H. Vesper (Eds.), *Frontiers of Entrepreneurship Research*. Wellesley, MA: Babson College.

Longenecker, J. G. and J. E. Schoen (1975), "The Essence of Entrepreneurship." *Journal of Small Business Management* 13:26–32.

Loucks, K. E. (1982), "Elaboration on Education in Entrepreneurship." In C. A. Kent et al. (Eds.), *Encyclopedia of Entrepreneurship*. Englewood Cliffs, NJ: Prentice-Hall.

Mace, E. R. (1980), "Entrepreneurs Adopt Modern Management Methods." *Management Focus* 27:34–37.

MacMillan, I. C. (1981), "Politics of New Ventures." In K. H. Vesper (Ed.), *Frontiers of Entrepreneurship Research*. Wellesley, MA: Babson College.

Macrae, N. (1980), "The New Entrepreneurial Revolution." *Policy Review* 12:79–88.

Madlin, N. (1985). "The Venture Survey: Probing the Entrepreneurial Psyche." *Venture* 7:24.

Maidique, M. A. (1980), "Entrepreneurs, Champions, and Technological Innovation." *Sloan Management Review* 21:59–76.

McClelland, D. (1969), *Motivating Economic Achievement*. New York: Free Press.

McGaffey, T. N. and R. Christy (1975), "Information Processing Capability as a Predictor of Entrepreneurial Effectiveness." *Academy of Management Journal* 18:857–863.

McGrath, M. D. (1974), "A Further Note on Entrepreneurial Behavior." *American Economist* 18:93–98.

McKendrick, J. (1985), "The Employee as Entrepreneur." *Management World* 14:12–13.

McMullen, W. E. (1976), "Creative Individuals: Paradoxical Personnages." *The Journal of Creative Behavior* 10:265–75.

McQueen, D. H. and J. T. Wallmark (1984), "Innovation Output and Academic Performance." In J. A. Hornaday, F. A. Tardley, Jr., J. A. Timmons, and K. H. Vesper (Eds.), *Frontiers of Entrepreneurship Research*. Wellesley, MA: Babson College.

Meehl, P. E. (1965), "The Creative Individual: Why it is Hard to Identify Him." In G. A. Steiner (Ed.), *The Creative Organization*. Chicago: The University of Chicago Press.

Mescon, T. S. et al. (1981), "The Personalities of Independent and Franchise Entrepreneurs: An Empirical Analysis of Concepts/Counterpoint." *Journal of Enterprise Management* 3:149–162.

Miller, D. (1983), "The Correlates of Entrepreneurship in Three Types of Firms." *Management Science* 29:770–91.

Miller, W. (1962), *Men in Business: Essays in the Historical Role of the Entrepreneur*. New York: Harper & Row.

Minkes, A. L. and G. R. Foxall (1980), "Entrepreneurship, Strategy, and Organization: Individual and Organization in the Behaviour of the Firm." *Strategic Management Journal* 1:295–301.

Mintzberg, H. and J. A. Waters (1982), "Tracking Strategy in an Entrepreneurial Firm." *Academy of Management Journal* 25:465–499.

Moeser, R. (1984), "Streamlining Operations: The Vertically Organized Unit at IBM." In R. W. Smilor and R. L. Kuhn (Eds.), *Corporate Creativity*. New York: Praeger Publishers.

Molz, R. (1984), "Entrepreneurial Managers in Large Organizations." *Business Horizons* 27:54–58.

Molz, R. (1985), "How to Nurture Entrepreneurs in Large Organizations." *Marketing News* 19:25–26.

Mueller, C. E. (1981), "Poverty and Entrepreneurship." In K. H. Vesper (Ed.), *Frontiers of Entrepreneurship Research*. Wellesley, MA: Babson College.

Murray, T. J. and M. Rozen (1984), "A New Heyday for Entrepreneurs." *Dun's Business Month* 123:40–46.

Murray, J. A. (1984), "A Concept of Entrepreneurial Strategy." *Strategic Management Journal* 5:1–13.

National Council for Urban Economic Development Information Service (1984), *The Industrial Incubator*. Washington, DC: National Council for Urban Economic Development.

Nelson, R. R. and D. Yates (Eds.), (1978), *Innovation and Implementation in Public Organizations* Lexington, MA: Lexington Books.

Obermayer, J. H. (1982), "Protection Strategies for the Technical Entrepreneur." In K. H. Vesper (Ed.), *Frontiers of Entrepreneurship Research*. Wellesley, MA: Babson College.

Olson, P. D. and D. A. Bosserman (1984), "Attributes of the Entrepreneurial Type." *Business Horizons* 27:53–56.

Owens, R. L. (1978), "Anthropological Study of Entrepreneurship." *Eastern Anthropologist* 31:65–80.

Pandey, J. and N. B. Tewary (1979), "Locus of Control and Achievement Values of Entrepreneurs." *Journal of Occupational Psychology* (UK) 52:107–111.

Park, J. C. (1983), "Entrepreneurial Corporations: A Managerial Assessment." *Journal of Small Business Management* 21:38–43.

Park, W. R. and I. B. Maillie (1982), *Strategic Analysis for Venture Evaluation*. New York: Van Nostrand Reinhold.

Paulin, W. L. et al. (1982), "Entrepreneurship Research: Methods and Directions." In C. A. Kent et al. (Ed.), *Encyclopedia of Entrepreneurship*. Englewood Cliffs, NJ: Prentice-Hall.

Pennings, J. M. (1982), "Elaboration on the Entrepreneur and His Environment." In C. A. Kent et al. (Eds.), *Encyclopedia of Entrepreneurship*. Englewood Cliffs, NJ: Prentice-Hall.

Pennings, J. M. (1982), "The Urban Quality of Life and Entrepreneurship." *Academy of Management Journal* 25:63–79.

Pennings, J. M., I. C. MacMillan, and A. Meshulach (1982), "The Urban Quality of Life and Entrepreneurship." In K. H. Vesper (Ed.), *Frontiers of Entrepreneurship Research*. Wellesley, MA: Babson College.

Perryman, M. R. (1982), "Commentary on Research Methodology in Entrepreneurship." In C. A. Kent et al. (Eds.), *Encyclopedia of Entrepreneurship*. Englewood Cliffs, NJ: Prentice-Hall.

Petrof, J. V. (1980), "Entrepreneurial Profile: A Discriminant Analysis." *Journal of Small Business Management* 18:13–17.

Porter, M. E. (1980), *Competitive Strategy Techniques for Analyzing Industries and Competitors*. New York: Free Press.

Powell, J. D. and C. F. Bimmerle (1980), "A Model of Entrepreneurship: Moving Toward Precision and Complexity." *Journal of Small Business Management* 18:33–36.

Quinn, J. B. (1979), "Technological Innovation, Entrepreneurship, and Strategy." *Sloan Management Review* 3:19–30.

Renas, S. R. and H. W. Fox (1978), "Proprietary Brands: Boon for the Entrepreneur." *Journal of Small Business Management* 16:27–30.

Richard, R. M. (1984), "Meeting the Challenge of Entrepreneurial Risk." *Risk Management* 31:22–27.

Richelson, J. (1973), "A Note on Collective Goods and the Theory of Political Entrepreneurship." *Public Choice* 16:73–75.

Robinett, S. (1985), "What Schools Can Teach Entrepreneurs." *Venture* 7:50–58.

Rodenberger, C. A. and J. McCray (1981), "Startups From Large University in a Small Town." In K. H. Vesper (Ed.), *Frontiers of Entrepreneurship Research*. Wellesley, MA: Babson College.

Ronen, J. (1983), "Some Insights Into the Entrepreneurial Process." In J. Ronen (Ed.), *Entrepreneurship*. Lexington, MA: D. C. Heath.

Ronstadt, R. C. (1981), "Entrepreneurial Careers." In K. H. Vesper (Ed.), *Frontiers of Entrepreneurship Research*. Wellesley, MA: Babson College.

Ronstadt, R. (1982), "Does Entrepreneurial Career Path Really Matter?" In K. H. Vesper (Ed.), *Frontiers of Entrepreneurship Research*. Wellesley, MA: Babson College.

Ronstadt, R. C. (1984), "Ex-Entrepreneurs and the Decision to Start an Entrepreneurial Career." In J. A. Hornaday, F. A. Tardley, Jr., J. A. Timmons, and K. H. Vesper (Eds.), *Frontiers of Entrepreneurship Research*. Wellesley, MA: Babson College.

Rosen, S. (1983), "Economics and Entrepreneurs." In J. Ronen (Ed.), *Entrepreneurship*. Lexington, MA: D. C. Heath.

Rothwell, R. (1975), "Intra-Corporate Entrepreneurs." *Management Decision* 13:142–54.

Russel, R. A. (1984), "The Managerial Entrepreneur." *Executive* 26:61–64.

Russell, C. (1981), "The Minority Entrepreneur." *American Demographics* 3:18–20.

Russell, S. (1984), "Design Entrepreneurs." *Venture* 6:46–55.

Sandberg, W. R. and C. W. Hofer (1982), "A Strategic Management Perspective on the Determinants of New Venture Success." In K. H. Vesper (Ed.), *Frontiers of Entrepreneurship Research*. Wellesley, MA: Babson College.

Sarachek, B. (1978), "American Entrepreneurs and the Horatio Alger Myth." *Journal of Economic History* 38:439–56.

Schell, D. W. and W. Davig (1981), "Community Infrastructure of Entrepreneurship." In K. H. Vesper (Ed.), *Frontiers of Entrepreneurship Research*. Wellesley, MA: Babson College.

Schendel, D. and C. Hofer (1979), *Strategic Management*. Boston: Little, Brown.

Schere, J. L. (1981), "Tolerence of Ambiguity as a Discriminating Variable Between Entrepreneurs and Managers." Ph.D dissertation, University of Pennsylvania.

Schollhammer, H. (1981), "Efficacy of Internal Entrepreneurship Strategies." In K. H. Vesper (Ed.), *Frontiers of Entrepreneurship Research*. Wellesley, MA: Babson College.

Schollhammer,, H. (1982), "Internal Corporate Entrepreneurship." In C. A. Kent, et al. (Eds.), *Encyclopedia of Entrepreneurship*. Englewood Cliffs, NJ: Prentice-Hall.

Schuyler, W. E., Jr. (1984), "Patents and the Entrepreneurial Environment." In C. A. Kent (Ed.), *The Environment for Entrepreneurship*. Lexington, MA: D. C. Heath.

Schwar, R. K. and U. Yucelt (1984), "A Study of Risk-Taking Propensities Among Small Business Entrepreneurs and Managers: An Empirical Evaluation." *American Journal of Small Business* 8:31–40.

Schwartz, R. G. and R. D. Teach (1984), "Primary Issues Effecting the Development and Growth of a Professional Infrastructure for Emerging Technology Start-ups: The State of Georgia Experience." In J. A. Hornaday, F. A. Tardley, Jr., J. A. Timmons, and K. H. Vesper (Eds.), *Frontiers of Entrepreneurship Research*. Wellesley, MA: Babson College.

Scott, D. S. and A. J. Szony (1979), "Evaluating the New Venture." In D. S. Scott and R. M. Blair (Eds.), *The Technical Entrepreneur*. Ontario, Canada: Press Porcepic Limited.

Sexton, D. L. (1980), "Characteristics and Role Demands of Successful Entrepreneurs." In R. C. Huseman (Ed.), *Academy of Management Proceedings*. Athens, GA: University of Georgia.

Sexton, D. L. (1982), "Research Needs and Issues in Entrepreneurship." In C. A. Kent et al. (Eds.), *Encyclopedia of Entrepreneurship*. Englewood Cliffs, NJ: Prentice-Hall.

Sexton, D. L. et al. (1981), "Directions for Future Research in Entrepreneurship." *American Journal of Small Business* 6:52–55.

Sexton, D. L. and C. A. Kent (1981), "Female Executives Versus Female Entrepreneurs." In K. H. Vesper (Ed.), *Frontiers of Entrepreneurship Research*. Wellesley, MA: Babson College.

Sexton, D. L. and P. Van Auken (1982), "Characteristics of Successful and Unsuccessful Entrepreneurs." *Texas Business Review* 56:236–239.

Sexton, D. L. and N. B. Bowman (1984), "Personality Inventory for Potential Entrepreneurs: Evaluation of a Modified JPI/PRF-E Test Instrument." In J. A. Hornaday, F. A. Tardley, Jr., J. A. Timmons, and K. H. Vesper (Eds.), *Frontiers of Entrepreneurship Research*. Wellesley, MA: Babson College.

Shapero, A. and L. Sokel (1982), "The Social Dimensions of Entrepreneurship." In C. A. Kent et al. (Eds.), *Encyclopedia of Entrepreneurship*. Englewood Cliffs, NJ: Prentice-Hall.

Shapero, A. (1984), "The Entrepreneurial Event." In C. A. Kent (Ed.), *The Environment for Entrepreneurship*. Lexington, MA: D. C. Heath.

Shapiro, M. (1983), "The Entrepreneurial Individual in the Large Organization." In J. Backman (Ed.), *Entrepreneurship and the Outlook for America*. New York: The Free Press.

Sheeran, L. R. (1985), "The Entrepreneur as Investor." *Inc.* 7:129–132.

Shils, E. B. and W. Zucker (1979), "Developing a Model for Internal Corporate Entrepreneurship." *Social Science* 54:195–203.

Sinetar, M. (1985), "Entrepreneurs, Chaos, and Creativity — Can Creative People Really Survive Large Company Structure?" *Sloan Management Review* 26:57–62.

Smith, N. R. and J. B. Miner (1983), "Type of Entrepreneur, Type of Firm and Managerial Motivation: Implications for Organizational Life Cycle Theory." *Strategic Management Journal* 4:325–340.

Smith, N. R. and J. B. Miner (1984), "Motivational Considerations in the Success of Technologically Innovative Entrepreneurs." In J. A. Hornaday, F. A. Tardley, Jr., J. A. Timmons, and K. H. Vesper (Eds.), *Frontiers of Entrepreneurship Research*. Wellesley, MA: Babson College.

Smith, S. A. (1981), "Psychology of Entrepreneurship: Culture, Motivation and Organization." *Antitrust Law and Economic Review* 13:45.

Soltow, J. H. (1968), "The Entrepreneurs in Economic History." *American Economic Review* 58:84–92.

Sommers, C. (1984), "What Keeps Entrepreneurs on a Fast Track." *Venture* 6:58–63.

Souder, W. E. (1981), "Encouraging Entrepreneurship in the Large Corporations." *Research Management* 24:18–22.

Snyder, C. W. (1985), "Independent Operations: Independents Revealed as Broad-Ranging Entrepreneurs." *Credit* 11:43–44.

Squires, G. D. et al. (1985), "Will Entrepreneurs Be America's Economic Saviors?" *Business & Society Review* (Spring): 4–14.

Stanford, M. J. (1982), *New Enterprise Management*. Reston, VA: Prentice-Hall.

Stevenson, H. H. and D. E. Gumpert (1985), "The Heart of Entrepreneurship." *Harvard Business Review* 63:85–94.

Stigler, G. J. (1976), "The Xistence of X-efficiency." *American Economic Review* 66:213–25.

Stoner, C. R. and F. L. Frey (1982), "The Entrepreneurial Decision: Dissatisfaction or Opportunity?" *Journal of Small Business Management* 20:39–44.

Thorne, J. R. and J. G. Ball (1981), "Entrepreneurs and Their Companies." In K. H. Vesper (Ed.), *Frontiers of Entrepreneurship Research*. Wellesley, MA: Babson College.

Thurston, P. H. (1981), "Commitment, Objectivity and Opportunism." In K. H. Vesper (Ed.), *Frontiers of Entrepreneurship Research*. Wellesley, MA: Babson College.

Timmons, J. A. (1982), "New Venture Creation: Models and Methodologies." In C. A. Kent, et al. (Eds.), *Encyclopedia of Entrepreneurship*. Englewood Cliffs, NJ: Prentice-Hall.

Timmons, J.A. (1979), "Careful Self-Analysis and Team Assessment Can Aid Entrepreneurs." *Harvard Business Review* 57:198–206.

Todd, J. (1977), "From 'Organization Man' to Entrepreneur — A Difficult Transition." *Journal of Small Business Management* 15:46–51.

Trombetta, W. L. (1980), "Post-Acquisition Product Liability: Potential Hazards Facing the Entrepreneur in a Buy-Out." *Business Law Review* 13:1–8

Troy, G. F. (1984), "The Entrepreneurial Spirit: Taking Risks at Control Data." In R. W. Smilor and R. L. Kuhn (Eds.), *Corporate Creativity*. New York: Praeger Publishers.

Twiss, B. (1980), "Creativity and Problem Solving." In B. Twiss (Ed.), *Managing Technological Innovation*. London: Longman.

United States Congress. Senate Committee on Small Business (1984), *Woman Entrepreneurs: Their Success and Problems: Hearing before the Committee on Small Business, United States Senate, Ninety-eighth Congress, Second session* Washington, DC: U. S. Government Printing Office.

United States Congress. House Committee on Banking, Finance, and Urban Affairs (1984), *The National Entrepreneurship Act: Hearing before the Subcommittee on Economic Stabilization of the Committee on Banking, Finance, and Urban Affairs, House of Representatives, Ninety-eighth Congress, Second session*. Washington, DC: U. S. Government Printing Office.

Uselding, P. (1981), "Measuring Techniques and Manufacturing Practice." In O. Mayr (Ed.), *The American System of Manufacturing*. Washington, DC: The Smithsonian Institution.

Van Andel, J. and R. M. DeVos (1979), "The Government versus the Entrepreneur." *Policy Review* 9:23–32.

Vesper, K. (1980), *New Venture Strategies*. Englewood Cliffs, NJ: Prentice-Hall.

Vesper, K. (1983). *Entrepreneurship and National Policy*. Chicago: Walter Heller International Institute for Small Business Policy.

Vesper, K. H. (1974), "Entrepreneurship, A Fast Emerging Area in Management Studies." *Journal of Small Business Management* 12:8–15.

Vesper, K. H. (1980), *New Venture Strategies*. Englewood Cliffs, NJ: Prentice-Hall.

Vesper, K. H. (1984), "Three Faces of Corporate Entrepreneurship: A Pilot Study." In J. A. Hornaday, F. A. Tardley, Jr., J. A. Timmons, and K. H. Vesper (Eds.), *Frontiers of Entrepreneurship Research*. Wellesley, MA: Babson College.'

Wallace, A. (1981), "The New Entrepreneurs." *Institutional Investor* 15:83–103.

Webster, F. A. (1977), "Entrepreneurs and Ventures — An Attempt at Classification and Clarification." *Academy of Management Review* 2:54–61.

Weick, K. E. (1979), "Cognitive Processes in Organizations." In B. Staw (Ed.), *Research in Organizational Behavior*. Vol. 1 Greenwich, CT: JAI Press.

Weintraub, R. (1979), "The Advantages of Becoming an Entrepreneur." *Vital Speeches* 46:8–10.

Welsch, H. P. (1982), "The Information Source Selection Decision: The Role of Entrepreneurial Personality Characteristics." *Journal of Small Business Management* 20:49–57.

Welsch, H. P. and E. C. Young (1982), "The Information Source Selection Decision: The Role of Entrepreneurial Personality Characteristics." *Journal of Small Business Management* 20:49–57.

Welsh, J. A. and J. F. White (1981), "Converging Characteristics of Entrepreneurs." In K. H. Vesper (Ed.), *Frontiers of Entrepreneurship Research*. Wellesley, MA: Babson College.

Welsh, J. A. (1984), "Entrepreneurial Characteristics: The Driving Force." In Raymond W. Smilor and Robert Lawrence Kuhn (Eds.), *Corporate Creativity*. New York: Praeger Publishers.

Welsh, J. A. and J. F. White (1978), "Recognizing and Dealing with the Entrepreneur." *Advanced Management Journal* 43:21–31.

Wetzel, W. E. (1982), "Risk Capital Research." In C. A. Kent et al. (Eds.), *Encyclopedia of Entrepreneurship*. Englewood Cliffs, NJ: Prentice-Hall.

Williams, E, F. (1981), "Innovation, Entrepreneurship, Brain Functioning." In K. H. Vesper (Ed.), *Frontiers of Entrepreneurship Research*. Wellesley, MA: Babson College.

Williamson, O. E.. (1970), *Corporate Control and Business Behavior*. Englewood Cliffs, NJ: Prentice-Hall.

Williamson, O. E. (1971), "The Vertical Integration of Production: Market Failure Considerations." *American Economic Review* 61:112–123.

Williamson, O. E. (1975), *Markets and Hierarchies*. New York: Free Press.

Williamson, O. E. (1983), "Organizational Innovation: The Transaction-Cost Approach." In J. Ronen (Ed.), *Entrepreneurship*. Lexington, MA: D. C. Heath.

Winter, R. (1980), *Government and the Corporation*. Washington, DC: American Enterprise Institute for Public Policy Research.

Wood, J. S. (1980), "Entrepreneurship and the Coordination of Expectations in the Stock Market." Ph.D. dissertation, New York University.

Wood, R. C. (1983), "Every Employee an Entrepreneur." *Inc.* 5:107–109.

Wyllie, I. G. (1966), *The Self-Made Man in America*. New York: Free Press.

SMALL BUSINESS REFERENCES

Albaum, G. and R. A. Peterson (1984), "Sources of Capital for Very Small Businesses." In Raymond W. Smilor and Robert Lawrence Kuhn (Eds.), *Corporate Creativity*. New York: Praeger Press.

Bannock, G. (1981), *The Economics of Small Firms: Return from the Wilderness*. Oxford: Basil Blackwell.

Berger, R. (1984), *The Small Business Incubator: Lessons Learned from Europe*. Washington, DC: Small Business Administration.

Birch, D. L. (1979), "The Role of Small Business in New England." In J. A. Timmons and D. E. Gumpert (Eds.), *A Region's Struggling Savior: Small Business in New England*. Washington, DC: Small Business Administration.

Blair, R. M. (1979), "Financial Management of a Small Technical Business." In D. S. Scott and R. M. Blair (Eds.), *The Technical Entrepreneur*. Ontario, Canada: Press Porcepic Limited.

Bracker, J. S. (1982), "Planning and Financial Performance Among Small Entrepreneurial Firms: An Industry Study." Ph.D. dissertation, Georgia State University.

Brandt, S. C. (1981), *Strategic Planning in Emerging Companies*. Reading, MA: Addison-Wesley.

Brophy, D. J. (1984), "Equity Participation Agreements and Commercial Bank Loans to Small Business Firms." In J.A. Hornaday, F. A. Tardley, Jr., J. A. Timmons, and K. H. Vesper (Eds.), *Frontiers of Entrepreneurship Research*. Wellesley, MA: Babson College.

Brown, J. (1972), *Social Responsibility and the Smaller Company*. New York: National Industrial Conference Board.

Bulow, J. and J. Shoven (1978), "The Bankruptcy Decision." *Bell Journal of Economics* 9:437–456.

Bunzel, J. H. (1979), *The American Small Businessman*. New York: Arno Press.

Burstiner (1979), *The Small Business Handbook*. Englewood Cliffs, NJ: Prentice-Hall.

Carland, J. W., Jr. (1982), "Entrepreneurship in a Small Business Setting: An Exploratory Study." Ph.D. dissertation, University of Georgia.

Chandron, R., D. D. Salvia, and A. Young (1977), "The Impact of Current Economic Forces on Small Business." *Journal of Small Business Management* 15:30–36.

Charan, R. et al. (1980), "From Entrepreneurial to Professional Management: A Set of Guidelines." *Journal of Small Business Management* 18:1–10.

Chilton, K. W. and M. L. Weidenbaum (1980), *Small Business Performance in the Regulated Economy*. St. Louis, MO: Washington University, Center for Study of American Business.

Christy, R. and B. M. Jones (1982), *The Complete Information Bank for Entrepreneurs and Small Business Management*. Wichita, KS: The Center for Entrepreneurship and Small Business Management, Wichita State University.

Churchill, N. C. and V. L. Lewis (1983), "The Five Stages of Small Business Growth." *Harvard Business Review* 61:30–50.

Chvotkin, A. (1984), "The Role of the Federal Government in Encouraging Small Business." In Raymond W. Smilor and Robert Lawrence Kuhn (Eds.), *Corporate Creativity*. New York: Praeger Publishers.

Comptroller General (1981), *Consistent Criteria Are Needed to Assess Small Business Innovation Initiatives*. Washington, DC: U. S. General Accounting Office.

Cooper, A. C. (1982), "The Entrepreneurship — Small Business Interface." In C. A. Kent et al. (Eds.), *Encyclopedia of Entrepreneurship*. Englewood Cliffs, NJ: Prentice-Hall.

Curran, M. and D. MacDonald (1983), "Small Business Incubators: A Tool for Local Economic Development." *Entrepreneurial Economy* (July):9–10.

Deeks, J. (1976), *The Small Firm Owner-Manager: Entrepreneurial Behavior and Management Practice*. New York: Praeger Publishers.

Deloitte Haskins and Sells (1981), *Cost-Benefit Study of the Small Business Investment Company Program*. New York: Deloitte Haskins and Sells.

Eisemann, P. and V. L. Andrews (1981), "The Financing of Small Business." *Federal Reserve Bank of Atlanta Economic Review* 66:16–20.

Ellin, E. (1979), "The Role of Small Business in Research, Development, Technological Change and Innovation in New England." In J. A. Timmons and D. E. Gumpert (Eds.), *A Region's Struggling Savior: Small Business In New England*. Washington, DC: Small Business Administration.

Fatzinger, G. B. (1982), "Federal Small Business Assistance: Review and Preview." *Journal of Small Business Management* 20:38–43.

Gartner, W. B. (1982), "An Empirical Model of the Business Startup, and Eight Entrepreneurial Archetypes." Ph.D. dissertation, University of Washington.

Gartner, W. B. (1984), "Problems in Business Startup: The Relationships Among Entrepeneurial Skills and Problem Identification for Different Types of New Venture." In J. A. Hornaday, F. A. Tardley, Jr., J. A. Timmons, and K. H. Vesper (Eds.), *Frontiers of Entrepreneurship Research*. Wellesley, MA: Babson College.

Gumpert, D. E. and J. A. Timmons (1982), *The Insider's Guide To Small Business Resources*. Garden City, NY: Doubleday.

Halperin, W. C. et al. (1983), "Exploring Entrepreneurial Cognitions of Retail Environments." *Economic Geography* 59:3–15.

Hand, H. H. and A. T. Hollingsworth (1979), *Practical Readings in Small Business*. Philadelphia, PA: W.B. Sauders.

Harrison, M. S. (1981), "Antitrust, Small Business and the Schumacher Movement: Seeds of a Common Cause." *Antitrust Law & Economic Review*. 13:25–38.

Hepburn, L. R. (1979), "Taxation and the Small Business." In D. S. Scott and R. M. Blair (Eds.), *The Technical Entrepreneur*. Ontario, Canada: Press Porcepic Limited.

Hollander, E. D. et al. (1979), *The Future of Small Business*. New York: Praeger Publishers.

Jones, R. G., Jr. (1979), "Analyzing Initial and Growth Financing for Small Business." *Management Accounting* 56:30–38.

Kiesner, W. F. (1984), "Higher Education and the Small Business Person: A Study of the Training and Educational Needs, Uses, and Desires of the Small Business Practitioner (Entrepreneurship)." Ph.D. dissertation, Claremont Graduate School.

Knight, R. M. (1984), "The Independence of the Franchisee Entrepreneur." *Journal of Small Business Management* 22:53–61.

MacFarlane, W. N. (1977), *Principles of Small Business Management*. New York: McGraw-Hill.

Mayer, K. B. and S. Goldstein (1961), *The First Two Years: Problems of Small Firm Growth and Survival*. Washington, DC: U. S. Government Printing Office.

Naums, W. (1978), *Entrepreneurial Manager in the Small Business: Text Readings and Cases*. Reading, MA: Addison-Wesley.

Rollins, H. M. (1979), "The Plight of the Successful Small Business." *Texas Business Review* 53:119–24.

Rotch, W. (1967), *Management of Small Enterprises, Cases and Readings.* Charlottesville, VA: University of Virginia.

Rothwell, R. (1978), "Small and Medium Sized Manufacturing Firms and Technological Innovation." *Management Decisions.* 16:362–70.

Schabacker, J. (Ed.), (1971), *Strengthening Small Business Management.* Washington, DC: U. S. Government Printing Office.

Schell, D. (1982), "Entrepreneurial Implications of Small Business Investment Incentives Act." In K. H. Vesper (Ed.), *Frontiers of Entrepreneurial Research.* Wellesley, MA; Babson College.

Schollhammer, H. and A. H. Kuriloff (1979), *Entrepreneuriship and Small Business Management.* New York: Wiley.

Scott, D. S. (1979), "Government Assistance to Small Business." In D. S. Scott and R. M. Blair (Eds.), *The Technical Entrepreneur.* Ontario, Canada: Press Porcepic Limited.

Scott, D. S. (1979), "So You Want to Run Your Own Business?" In D. S. Scott and R. M. Blair (Eds.), *The Technical Entrepreneur.* Ontario, Canada: Press Porcepic Limited.

Sexton, D. L. and P. M. Van Auken (1982), *Experiences in Entrepreneurship and Small Business Management.* Englewood Cliffs, NJ: Prentice-Hall.

Shatto, G. M. (1980), "Credit and Venture Capital for Small Business Investment." *Texas Business Review* 54:267–71.

Siropolis, N. C. (1977), *Small Business Management: A Guide to Entrepreneurship.* Boston: Houghton Mifflin.

Smith, W. J. and D. Creamer (1968), *R&D and Small Company Growth.* New York: Wiley.

Smollen, L. E. and M. A. Levin (1979), "The Role of Small Business in Research, Development, Technological Change and Innovation in Region I." In J. A. Timmons and D. E. Gumpert (Eds.), *A Region's Struggling Savior: Small Business In New England.* Washington, DC: Small Business Administration.

Stewart, M. D. (1979), "The Case for 'Smallness': Entrepreneurship, Conglomerates and the Good Economic Society." *Antitrust Law & Economics Review* 11:67–82.

Timmons, J. A. and D. E. Gumpert (Ed.), (1979), *A Region's Struggling Savior: Small Business in New England.* Washington, DC: Small Business Administration.

Trippi, R. R. and D. R. Wilson (1974), "Technology Transfer and the Innovative Process in Small Entrepreneurial Organizations." *Journal of Economics & Business* 27:64–68.

United States Congress. Senate Committee on Small Business (1983), *Special Problems Facing Small Business in the Midwest: Hearing Before the Subcommittee on Entrepreneurship and Special Problems Facing Small Business of the Committee on Small Business, United States Senate, Ninety-eighth Congress, First session.* Washington, DC: U. S. Government Printing Office.

United States, Small Business Administration (1981), *Economic Research on Small Business: The Environment for Entrepreneurship and Small Business: Summary Analysis of the Regional Research Reports.* Washington, DC: Small Business Administration.

United States, Small Business Administration (1984), *Small Business Incubators—Resource Summary.* Washington, DC: Small Business Administration.

Van Voothis, K. R. (1979), *Entrepreneurship and Small Business Management.* Boston: Allyn & Bacon.

Watkins, D. S. (1982), "Use of Business Competitions to Stimulate Business Formations." In K. H. Vesper (Ed.), *Frontiers of Entrepreneurship Research.* Wellesley, MA: Babson College.

White House Commission on Small Business (1980), *America's Small Business Economy: Agenda for Action.* Washington, DC: U. S. Government Printing Office.

Young, J. F. (1977), *Decision Making for Small Business Management.* New York: Wiley.

Research Annuals and Monographs in Series in
BUSINESS, ECONOMICS AND MANAGEMENT

Advances in the Economics of Energy and Resources
Edited by John R. Moroney, *Department of Economics, Texas A & M University*

Applications of Management Science
Edited by Randall L. Schultz, *School of Management, The University of Texas at Dallas*

Perspectives on Local Public Finance and Public Policy
Edited by John M. Quigley, *Graduate School of Public Policy, University of California, Berkeley*

Public Policy and Government Organizations
Edited by John P. Crecine, *College of Humanities and Social Sciences, Carnegie-Mellon University*

Research in Consumer Behavior
Edited by Jagdish N. Sheth, *School of Business, University of Southern California*

Research in Corporate Social Performance and Policy
Edited by Lee E. Preston, *Center for Business and Public Policy, University of Maryland*

Research in Domestic and International Agribusiness Management
Edited by Ray A. Goldberg, *Graduate School of Business Administration, Harvard University*

Research in Economic History
Edited by Paul Uselding, *Department of Economics, University of Illinois*

Research in Experimental Economics
Edited by Vernon L. Smith, *Department of Economics, University of Arizona*

Research in Finance
Edited by Haim Levy, *School of Business, The Hebrew University and The Wharton School, University of Pennsylvania*

Research in Governmental and Non-Profit Accounting
Edited by James L. Chan, *Department of Accounting, University of Illinois*

Research in Human Captial and Development
Edited by Ismail Sirageldin, *Departments of Population Dynamics and Policital Economy, The Johns Hopkins University*

Research in International Business and Finance
Edited by H. Peter Grey, *Department of Economics, Rutgers University*

Research in International Business and International Relations
Edited by Anant R. Negandhi, *Department of Business Administration, University of Illinois*

Research in Labor Economics
Edited by Ronald G. Ehrenberg, *School of Industrial and Labor Relations, Cornell University*

Research in Law and Economics
Edited by Richard O. Zerbe, Jr., *School of Public Affairs, University of Washington*

Research in Marketing
Edited by Jagdish N. Sheth, *School of Business, University of Southern California*

Research in Organizational Behavior
Edited by Barry M. Staw, *School of Business Administration, University of California, Berkeley* and L.L. Cummings, *J.L. Kellogg Graduate School of Management, Northwestern University*

Research in Personnel and Human Resources Management
Edited by Kendrith M. Rowland, *Department of Business Administration, University of Illinois* and Gerald R. Ferris, *Department of Management, Texas A & M University*

Research in Philosophy and Technology
Edited by Paul T. Durbin, *Philosophy Department and Center for Science and Culture, University at Delaware.* Review and Bibliography Editor: Carl Mitcham, *New York Polytechnic Institute*

Research in Political Economy
Edited by Paul Zarembka, *Department of Economics, State University of New York at Buffalo*

Research in Population Economics
Edited by T. Paul Schultz, *Department of Economics, Yale University* and Kenneth I. Wolpin, *Department of Economics, Ohio State University*

Research in Public Sector Economics
Edited by P.M. Jackson, *Department of Economics, Leicester University*

Research in Real Estate
Edited by C.F. Sirmans, *Department of Finance, Louisiana State University*

Research in the History of Economic Thought and Methodology
Edited by Warren J. Samuels, *Department of Economics, Michigan State University*

Research in the Sociology of Organizations
Edited by Samuel B. Bacharach, *Department of Organizational Behavior, New York State School of Industrial and Labor Relations, Cornell University*

Research in Transportation Economics
Edited by Theordore E. Keeler, *Department of Economics, University of California, Berkeley*

Research in Urban Economics
  Edited by J. Vernon Henderson, *Department of Economics, Brown University*

Research on Technological Innovation, Management and Policy
  Edited by Richard S. Rosenbloom, *Graduate School of Business Administration, Harvard University*

Monographs in Series

Contemporary Studies in Applied Behavioral Science
  Series Editor: Louis A. Zurcher, *School of Social Work, University of Texas at Austin*

Contemporary Studies in Economics and Financial Analysis
  Series Editors: Edward I. Altman and Ingo Walter, *Graduate School of Business Administration, New York University*

Contemporary Studies in Energy Analysis and Policy
  Series Editor: Noel D. Uri, *Bureau of Economics; Federal Trade Commission*

Decision Research - A Series of Monographs
  Edited by Howard Thomas, *Department of Business Administration, University of Illinois*

Handbook in Behavioral Economics
  Edited by Stanley Kaish and Benny Gilad, *Department of Economics, Rutgers University*

Industrial Development and the Social Fabric
  Edited by John P. McKay, *Department of History, University of Illinois*

Monographs in Organizational Behavior and Industrial Relations
  Edited by Samuel B. Bacharach, *Department of Organizational Behavior, New York State School of Industrial and Labor Relations, Cornell University*

Political Economy and Public Policy
  Edited by William Breit, *Department of Economics, Trinity University* and Kenneth G. Elzinga, *Department of Economics, University of Virginia*

Please inquire for detailed brochure on each series

 **JAI PRESS INC.**